T0365755

Sexual Addiction:
Understanding and Treatment

Textbook and Reference Manual

Paul Becker, MAEd, LPC

authorHOUSE®

AuthorHouse™
1663 Liberty Drive
Bloomington, IN 47403
www.authorhouse.com
Phone: 1 (800) 839-8640

© 2015 Paul Becker, MAEd, LPC. All rights reserved.

No part of this book may be reproduced, stored in a retrieval system, or transmitted
by any means without the written permission of the author.

Published by AuthorHouse 02/21/2015

ISBN: 978-1-4969-6987-3 (sc)
ISBN: 978-1-4969-6988-0 (e)

Library of Congress Control Number: 2015902509

Print information available on the last page.

Any people depicted in stock imagery provided by Thinkstock are models,
and such images are being used for illustrative purposes only.
Certain stock imagery © Thinkstock.

This book is printed on acid-free paper.

Because of the dynamic nature of the Internet, any web addresses or links contained in this book may have changed
since publication and may no longer be valid. The views expressed in this work are solely those of the author and do
not necessarily reflect the views of the publisher, and the publisher hereby disclaims any responsibility for them.

CONTENTS

FIGURES

Acknowledgement

I thank and acknowledge Sherry Hart, Richard Vann, and Corrine Casanova who made valuable and appreciated contributions to this book.

PREFACE

Helping the sexually addicted recover is my vocation, my passion. Being of service confers meaning and purpose to my life.

In 1981, I canvased all of Harvard University's libraries in search of information on sexual addiction. The effort was futile. When Dr. Carnes published, *Out of the Shadows* in 1983, his research filled a virtual void. His work was new, exciting, and enlightening. While his books favored the mental health community, I awaited the day when his work would be presented in a literary style pleasing to the average person.

A few years later, I began to restate some of Dr. Carnes' work. Dr. Carnes read drafts of my first two books and approved them for publication by Gentle Path Press, a publication company owned by Dr. Carnes. In addition to the first two books, *In Search of Recovery: A Christian Man's Guide*, (Becker, 2012b) and *In Search of Recovery* Workbook (Becker, 2012c), I have written several other self-help books including one for spouses or significant others of sexually addicted men.

Dr. Carnes' professional research standards are impressive. He was the first in the field of sex addiction to apply statistical analysis to validate his hypotheses. His work is based on statistically significant populations. His research findings are reliable and applicable in the clinical setting. His books have inspired a new breed of therapist who has selected sexual addiction therapy as their primary focus.

Over time, I developed a recovery program based on Dr. Carnes' work. The program has assisted clients achieve their quest for sexual sobriety. The recently published book, *Clinical Guide for the Treatment of Male Sexual Addiction*, (Becker, 2013) is a syllabus for group therapy that uses the *Recovery from Sexual Addiction* books (Becker, 2010b and c) as the foundation for a recovery program. *In Search of Recovery Workbook* (Becker, 2010c) featured some of the exercises contained in this new book. *Sexual Addiction: Understanding and Treatment* significantly expands the content, refines, and recasts the structure of the earlier recovery program. It too was tested in a group setting and found to be effective.

Rephrasing Dr. Carnes' work opened new publication opportunities. His fundamental concepts were not changed, only the style of presentation was modified. The senior editor at Gentle Path Press and the *International Institute for Trauma and Addiction Professionals* (ITAP) has approved, on behalf of Dr. Carnes, my use of his concepts and adaptations for all of my books, including this one.

The intended audience for *Sexual Addiction: Understanding and Treatment* is unlike my previous books. It is more than a self-help book. This book is authored primarily for the mental health and academic communities. My goal is to share Dr. Carnes' research and my own work with therapists and to invite all to use the program presented here in a clinical setting. In a conversation with a professor who teaches counseling education, we agreed that a textbook is needed to introduce graduate level students to the field of sexual addiction—a growing service area for therapists and counselors. It is my expectation that graduate schools will elect to use this book to further the education of students who, in turn, will elect to minister to sexually addicted men and women.

This book contains *36 therapeutic exercises* to help sexually addicted men and women, in conjunction with sex addiction therapy, to achieve long-term sobriety. Copies of the exercises are available for download or printed from the web site: sexaddictionhelpbooks.com

I welcome your comments. Please send them to me at hh8326@gmail.com

Other Books by Paul Becker, LPC

Letters from Paul

In Search of Recovery: A Christian Man's Guide

In Search of Recovery Workbook: A Christian Man's Guide

In Search of Recovery: Clinical Guide

The Christian Guide books are published by Gentle Path Press.

Why Is My Partner Sexually Addicted? Insight Women Need

Recovery From Sexual Addiction: A Man's Guide

Recovery From Sexual Addiction: A Man's Workbook

Clinical Guide for the Treatment of Male Sexual Addiction

The Recovery Series books are published by Author House. The *Clinical Guide* is for therapists who wish to use the recovery series in a therapy setting.

The book, *Recovery from Sexual Addiction: A Man's Guide,* is a revised edition and replaces, *In Search of Recovery: A Christian Man's Guide. Recovery from Sexual Addiction: A Man's Guide,* adds substantial new material.

The book, *Recovery from Sexual Addiction: A Man's Workbook,* is a revised edition, and replaces *In Search of Recovery Workbook: A Christian Man's Guide.*

The book, *Clinical Guide for the Treatment of Male Sexual Addiction*, is a revised edition, and replaces *In Search of Recovery: Clinical Guide.*

INTRODUCTION

Let us begin with Jake's story.

Around age seven, I found my brother's pornographic magazines. I remember it well. My brother, Jacob, was at basketball practice and I went to his room to look for my Nintendo game. Jacob had borrowed it and I thought it might be under his bed. It was not but several copies of a magazine were there. I wondered why Jacob would hide his magazines under his bed. I began to look at them. I could not believe it had pictures of naked ladies. What's more, I wondered how they could pee—they weren't like me.

I took one magazine but Jacob discovered it was missing. He hit me so hard—I wanted to tell dad but I would have had to tell him about the magazines, too. I was more afraid of dad than of Jacob. I thought he would beat me even more. Dad had a terrible temper.

During grade-school years, I often went to Joey's house after school. One day we found his dad's magazines. From then on, we couldn't stop ogling those pictures. I also found that when I was in bed at night, I could touch myself and think about one or more of the pictures. My first orgasm occurred around age 14. I began messing with myself several times a week. I thought maybe that doing so was wrong and I tried to stop, but I didn't.

I continued to view pornography and masturbate all through high school. I was shy and didn't date much. In college, I discovered internet pornography. I began to date and in my junior year, I had intercourse for the first time.

I met Jane in college. We had a fast track relationship, which turned sexual within a few months. We both felt it was ok since we planned to marry after college. I was so happy to marry. I thought that my pornography and masturbation habits would end since sex was readily available. I was dead wrong. I began to live two lives. One was my married life and the other was my secret life. Jane caught me viewing pornography one evening and I assured her she didn't need to worry. I told her all men do it. I also told her that I didn't do it very often—and several other lies. The truth was my secret life was out of control. I didn't know how to stop; I was obsessed with finding the perfect image, just like the one in Jacob's Playboy.

About a year later, when Jane was out with her friends, I went online to view Internet pornography. I didn't hear her come in. She was shocked to see me masturbating to an Internet porn film. We had a very long conversation during which I admitted to my problem. I agreed to seek counseling.

Jake's story raises several points. Before entering into recovery counseling:

- Jake's sexual behavior began in early childhood long before he had the capacity to recognize the consequences of his behavior or to make a choice.

- Jake was drowning in his unwanted compulsive behavior. He was obsessed with viewing pornography in search of the perfect image.

- His life was unmanageable.

- He lived a dual existence: one part of him was married and the other lived a secret life.

- Jake was discovered viewing pornography and masturbating.

- Jake confessed his behavior to his wife.

- His wife was devastated and their marriage was in crisis.

- Without counseling, his efforts to change his behavior would not be successful.

Jake's story, in one form or another, is repeated by those who are addicted to uncontrollable sexual behavior. The challenge for the mental health community is to comprehend the nature of sexual addiction and to engage men and women in effective treatment programs. This book, *Sexual Addiction: Understanding and Treatment*, provides tools to do both.

Humanity has experienced aberrant sexual behavior throughout history. However, the modern day sex addict can view more stimulating sexual material in one Internet session than his or her forbearers could digest in a lifetime. Modern technology has brought the availability of sexual stimulation and the propensity to become addicted into the home through DVD videos, TV, web cam, and online pornography. The Internet has generated access to pornography, sexual chat rooms, and a means to meet willing partners in a way society never fathomed in the past. The Internet is a blessing to many but a curse to those who have a weakness for sexual stimulation. Jake is a typical example of how the Internet has become more of a curse than a blessing. Jake was overwhelmed by technology-aided wonderment.

Compared to other addictions, sexual addiction is the least talked about and perhaps the least understood. It is as if the leaves Adam and Eve placed on their bodies after the *Fall* were also placed on their descendants' minds and hearts. The lack of knowledge and understanding comes from society's unwillingness to recognize the impact that sexually addictive behavior has on its morals. This is beginning to change, as many sex addiction therapists and help books are available today. Sexually addicted men and women can now seek a therapist to help them identify the various factors that nurture their addiction and to assist them achieve long-tern sexual sobriety.

Challenge

Sexual addiction and other addictions share some characteristics. Whereas, all addicts are vulnerable to temptation, sex addicts, unlike the alcoholic or drug addicts, carry a bottle or fix in their head. To begin stimulation sex addicts merely engage in sexual thinking or fantasy. Addicts, who also were afflicted with alcoholism, say that sexual addiction is much more difficult to address, particularly because their attachment to sexual behavior, for most, began so early in life.

No other addiction resides in our brain as does sexual addiction. Repetitive sexual thinking and fantasies are the addict's rehearsal for physically acting out. Previous sexual encounters and pornographic images are the living in the moment precursors to orgasmic pleasure. The battleground for sexual addiction is in each man or woman's head.

What this Book Provides

Sexual Addiction: Understanding and Treatment, is divided into four parts. The first three parts are educational and part four provides a framework for 36 therapeutic exercises.

- PART ONE presents a comprehensive definition of sex addiction and its characteristics.

- PART TWO presents the factors that nurture sexual addiction.

- PART THREE describes the conditions that join a man or woman to sexual addiction.

- PART FOUR introduces recovery—modifying aberrant sexual behavior.

PART FOUR presents, *Five Stages of Enlightenment,* a comprehensive recovery program comprised of *36 therapeutic exercises*. The exercises form a logically ordered sex addiction therapy program. (Refer to the *Table of Contents* for a listing of the exercises.)

The *Five Stages of Enlightenment* program is found in the last five chapters of the book. The outline of *Five Stages of Enlightenment program* by chapter follows:

Chapter Eight - *Stage I - Expose Addictive Behavior, Denial, and Shame to the Light of Day.* Recovery depends on a greater self-awareness, an understanding of how and why addictive sexual behavior became ingrained, and why addiction continues despite adverse consequences.

Chapter Nine - *Stage II - Address Factors that Bind an Addict to Sexual Addiction.* Multiple factors keep an addict steeped in sexual addiction. They include sexual thinking and fantasy, acting-out cycle and rituals, depressed mood and anxiety, anger, habit, isolation, loneliness, and pornography.

Chapter 10 - *Stage III - Recovery—Modifying Behavior.* The core of recovery is eliminating addictive behavior.

Chapter 11 - *Stage IV - Live a Healthy Life Style.* The gateway to changing the addiction torment is living a healthy life style.

Chapter 12 - *Stage V - Relapse Prevention.* Continuing sexual sobriety depends on planning for the inevitable future temptation.

Clinical groups tested this book's content and effectiveness of presentation. Group members found it a very effective adjunct to therapy. Chapter Seven, written specifically for the therapist, addresses counseling dynamics that promote effective sex addiction therapy. Chapters Eight through 12, *Five Stages of Enlightenment,* serve to organize the presentation of *36 therapeutic exercises.*

Sexual Addiction: Understanding and Treatment is, in part, an expansion of subject material and exercises presented in the author's earlier books. Exercises were tested in a clinical setting (Becker, 2012c, pp. 69-92). The text is prepared in a modified APA style and includes relevant source citations. However, since the therapeutic exercises are targeted for use by a client, for the most part, citations are not included.

PART ONE: UNDERSTANDING SEXUAL ADDICTION

Includes a guide
for understanding the nature
and characteristics of sexual addiction.

CHAPTER ONE: BEHAVIORS PRACTICED
BY SEXUALLY ADDICTED PEOPLE

This chapter explores the diagnostic criteria (or the lack of specific sex addiction criteria) found in the *Diagnostic and Statistical Manual of Mental Disorders* (5th ed. DSM-V). It also provides descriptions of aberrant sexual behaviors for which therapy is appropriate (American Psychiatric Association, APA, 2013).

The authority for defining mental disorders is the *DSM*-V. The manual classifies and establishes common definitions and diagnostic standards for use by the mental health community, insurance industry, and researchers. It is the product of considerable professional study and represents the *American Psychiatric Association*'s guidance to the mental health community at large.

The 2013 version of the DSM does not recognize sexual addiction as a disorder. Discussion continues in the mental health community and by others to ascertain if sexual addiction is better described as hyper-sexuality. Other experts believe that sexual addiction is actually a form of an obsessive-compulsive disorder and refer to it as sexual compulsivity. Still other experts believe that sex addiction is a myth, a by-product of cultural influences (Goodman, 2001, Abstract). Some therapists would classify typical sex addiction behavior under the heading, *Other Specified Paraphilic Disorders* (APA, 2013, p. 10).

Sexual addiction is diagnosed by adapting the DSM-V criteria for substance dependence. The brain chemistry of a sex addict is nearly the same as that of a drug addict. Sex addicts demonstrate similar abuse characteristics as those who are dependent on alcohol or drugs (APA, 2013, p. 10-11).

The previous version, DSM-IV, provided a *not classified elsewhere* category entitled *Sexual Disorders Not Otherwise Specified*. Such behaviors as compulsive searching for multiple partners, compulsive fixation on an unattainable partner, compulsive masturbation, compulsive love relationships, and compulsive sexuality in a relationship were included here. This section has not been included in the DSM-V.

The DSM-V does address multiple sexually aberrant behaviors under the title of *Paraphilia*. However, the DSM-V does not specifically classify paraphilias as sexually addictive behaviors. Nevertheless in the normal course of events, sex addiction therapists would consider these behaviors as sexually addictive disorders (APA, 2013, pp. 685-705).

Paraphilias

The DSM-V includes and classifies a small proportion of aberrant sexual behaviors and labels them as *paraphilias*. According to the DSM-V, they are characterized by reoccurring, intense sexual urges, which have occurred over at least 6 months. To make a diagnosis, they must also cause significant stress or impair social, occupational, or everyday functioning. The individual also experiences a sense of distress. Typically, addicts recognize the symptoms as negatively affecting their lives but believe they are unable to control them (APA, 2013, pp. 685-705).

Paraphilia included in the DSM-V are:

- **Voyeurism.** Involves observing an unknowing and non-consenting person, usually a stranger, who is naked or in the process of becoming unclothed and/or engaging in sexual activity. The act of looking (peeping) produces sexual excitement and is usually accompanies masturbation. Fantasies arising from voyeurism fuel future masturbation.

- **Exhibitionism.** Involves the surprise exposure of genitals to a stranger. Exhibitionism may coincide with masturbation and a fantasy expectation that the stranger will become sexually aroused.

- **Frotteurism.** Involves touching and rubbing genitals against a non-consenting person. The behavior may also involve fondling. During the act, the perpetrator usually fantasizes an exclusive and caring relationship with the victim. The behavior generally occurs in crowded places.

- **Masochism.** Involves the acts of humiliation such as beatings, being bound, or otherwise made to suffer physical abuse in order to enhance or achieve sexual excitement. In some cases, the act is limited to a fantasy of rape while bound with no possibility of escape. Sexual masochism may involve a wide range of devices to achieve the desired effect, including some devices that may cause death.

- **Sadism.** Involves an act in which the individual derives sexual excitement from the psychological or physical suffering, including humiliation, of the victim. The partner may or may not be consenting. Sadism may involve a wide range of behaviors and devices to achieve the desired effect.

- **Pedophilia.** Characterized by sexual activity against a child by a pedophile. The sexual interest of a pedophile is solely for children age 13 or younger, or in the case of an adolescent, a child five years younger than the pedophile. The sexual interest of a perpetrator may include asking or pressuring a child to engage in sexual activities (regardless of the outcome), indecent exposure of genitals to a child, exposing a child to pornography, actual sexual contact with a child, physical contact with the child's genitals, viewing the child's genitalia without physical contact, or using a child to produce pornography.

- **Fetishism.** Involves the use of nonliving objects, for example, a man/woman's underwear or other male/female apparel to achieve a state of arousal. The addict may masturbate while holding, rubbing, or smelling the apparel. The spouse may wear the apparel during sexual encounters. The fetish is either preferred or required for sexual excitement. Sexual arousal from a particular body part is classified as *partialism*.

- **Transvestic fetishism.** Involves mostly heterosexual males who dress in female clothing (cross-dressing) to achieve or enhance their sexual arousal. The fetish is based in fantasy when the male portrays himself as the female partner. Women's garments are arousing primarily as symbols of the individual's femininity.

- **Other Specified Paraphilic Disorders.** Classifies recurrent and intense sexual arousal involving telephone scatologia (obscene phone calls), necrophilla (corpses), zoophilla (animals), corprophilia (feces), kilsmaphilia (enemas), or urophilia (urine) (APA, 2013, pp. 685-705).

Aberrant Sexual Behaviors not Found in DSM-V

The following aberrant sexual behaviors are not included in the DSM-V but may result in significant stress or impair social, occupational, or everyday functioning.

- **Extramarital affairs.** Involve single or multiple sexual relationships with partners outside the marriage that cause significant stress to the marriage relationship. The addict may justify an affair because of unfulfilled sexual expectations within the marriage. Swinging and partner swapping are forms of extramarital affairs that include the participation of both marriage partners.

- **Multiple or anonymous sexual partners and/or one-night stands.** The sexual acts often are anonymous, situational, and intended to provide sexual experience. Behavior may be habitual when repeated often with new partners. The sexual activities are dangerous to the parties if practiced without the protection of a condom.

- **Prostitution.** Involves the solicitation and procurement of various types of sexual behavior from male or female escorts or prostitutes. Sexual massage involves the solicitation and procurement of sex, most often oral sex, or masturbation, from a male or female masseuse. In most cases, those who seek such services have an attraction to other aberrant sexual behaviors.

- **Obscene phone calls.** (scatologia). The caller receives sexual pleasure by delivering sexual or foul language to an unknown called party. Making obscene telephone calls for sexual pleasure is a form of exhibitionism. The obscene telephone calls are unsolicited.

- **Rape.** Defined as a sexual assault by a man or woman against another person without that person's consent. Rape by a male involves penetration.

- **Sexual anorexia.** Involves an obsessive state in which the physical, mental, and emotional tasks of avoiding sex dominate life. Preoccupation with the avoidance of sex masks or avoids relational problems. The obsession can then become a way to cope with all stress and all life difficulties (Carnes, 2001 p. 34-36).

- **Sexual harassment.** Involves intimidation, bullying, sexually demeaning language, or coercion of a sexual nature, or the unwelcome or insensitive promise of a reward in exchange for sexual favors.

Other Sexual Behaviors

Today's society judges some sexual behaviors as reasonably normal. Little stigma is attached to them. Common excuses are "Everyone does it" or "It doesn't hurt anyone." This kind of thinking justifies the behavior. What changes a behavior from acceptable to unacceptable is *compulsivity*. The sexual behavior is excessive and time consuming; interferes with a person's daily routine, work, or social functioning; continues despite a lack of pleasure or gratification; places the individual at risk of physical harm; or has legal or personal consequences such as financial debt (Carnes, 2001b, p. 86-87, 143).

Examples of compulsive sexual behaviors include:

- **Masturbation.** Involves self-stimulation, most commonly, by touching, stroking, or massaging the penis, clitoris, or vagina or other body parts until orgasm is achieved. Masturbation is subject to compulsive repetition and is the most common form of sexually addictive behavior practiced by both men and women.

- **Pornography.** Any material that depicts or describes sexual functions for fostering sexual arousal upon the part of the consumer. Pornography, found in all types of media, includes pay-for-view channels, magazines, video cassettes, motion pictures, and on the Internet. An addict may be stimulated when watching network or cable programs.

- **Cybersex.** Use of a computer, Internet access, expected anonymity, and sexually provocative material to generate arousal and is usually followed by masturbation. Multiple cybersex venues exist such as dial-a-porn, email, chat rooms, live video streams, instant messaging, postings to social networks (like Facebook), visual images of real or graphically generated persons, and interactive sex through a web cam.

- **Phone sex.** Involves the use of a phone to talk or listen to a provocative discourse to generate arousal followed, most often, by masturbation.

- **Obsessive dating through personal ads.** Preoccupation with making relational contact with another person to engage in some form of sexual behavior (Carnes, 2001, pp. 38-48).

Which term, *sexual addiction* or *hyper sexuality*, better describes sexually deviant behavior? (Rettner, 2012). In reality, both terms essentially define the same sexual conditions although hyper sexuality is a more apt description of a male sexual disorder. In contrast, healthy sexual relations consist of a mutual expression of love that ideally results in healthy sexual activity (para. 6).

CHAPTER TWO: WHAT IS SEXUAL ADDICTION?

This chapter explores aberrant sexual behaviors that share common characteristics and consequences.

The following are representative examples of the definition of sexual addiction.

The *Society for the Advancement of Sexual Health* (2014) defined sexual addiction as a "persistent and escalating pattern or patterns of sexual behaviors acted out despite increasingly negative consequences to self or others" (screen 2).

Ferree (2010) defined sexual addiction as an "intimacy disorder." Sex is the most intimate of connections between a man and woman but childhood experiences may serve to sever relational intimacy and substitute a false intimacy based on the primacy of getting their sexual needs met (p.72).

Sex Addicts Anonymous (SSA, 2014) defined sex addition by presenting characteristics.

- Powerlessness over addictive sexual behavior.

- Results in unmanageability of his/her life.

- Feelings of shame, pain, and self-loathing.

- Failed promises and attempts to stop acting out.

- Preoccupied with sex leading to ritual.

- Progressive worsening of adverse consequences. (para.4)

Carnes (1994), the foremost researcher and writer in the field of sexual addiction in the United States, defined sexual addiction as a "pathological relationship with a mood-altering substance or behavior" (p. 4). *Pathological* means a very unhealthy or diseased relationship during which an addict alters mood by sexual stimulation as an intended outcome.

If recovery from sexual addiction just entailed transforming behavior to preclude a pathological relationship with a *mood-altering* entity, recovery would be incomplete. Behavior modification is only one aspect of recovery. Sexual addiction has underlying psychological attributes that need to be addressed if a wounded man or woman is to be made whole. For example, sexual addiction is a *shame*-based disease. In recovery, the specific source of the addict's shame is identified and resolved.

Shame has a corollary. *Feelings* underlie the addict's perception of his or her adequacy as a human being. As a defense mechanism against exposure and shame, the addict often shuns normal feelings. Addicts also engage in other behaviors to obscure feelings. For example, a sex addict who is also a workaholic focuses on work objectives to the extent that feelings, relational or otherwise, are only distractions. Restoring the addict's ability to enjoy normal feelings is a requisite recovery task.

A sex addict often presents with co-existing *mental illnesses* or personality deficiencies. For example, it is very common for an addict to live life in low-grade depressed mood. Other potential co-existing deficiencies include life controlling anxiety, unreasonable anger, alcohol and drug abuse, personality and bi-polar disorders, and the inability to give and feel loving intimacy. Co-existing deficiencies must to be recognized and remedied.

This book addresses the recovery triad: behavior modification, restoration of normal feelings, and attending to co-existing deficiencies. Supplemental therapy, such as an eating disorder, may be required to address fully all of the addict's issues. For some, it is a life-long endeavor.

Addiction - Multiple Characteristics

Sexual addiction has defining characteristics, of which the following are the most definitive.

• The addict *compulsively* repeats sexual behavior.

• The addict is *obsessed* with sex.

• *Behavior continues* despite adverse consequences

• Sex addiction is subject to *tolerance*, that is, the flow of neurochemicals must increase in order to maintain the addict's same level of interest.

Compulsion. Compulsivity is an irresistible and persistent impulse to perform an act *repeatedly*. It characterizes all addictions. Addiction forms such a choke hold that the addict no longer has the ability to refrain from addictive behavior. An addict acts out without regard to consequences. Over time, acting out becomes a habitual repetition of a means to escape reality. Ultimately, an addict forfeits his or her ability to choose, that is, to exercise free will. Normal control mechanisms become impaired or disabled. The addict develops a psychological dependency based on the flow of the brain chemical, dopamine. The hyper chemical flow creates *neuropathways*, which take prominence in determining the addict's behavior. In other words, the brain forms *highways* to facilitate the onset of sexual fantasy, thinking, and activities, which lead to emotional euphoria or orgasm (Carnes, 1997b, pp. 11-13, 28).

According to Hastings (1998):

While (aberrant sexual) behaviors distract from healthy sexuality, they are only addictive if they are also obsessive or compulsive; in other words, if the person has difficulty interrupting thoughts about sex, searching for sex, or acting sexually. While sexual addiction recovery tends to focus on behaviors, the trance state can begin many hours or days before the sexual activity. This is the obsessive part of the addiction. The sexual act can be brief and is often unsatisfying. Alternatively, it can go on for hours, to the point of damaging tissues of the penis or vagina. This is the compulsion. (p. 71)

A common misconception is that acting-out sexually is always a frequent event—daily or at least weekly. Not necessarily so, every addict has his or her own repetition cycle. For some it is opportunity based. For most, the frequency of sexual thinking and fantasy determine sexual urges. Although timing varies for each addict, compulsivity underlies the craving to repeat the sexual event.

Ted's story. Ted came to counseling after he visited a house of ill repute. Although he expressed considerable remorse for having fallen, he was particularly concerned that he may have been exposed to a venereal disease. He spent most of the session talking about how sorry he was. Because of finances, Ted scheduled his next counseling appointment for a month later.

Ted did not return for his second session. In a follow-up telephone conversation, Ted declared he was not sexually addicted. He said his behavior was under control and he would not fall again. About six months later Ted revisited the same house of ill repute. Ted's acting-out cycle was lengthy.

Ted is not a daily abuser of sexual stimulation, but he engages in sporadic binges. A sex addict invariably feels compelled to replicate his or her behavior. An addict is powerless to take or leave sexual urges.

For the male addict, sexual behavior is not about love; it is about achieving sexual satisfaction. A male sex addict is compelled to act out sexually notwithstanding his greater or lesser biological hyper-sexuality.

Although a woman experiences a similar sex addiction cycle, as does a man, she may be satisfied without an orgasmic conclusion. Alternatively, she may seek an emotional relationship with a man to satisfy her desire for intimacy (Carnes, 2001b, p. 209). In other words, a woman may be addicted to the exhilaration of the hunt but may not be interested in sex after she has tagged her prey (Ferree, 2010, p. 60).

Obsession. Obsession means to be "intensely and abnormally preoccupied with something. The object of obsession is all consuming" (Ferree, 2010, p. 48). The obsession of a sexually addicted person is to experience multiple acting out opportunities. As such, the addict focuses attention on addictive behavior to the detriment of other healthy activities. Left unchecked, an addict dedicates much time to the behaviors that give significant pleasure or temporarily shields him or her from social or mental health deficiencies (Ferree, 2010, pp. 48, 144).

An addict is obsessed with achieving greater sexual satisfaction each time s/he repeats the four phases of the *sex addiction cycle* (See Exercise Six).

Randy's story. After my wife goes to bed for the night, I spend hours viewing explicit and tantalizing images. I search for the perfect image that matches my unique mental concept of perfection. However, my continual searches never meet with success. Each successive image, while stimulating, never satisfies me.

When Randy becomes aroused so that orgasm follows, he has completed three of four phases of his sex addiction cycle. During the last phase, Randy tells himself, *and he believes*, he will not repeat his acting-out behavior but obsession leads him to repeat his cycle time and again (Carnes, 2001b, pp. 28-33).

A woman will obsess more on sexual thinking and fantasy than a man will. For example, a sexually addicted woman may become engrossed in a fantasy of a man who meets her mental image of *Mr. Perfect* (Carnes, 2001, p. 209). Sex addiction for a woman is referred to as *female sex and love addiction* (FLSA) because her addiction is often related to dysfunctional relationships. A woman with a sex and love addiction has great difficulty bonding with other humans. She falls in love with love and not with a person (McDaniel & Valenti-Anderson, 2012, p. 27).

Destructive consequences continue. Why would anyone take aim at his or her foot and pull the trigger? To the healthy person, it just does not make sense. Nevertheless, an addict engages in behavior with adverse outcomes even when experience clearly predicts what will happen.

John's story. I continue to do what I know is wrong and I don't know why. Gambling has taken hold of my life. I know I have the key to cash in the big win.

His counselor asked John how long he has been seeking the big win. He refused to answer. John's family was facing bankruptcy. John finally admitted that his gambling had become a terrible burden on his family. Nevertheless, he told his counselor that nothing was more important to him than experiencing the thrill of winning. He cried as he told of a car accident he witnessed. The man in the car in front of him clearly needed assistance but John passed him by because it would have made him late for the first race. He had become psychologically dependent on the adrenaline rush related to his anticipation of winning. Even the survival of a human life was of lesser consequence to John.

Although acting out creates a euphoric feeling, it is short lived. Over time addictive sex becomes less satisfying and, for some, acting out just satisfies habitual behavior. It may even become boring. An addict knows that addictive behavior fails to yield a satisfying lifestyle but is powerless to change (Weiss 1998, pp. 23-24). S/he will stop for a short time, but invariably s/he caves into sexual urges and returns to old habits.

Addictions restrict our ability to dream beautiful dreams. Untold hours are squandered by aimless searching for, for what? Lost is a sense that the real world brings wonder, challenge, risk, and exquisite beauty. Addictions create problems that lead to desperation. Couples separate. Families dissolve. Dreams die. (Morris, 2001, n.p.)

Tolerance. The addict's brain becomes accustomed to higher levels of neurochemicals produced during sexual stimulation. To experience the same level of arousal over time, the flow of neurochemicals must increase. Addiction to pornography is a case in point. An image that stimulates today will not do so in a week or month from now. An addict requires new and more enticing images to generate the same level of arousal. Classic tolerance is the necessity to experience ever-increasing levels of neurochemicals to maintain the same level of addiction (Becker, 2012b, p. 6).

Janet's story. I have painful memories of terrible beatings inflicted on me by my former husband. I found I needed to banish my fearful thoughts so I could work at my desk. To medicate my painful feelings I positioned my foot under me so that I could masturbate. Over time I masturbated so frequently that, it interfered with my work. I was in a double bind. Either way, I did not either relieve or solve my problem.

Jeff's story. I like to visit massage parlors. I continually search for new establishments in hopes that I would find a masseuse with a new way of stimulating me. After having tried every massage parlor in his city, I decided to see if a prostitute could improve upon my experiences with masseuses. I continued to look for more and better sexual encounters, even trying sexual sadism. Massage parlors and prostitutes no longer did it for me.

Other characteristics of sexual addiction. The mental health community has identified other characteristics of sexual addiction including:

- The addict's life becomes *unmanageable.*

- Compulsions become stronger due to the *progressive* nature of addiction..

- An addict *procrastinates* in work or other necessary activities.

- The addict uses sexual behavior to *escape feelings.*

- The addict feels *entitled* to sex as a *reward* for a period of sobriety.

- Sexual *power* is used to form relationships.

- The addict *denies* the illness. He or she is plagued with *shame.*

- Destructive *core beliefs* keep sex addiction alive.

- *Withdrawal* symptoms occur after an addict ends addictive behavior.

Practices become unmanageable. What began as an occasional practice may progress to the point where behavior becomes unmanageable. All the best pledges to alter behavior become a long series of failed intentions. Unwanted sexual practice becomes part of the addict's life. Eventually the addict's sexual practices are out-of-control and life-damaging consequences follow (Becker, 2012b, p. 6).

Carnes (1994) said it this way:

Perhaps the best test of the presence of an addiction is its unmanageability. The therapist makes a thorough effort *to search for out of control behavior.* Chaos, which results from the addict's pursuit of the addiction scenario, provides many clues to the internal conflict that the addict experiences due to distorted priorities. Perhaps the surest sign is the addict repeatedly makes efforts to stop and fails, despite the obvious consequences of the behavior. Tapping into the addict's desire to quit is key to the assessment and recovery. (pp. 214-215)

Gene's story. I am a successful executive but I have difficulty coping with anxiety. Doubts that my business decisions are correct or if they will make me money, causes me considerable anguish. Each day I experienced distressing anxiety. I learned at some point, if I masturbated, my anxiety level dropped. Unfortunately after I masturbated, my reduced anxiety level lasted but a few hours and then I needed to repeat my behavior. I masturbated four and five times a day, not for the pleasure but to reduce my anxiety.

Gene's life became unmanageable because he had no idea how to lower his anxiety other than by masturbating. Despite advice to the contrary, he felt only weak men took anti-anxiety medication. Gene came to counseling, not to deal with his anxiety, but because he could no longer perform in the marital bed. His partner told him to seek counseling or pay alimony. In therapy, he dealt with his underlying anxiety disorder and his compulsive masturbation ended. His life became manageable once again.

A characteristic of unmanageability is the risk that addicts takes.

Joe's story. I am an assistant pastor at a local church. One day my church-issued laptop froze. I turned my laptop over to our IT contractor. The IT contractor discovered that my hard disk was full of pornography and my computer had no storage memory left. The IT contractor told the pastor. My pastor called me to his office and we had a long discussion about the possibility of me finding employment elsewhere. I risked my employment, my marriage, and my covenant with God to satisfy my sexual needs.

Joe and his pastor agreed that he would enter counseling. During therapy, Joe discovered a long-term benefit. He could now share knowledge of his sexual addiction with his young men's groups. His words conveyed authenticity to the young men in his church because he dealt with sexual temptation as they did. He was able to bond with young men who needed to know that clergy are real people and have the same failings.

One more example of an unmanageable life is the ability of an addict to delude self, that is, tell lies to self, and actually believe his or her lies (Becker, 2012b). While telling self lies and believing them is addressed later, a short illustrative scenario follows (p. 6).

Seth's story. Going online is my first acting-out step, but no more. In a group program, I shared that I planned to change my approach to my computer use. I told them I would move my computer to the living room so I would no longer access porn in my home. (I didn't want to put an Internet blocker on my computer in case I needed a fix.) I knew I didn't tell my group the whole truth.

At the next session I told the group what happened. I moved the computer to the living room and I firmly believed I would not go to a porn site when I turned on my computer to check my email. However, once I turned on my computer it was like going into a trance. I checked email, went to a sports page, saw an attractive image of a singer, checked out the singer's web page, and then I viewed pornography.

I lied to my group because I knew that on Saturday mornings my wife and son would not be in the house. With the support of my group, I admitted my strategy was purposely flawed. I needed to put an *Internet blocker* on my computer.

Behavior is unmanageable when it becomes a conditioned response. Pavlov conditioned a dog to respond to the sound of a bell. Seth's bell was a conditioned response to turning on his computer that led him to act out (Weiss, 1998, pp. 20-21).

Progressive. Progression drives an addict to seek more titillating images or experiences. For example, when an addict becomes bored with one class of pornography, s/he will seek new stimulating subject matter. With time, the addict views images that s/he would never have viewed in the past. He or she continually seeks more, better, and often more degrading. It may begin out of curiosity, but in reality, viewing new exotic images is part of the progressive nature of addiction (Becker, 2012b, p. 7).

A woman in a recovery group talked about how she searched for more stimulating pornographic images and doing so took her to a *kinky* web site. At first, she was repulsed by what she saw on the kinky web site but that only lasted a few days. She had progressed to more bizarre images and videos.

Progression may include dedicating more time, money, and risk to meeting sexual needs. It is like falling into quicksand. It is a downward spiral of degradation.

Sexual addiction is progressive and it rarely gets better. Over time, it gets more frequent and extreme. At other times when it seems under control, the addict is merely engaging in one of the common traits of the disease process in which he switches from sexual release to the control of it. The control phase inevitably breaks down over time and the addict is back in the behavior again. When the ecstasy of the release is spent, the addict will feel remorse at his failure and will switch back to another *white-knuckle* period of abstaining from the behavior until his resolve weakens again (Ewald, 2003, para. 6).

Procrastination. Procrastination coexists with other addictions but it is particularly troublesome when symptom relief only occurs by acting out. Almost by definition, addicts are plagued by low self-esteem, feel inadequate, and fear they cannot produce a successful product. Because they fear failure, they have a propensity to delay work assignments until there is no other choice. From clinical experience, one concludes that sexually addicted people are usually bright and failure to produce is not due to a lack of intelligence or skill. Addicts believe that failure will bring unbearable shame.

Procrastination is a form of anxiety. Acting out relieves anxiety and the necessity to procrastinate, at least for a while. Procrastination is manifestation of an unmanageable life (Becker, 2012b, p. 6).

Monica's story. My IT friend told me that data from the company's computer server showed I spend considerable time online. My friend suggested I curtail my usage before upper level management is informed. Although I am a very talented engineer, I procrastinate much of my day. I am capable of producing high quality work in a short period when I need to do so.

I was depressed. I was on the verge of discovery because I wasted far too much time and I did not know how to stop.

My sister suggested that I talk to a therapist. I told my therapist I did not know why I felt such a strong urge to play solitaire. I thought that procrastination was a family trait.

After several sessions, during which Monica made little progress, she blurted out that solitaire was not her problem. It was viewing pornography. Procrastination was her way of dealing with a compulsive desire to view pornography. Although she no longer viewed pornography at work, she shifted her search for titillating pornography to the evenings. Monica, cradling her head in her hands, cried, "My life is a mess—I feel so ashamed—I feel like I am drowning."

Acting out to escape feelings. Because of shame and low self-esteem, the addict experiences feelings of hopelessness, despair and, at times, urges to consider suicide. The addict also experience feelings of guilt and remorse over lost relationships and opportunities. Acting out sexually is a way to escape feelings, if only for a short time (Sbraga & O'Donohue, 2003, pp. 130-131).

A woman uses sex to soothe the ache of loneliness. Sexual stimulation is a powerful mood-altering agent. To escape her adverse feelings, a woman may become self-absorbed in the pursuit of an altered mind state (Ferree, 2010, P. 44). She shrouds her normal feelings to make room for sexual fantasy and thinking.

Entitlement and reward. An addict alternates between recovery thinking and excuses to act out. After a period of celibacy, it is common for an addict to feel entitled to act out as a reward for sobriety. Faulty thinking is an expected characteristic of living with sexual addiction (Becker, 2012b, p. 42).

The brain rewards addictive behavior (Weiss, 1998, p. 23). Addictive drugs provide a shortcut to the brain's reward system by flooding the nucleus accumbens with dopamine. The hippocampus lays down memories of this rapid sense of satisfaction, and the amygdala creates a conditioned response to certain stimuli. In addition, dopamine relieves adverse feelings from which the addict desires to escape (Harvard Mental Health Letter, n.d., Pleasure principle, para. 4).

Power. Sex is used to create a *feeling of power* over that which addicts have no power—their own lives. Through seduction and romance, she uses sex to gain power over her target. Sexual power is the use of physical beauty to attract men. She flaunts her femininity by flirting, wearing provocative clothing, or displaying suggestive body movement to gain sexual power over a male of her choice. Lastly, she may seek a relationship with an influential or powerful person to boost her ego. Any relationship that raises the perception of self-worth above that normally felt by an addict is an exercise in use of sexual power (Ferree, 2010, pp. 70-71, 35; McDaniel & Valenti-Anderson, 2012, p. 33).

"Women sex addicts…tend to use sex for power, control, and attention. They score high on measures of fantasy sex, seductive role sex, trading sex, and pain exchange" (O'Hare, 2012, para. 6).

Denial and shame. Fear of abandonment is fundamental to a person who is deeply ashamed. Abandonment seems quite probable to anyone who believes that s/he is worthless and unlovable. *Why would anyone stay with me when so many better people inhabit the world?* Excessive shame prevents a person from believing that s/he is valuable enough to be cherished (Potter-Efrom, R. & Potter-Efrom, P., 1989, pp. 42-43). Because of shame, the addict is in denial of his or her God given worth. Feelings of degradation enhance shame. Denial and shame are *thinking disorders* (Carnes, 2001b, p. 17).

A primary characteristic of both denial and shame is secrecy. An early recovery step for a sex addict is to address his or her secret world. Disclosure of aberrant sexual behavior is a catalyst to resolve denial.

Rarely does an addict fully disclose the extent of his or her aberrant sexual behavior early in therapy. The addict may convince self that some or all of his or her behavior is normal or at least not that bad. Self-delusion may come in the form, "I am not hurting anybody." An addict minimizes the consequences of addictive behavior to family, self, job, and social life. Denial to escape reality is common. Denial is a subterfuge behind which the addict hides his or her behavior (Carnes, 2001b, pp. 126-127, 2).

Shame has its roots in childhood exposure to sexual behavior. Unwanted sexual behavior usually took place between the ages of four and 12 (Carnes, 2001a, p. 206-207). Shame reduction occurs when an addict understands that childhood abuse was outside his or her ability to control.

Hastings (1998) clarified how shame becomes part of the child's physic.

Shame is introduced to individual children and young people in countless ways. Some of these are sexual shame, emotional abuse of sexuality, sexual secrecy, exposure to pornography in a sexualized manner, religious shaming, taking on the disowned sexual shame of a parent, being dressed to hide the body, and leading a promiscuous lifestyle. Shame is focused on sexuality more than any other human quality—worldwide. (pp. 16-17)

Shame is a characteristic of addiction, reinforces addictive behavior, and keeps the addict attached to addiction. Shame is addressed again later.

Core beliefs. Carnes' (1994) identified an addict's core beliefs that either promote addiction or inhibit recovery. Shame-based core beliefs are:

- I am a bad and unworthy person.

- No one would love me as I am.

- My needs will never be met if I have to depend on others.

- Sex is the most important sign of love (p. 127).

Core beliefs are detrimental to clear thinking. A child raised in a dysfunctional family is subject to physical, emotional, sexual, or spiritual abuse. However, a child is unable to recognize that his or her parents are at fault. Doing so is contrary to a child's developmental instincts. For example, when parents' divorce, the child's reaction often is "If I had been more obedient (or any other illogical conclusion), my mother or father would not have left me." An addict believes: "I am not loveable; sex is the only way to get my intimacy needs met." All survivors of dysfunctional families share illogical thinking. If the brain were purged of thinking disorders, sexual behavior would diminish.

Withdrawal. Psychological and physical withdrawal symptoms inhibit efforts to stop or change behavior. Withdrawal symptoms include depressed mood, headaches, irritability or restlessness, sleep or eating disturbance, itchy skin, and anxiety.

Fear of losing a cherished friend is part of psychological withdrawal. The number of years an addict has been in a relationship with his or her addiction usually spans decades. Pleasurable experiences from the *hunt* and *orgasm* are fully encoded into an addict's brain (Struthers, 2009, p. 59). Giving up cherished behavior is like experiencing the cold terror of the night. Therapy participants talk about loss as one of the more painful experiences in recovery. At the beginning of recovery, victories over temptation are counted in hours and perhaps weeks. Each victory becomes a triumph over withdrawal. Each milestone becomes an investment in sobriety (Carnes, 2001b, p. 133).

Similar to substance and drug addictions, withdrawal from sexual addiction has many of the same physical characteristics. Brain chemicals foster withdrawal symptoms and thus inhibit the transition from addiction to sobriety. However, withdrawal *must* be experienced and tolerated. Withdrawal symptoms may be reduced with medication (Becker, 2012b, p. 7).

Male and Female Sexual Addiction

For the most part, the attributes of male and female sexual addiction are similar. That is, they are not gender specific. Both genders compulsively repeat aberrant sexual behavior despite good intentions to reduce or end such activities. Unmanageability, progression, denial, tolerance, and withdrawal are common to both. An addict may be co-addicted to alcohol and or drugs. Substance abuse in conjunction with risky acting-out behavior and emotionless sex serve to mask underlying relationship disconnects (Ferree, 2010, pp. 57-68; McDaniel, Valent-Anderson, Ferree, Hudson, & Katehakis, (2012), pp. 19, 40-41).

"Addicts typically inherit a genetic structure which predisposes them to addiction in general" (Carnes, 2001b, p. 44). When a genetic predisposition to addiction is likely, acting out shows up early in life. Youth often begin alcohol consumption, experiment with drugs, and engage in sexual behaviors during teen years. It is far more common for an addict to carry sex addiction forward from early life than to begin addictive behavior as an adult (Becker, 2012b, p. 36, 42).

Sex addiction characteristics apply to the male and female addict in varying degrees. For example, both experience sexual shame. However, society holds a woman to a higher standard and thus she is perceived to experience shame to a greater degree than does a man (Ferree, 2010, p. 30).

A common sexual activity shared by both men and women is masturbation. Zoldbrod (1998) found that "one-third of women and two-thirds of men reported as having masturbated by the age of 13" (p. 147).

Carnes (2000, slide 3, 7) found that sexual addiction participation rates for women have increased. In the year, 2000 Carnes found:

[F]or every three men with sexual compulsivity, there is one woman with the disorder. (p. 3)

Ten years later Carnes (2010) found, "in treatment, our female patient population has equaled and sometimes exceeded our male patients" (slide 3, 7).

Differences exist between male and female sexual addiction. For a man sexual addiction is embodied at the core by arousal and orgasm in whatever way he seeks fulfillment. Female sexual addiction is characterized by real or fantasy sexual relationships.

Struthers' (2009) found that a man's brain process sexual stimuli differently than does the brain of a woman.

"A man's brain is a sexual mosaic influenced by hormone levels in the womb and in puberty and molded by his psychological experience. Male brains can be very different from female brains because of this. Although neither superior nor inferior they are very different in the way, they detect stimuli, process information, and respond to emotions. This is important because men detect sexual cues rapidly when it comes to nakedness or sex related stimuli." (pp. 84) This particular proficiency [explains why men have difficulty] looking away. All women become potential porn stars in the minds of men. "They have created a neurological circuit that imprisons their ability to see women rightly as created in God's image." (Struthers 2009, pp. 84-85)

A woman's brain, unlike that of a man, seeks attachment and feelings of well-being. Sex and love addiction (SLA) is, at the core, a brain disease.

Post-coital release of the neurohormones oxytocin and serotonin create feelings of attachment and well-being and further attaches the female to the sexual experience. Along with brain structure and early relational injuries, women's bodies may also intensify vulnerability to SLA. Every 28-32 days, the menstrual cycle alters levels of neurohormones including estrogen, which shapes brain structure and chemistry and may regulate arousal and make female SLAs likely to cheat when ovulating. The female brain seems deeply involved in orgasm…. [W]omen reported that the more in love they were the stronger their orgasms were. (Ferree, Hudson, Katehakis, McDaniel, & Valenti-Anderson, 2012, pp. 50)

Socialization is also different, that is, in the way a woman interacts with others in relationships. Corley (2012) holds that a therapist needs to be sensitive to a woman's attachment experience, trauma, and relational injuries. A woman must feel safe, secure, and in particular, *heard*. A woman benefits when she shares her recovery experience with other sex and love addicted women (p. 19).

Another difference is the unique ability of a woman to become pregnant. Pregnancy that results from addictive behavior causes a crisis in the life of a woman. The crisis cries for empathic counseling. A woman may present with co-existing mental health issues, substance abuse, or other illnesses. A woman is less likely to self-identify as an addict and will describe her relational sex addiction as, "I'm love addicted to him" (McDaniel et al., 2012, p.40).

Male Sexual Addiction

A male sex addict desires a relatively sparse emotional involvement with the woman with whom he is sexual (Carnes, 2010, slide 5). The addict lacks the ability to trust others sufficiently to form a bond (Weiss, 1998, pp. 73-74). Usually an addict lacked a parental model that taught trust. For an addict, intimacy meant sex and most often sex outside of a committed relationship. For example, a consequence of a lack of marital connectivity is his inability to maintain an erection without recalling past encounters with other sex partners or pornographic images stored in his brain. According to Ferree (2010), sexual addiction is an *intimacy* deficit (p. 72). Carnes (2001b) agreed: "One of the primary failures that plays a role in making an addict is the inability to sustain intimacy" (p. 44).

Carnes (1992) said it this way:

Nowhere is this fact of addictive life more clear than in the addict's relationships. As their illness progresses, sex addicts put energy only into relationships with sexual potential. They invest in few or no nonsexual relationships. Relationships are neglected that once had meaning. Long-term relationships of active sex addicts are often stormy and unsuccessful... Addicts, because of their...avoidance of intimacy, tend to leave interpersonal transactions...left to wilt or die. Further, addicts typically search for people who will take care of their neediness or for people who will be vulnerable or dependent upon them. Finally, the quality of emotion is affected. The degree of shame surrounding the double life prevents addicts from being emotionally present, especially at critical or meaningful times. (p. 27)

A greater feeling of intimacy occurs when an addict engages in self-sex in contrast to marital sex. In self-sex, the addict calls on sexual thinking and fantasy to frame an erotic environment. He controls the sex act, both its content and duration. A young male addict, chronically exposed to pornography and masturbation, finds he cannot engage in intercourse with a woman because of fear he will be unable to perform (Wilson, 2012, p. 3).

A sex addict engages in non-relational sex in conjunction with pornography, voyeurism, frequenting prostitutes, or by anonymous sex. An addict acts as if he is fitted with a permanent pair of eyeglasses and each lens has a built-in *sex prism*. The sex-prism blocks normal vision in favor of anything sexual. A woman is just body parts over which the addict lusts. The addict sees a woman as an object, not a God-made person (Sbraga & O'Donohue, 2003 pp. 155-157). Body parts which draw attention are breasts, buttocks, genitals, hair color, moles, stretch marks, legs and for some necks, hands, and armpits or feet (Carnes, 2001b, p. 239). In other words, men as a whole, lust over every conceivable body part or body function. Internet pornography provides today's addict with a continuing supply of sexual food. Sadly, the Internet has become the addict's food market. "This may be seen as a logical extension of the way men in our culture are raised to view women and sex" (Carnes as cited by O'Hare, 2012, para. 2).

A male addict's life becomes a perpetual sexual existence. For example, when he sees a woman, man, or (sadly) a child, he surveys body parts for a match to his internal concept of what is sexually stimulating. Rarely does he focus on a whole person or a person's eyes or face. The habit of checking out bodies becomes so ingrained that it defines how he views humanity. To an addict, people are opportunities for sexual gratification, that is, his "relationship is with sex—and not with people" (Carnes, 2001a, p. 16). So too, when an addict picks up a book, magazine, or newspaper, his first instinct is not for the intellectual content of the publication but for images that sexually stimulate his mind. Sex is his number one focus and his number one requirement (Becker, 2012b, p. 3).

Marcel is fixated with women's breasts. Every woman is an *object* for his gratification. He needs a front row seat at a ball game to preclude every female within eyeshot from distracting him. Although he tried multiple interventions, he could not stop objectifying female body parts

Objectification is a result of inadequate infantile attachment or abandonment arising from a dysfunctional family of origin. Abandonment is experienced by 100 % of men and women who struggle with sex addiction (Ferree, 2010, p. 133). It is hard for an addict to respond in a way that his or her childhood maturation process ignored.

Today's society places value on competition and autonomy. Career and financial success, achieving status, and successful sexual conquests reflect the American way. Negative relational consequences are isolation, objectification of sex partners, an inability to express feelings, and a strong sense of entitlement at the expense of others—all fertile breeding ground for addictive behaviors.

Sex addiction is a curse and many men feel cursed by it. An estimated half of the male population is sexually addicted. Many therapists regard some sexual activities as severe antisocial behavior. Sex addicts, and particularly sex offenders, are analogous to the lepers of days gone by. Politicians and the press vilify sexual misconduct. *Sex Offender Registries* add to shame by disclosing the name and residential address of the sex offender population—even those with long-term sobriety. Sexual addiction has no friend.

Female Sexual Addiction

The male sex paradigm is not foreign to all female sex addicts. In recent years, exposure to Internet pornography and masturbation serve to blend the characteristics of male and female sexual addiction. Carnes (2010) has found more male type behavior by women in treatment, that is, compulsive use of prostitutes, aggressive approach to prospective sex partners, and maintaining pornography collections (slide 6).

However, some aspects of female sex addiction still present differently. Because a woman is biologically unique and her socialized is to seek connection, her sexual disposition communicates a desire for a relationship with a partner. Seeking a fulfilling romantic connection is more to the core of addiction for a woman, that is, romance is the build-up to sex. The build-up, the hunt, the high, often begins hours and even days before the sexual encounter. Sexual fantasy or experiences are the fuel that keeps desire-burning (Ferree, 2010, pp. 37-38, 57-59).

Female sexual desire relates to both a psychological as well as physiological arousal. As such, healthy women lose desire if their partner is not psychologically and physiologically aroused. On the other hand, a sex and love addict who suffered early relational trauma will stay in a painful relationship because the fantasy of romance is more compelling than real suffering (Ferree, et al., 2012, p. 50). A love and sex addict often looks to a sex partner for feelings of well-being. An addicted woman lacks an internal barometer that measures her satisfaction or happiness as an outcome of her behavior (McDaniel et al., 2012, pp. 28-30). The expectation of many is that women (especially moral or religious women), do not have problems with sex addiction, helps to keep addiction secret. A female patient suffers the shame of having a sexual disorder and from being a woman who has lost control (Carnes, 2000, p. 3).

A woman, like a man, experiences remorse after an illicit sexual encounter. Remorse occurs, in part, due to the depletion of brain chemicals that cause desire during sexual relations.

A love addict will accept a significant distortion of reality rather than face any form of abandonment. For example, she will stay in a dysfunctional relationship even when she is battered, abused, or when normal support is withheld. This type of relationship is *codependent*, that is, a compulsive relationship over which she has no control (Carnes, 2001b, p 209).

Kasl, (as cited in O'Hare, 2012) defined female sexual codependency:

[L]etting their body be used in order to hold onto a relationship, regardless of whether a woman really wants to have sex. In general, sex addicts tend to use [manipulate] relationships in order to have sex; whereas sexual codependents use [manipulation] sex in order to keep relationships. Neither group has a clue as to the true meaning of intimacy. (para.7)

Ferree (2010) addressed eight presentations of female sexual addiction. The following is a synopsis of her findings:

Relationship or love addict. The life of the female sex addict is often one of serial or simultaneous relationships. She seeks to fill the hole in her soul through multiple affairs. She forms an intense (as opposed to intimate) emotionally dependent relationship but only a temporary attachment. She focuses on her partner to the loss of self. Her relationships are enmeshed (she has no healthy boundaries). No relationship is satisfying because it fails to provide real love. The addictive relationship is possessive and consuming.

Romantic addict. The addict is tethered to the thrill of the *chase* that is, pursuing or being pursued. Once the hunt is over, so is the relationship. Finding a new partner is more exciting. She doubts her worth as lovable, needs constant reassurances, and is high maintenance.

Fantasy addict. Her compulsive relationship is all in her head—and she falls in love with many men. She interprets any kindness as a sign of his interest. The *magical man* captures her focus but *not reality*—no human can live up to a fantasy (Ferree, 2010, p. 61). Like some men, she may be unable to honor the marital bed without recalling past encounters with other sex partners or pornographic images stored in her brain.

Pornography or cybersex addict. Because of perceived privacy and feelings of autonomy, an addict may find the Internet a safe haven to search for pornography, engage in chat rooms, web cams, cybersex, and the like. Because of her secret behavior, she feels shame—for nice girls do not view porn. A woman, who is involved in chat rooms, may meet her chat room partner for sex, often-unsafe sex, but she continues nevertheless. "Twice as many women favor chat rooms as do men" (Ferree, 2010, p. 63).

Masturbation. Self-sex is a partner to stimulation engendered by pornography or fantasy. As an addiction, it alters one's mood in an unhealthy way. A woman who favors pornography and masturbation presents similarly to a male addict.

Exhibitionism. Society condones exhibitionism in multiple ways. The addict uses her body to seek attention. She sells lust in the way she flaunts herself. She experiences a *rush* when she feels coveted or seen. In a way, she lives in a fantasy world.

An addict who sells or trades sex. A woman may trade sex for favors, alcohol, or drugs. Unfortunately, she believes she has no choice but to engage in barter. She feels she is not worthy of seeking a committed relationship.

Partnering with another addict. A common manifestation of sex addiction is the addict who partners with another sex addict. She seeks to create an environment where her co-partner will see her worth and remain in the relationship (pp. 57-67).

All female presentations of sexual addiction include a powerlessness of a woman to control her behavior and at the core of her addiction is an intimacy disorder. It is not about sex but a desperate search for love, touch, affirmation, and acceptance (Ferree, 2010, pp. 71-72).

According to McDaniel et al., (2012):

In addition to a psychological and cultural disease, sex and love addiction is also a brain disease. We're all addicts when we first fall in love—highlight's the powerful chemical process involved with mate selection. For women who find themselves addicted to sex and love, mate selection has gone awry. In the brain of a sex and love addict, the relationship is unconsciously formed with the experience of a chemical high rather than with an individual. In essence, brain chemistry becomes the mate. (p. 28)

Counseling a male sex addict is complex but working with a female addict is even more challenging. A woman often does not know she is sexually addicted, and if she did, her profound shame would cause her to hide her distress in therapy. Female sexual addiction becomes a concern subsequent to a crisis or when a skillful therapist, who is in tune with subtle messages, pursues a line of questioning that leads to disclosure of deeper relational issues.

If you plan to counsel sexually addicted women, a resource essential to your work is *Making Advances: A Comprehensive Guide for Treating Female Sex and Love Addicts*, edited by Marnie Ferree. However, most therapists in private practice will not experience a significant caseload of sexually addicted women (McDaniel et al., 2012, p. 27).

Character of a Sex Addict

In Chapter 1, the characteristics of sexual addiction are defined. Carnes, on the other hand, addressed the character anomalies of those affected by sexual addiction.

The following is a shortened version of the results of his research:

- **Distrust of authority.** A future sex addict is usually born into an extremely rigid and controlling dysfunctional family of origin. A child lacks self-limitation and responsibility. For a child to comply with authority means a loss of self and, as an adult, resistant to accountability.

- **Intimacy deficit.** Families are detached, uninvolved, or emotionally absent. Sexual behavior reflects an intimacy disorder and lack of emotional nurturing during childhood.

- **Post-traumatic stress disorder (PTSD).** An addict with a history of sexual, physical, and/or emotional abuse may suffer from PTSD. Addictive behavior relieves stress, which may cause the compulsive repetition of the trauma.

- **Extreme eroticization**. A consequence of sexual abuse and/or a dysfunctional family is all thinking and images become sexual stimulus.

- **Shame-based sense of self.** An addict lacks a positive sense of self-worth. The inability to control sexual behavior confirms to the addict that s/he is flawed and unlovable.

- **Compartmentalization.** An addict compartmentalizes his or her life to avoid reality. Work, marriage, hobbies are mentally separated from their acting-out behavior. Compartmentalization allows the addict to ignore the impact that his or her sexual addiction has on the other aspects of his or her life (Carnes, 2001, pp. 2, 202). (See Exercise 27).

- **Compulsive cycles.** According to Carnes (2000), 72 % of addicts binge, feel depressed, or despair after acting out. An addict has two faces, one is presented to the world, (good person), and one is hidden (bad person). Presenting the bad person is bingeing (acting out) and the good person is (abstaining) purging unwanted sexual behavior (p. 5). (See Exercise 27).

- **Self-destructive behavior.** An addict, who was abused as a child, is more likely to engage in high-risk behavior and integrate fear into his or her acting-out behavior. An addict usually knows the consequences of sexual behavior but does it anyway.

- **Other addictions or compulsions.** To manage the stress of addictive behavior, an addict adopts other compulsions. For example, Carnes (2000) found that "41 % of sex addicts had problems with alcohol or drugs and 38 % had an eating disorder. Co-addictions include compulsive gambling, substance abuse, excessive work or play, spending, and nicotine. An addict may replace one set of addictive behaviors with an alternative set" (p. 6).

- **Concomitant mental health disorders.** Conditions, such as depression, anxiety disorders, and abnormal personality traits cause and, in turn, are caused by sex addiction and complicate treatment (Carnes, 2000, p. 5-6).

Damaging Consequences

Sexual addiction gives birth to multiple adverse consequences (Sbraga & O'Donohue, 2003, pp. 13, 31). On the other hand, when addicts realize that sexual behavior causes damaging consequences, they may seek counseling. However, only a small percentage of addicts self-refer. Persuasion is more often at the hands of a spouse who delivers the message, "*If you don't get therapy; I am taking the children, and leaving.*"

An addict often hides egregious or embarrassing sexual behaviors. Conversely, an addict often seeks therapy to address socially acceptable symptoms like depressed mood, bulimia, stress, acute anxiety, and substance abuse. Although these symptoms are of concern, underlying romantic and sexually addictive life styles need to take precedent in therapy. One way for a therapist to uncover deeper sexual issues is to explore adverse consequences, that is, what is going wrong in client's life. Questions, which expose negative behaviors, serve to break through denial. Core addiction issues along with co-existing mental health deficiencies form two-thirds of the recovery journey. The other third is addressing shame (Becker, 2012b, p. 7).

Marriage and family. An addict may seek counseling because of a relational crisis. For example, if a woman becomes pregnant the family system will be in stress. Other stressors include loss of a job, divorce, discovery, or arrest.

When an addict's partner discovers previously unknown aberrant sexual behavior, a crisis of trust is at hand. Although the dictum, "*get help or else,*" is not the ideal motivation for seeking counseling, it is the most common reason for an addict to enter therapy. It also underscores that the family is a primary causality in sexual addiction. An addict often has difficulty understanding why he or she engages in aberrant sexual behavior. The partner of an addict also lacks understanding. For example, it is very difficult for a partner to understand how his or her spouse could engage in aberrant sexual behavior and, at the same time, pretend to be happily married. Likely, the innocent partner will experience significant trauma and stress upon learning of the spouse's aberrant sexual behavior (Becker, 2012b, p. 56).

Sexual addiction makes *love* with another person impossible. The addict is in love with self. The addict loses the ability to regard his or her partner as the most important person in his or her life. The innocent partner takes second place to the addict's requirement for sexual satisfaction. Even when an addict is addicted to sexual behavior with his/her partner, it is sex, not the partner, who the addict loves. A sexually addicted person cannot understand the meaning and the beauty of self-sacrificing love. The addict cannot put another person first when his or her sexual interest is always first. Thus, the addict manipulates the marriage relationship but does not honor it. Addiction blocks the capacity to experience true marital intimacy (Sbraga & O'Donohue, 2003, pp. 185-196).

The addict deludes self into believing that his or her sexual needs can be met outside the marriage, while at the same time, joining the partner in the marriage bed. Ultimately, such a rationalization leads to distancing between the partners. Both partners become lonely in the marriage because intimacy is lacking. Secrecy compounds delusion and the mask the addict wears to hide the addicted self.

Laaser (2006) added:

Even people who have sex only in their marriages can be addicted to sex if they are using it as an escape from the loneliness of their relationship (para. 9).

The family suffers since the spouse and children are not the addict's primary relational focus. Sex outside the home takes attention, time, and money away from the family. The addicted parent is often absent from the home or emotionally distant when with the family. The marital relationship is adversely affected because the addict is unable to engage in the intimacy of self-sacrificing love. Often the partners in such a relationship live separate lives under the same roof.

Other relationships are also in jeopardy. Because the addict withdraws and becomes isolated, relationships with parents, siblings, and friends often are affected.

Once his secrets are divulged, the male addict feels relief. After disclosure, he usually seeks forgiveness. He then wants to move on with his life and he expects his partner to follow. His thinking is badly distorted. Trust is shattered (Carnes, 2001b, pp. 126-128). It takes a considerable period of time, months, and even years to rebuild trust into a compromised relationship. Not only will the addict want to enter into counseling but also will the innocent partner. The family has been shaken to the quick and it will not heal overnight (Maltz, 2001, pp. 75-76).

A spouse may be relieved when she confirms her partner's addiction. Often the partner feels guilty when s/he suspects her spouse is not emotionally engaged in the marriage. When the truth is told, the innocent partner's mind is allayed to learn that his or her suspicions were valid.

If left unchecked, the addict who specializes in clandestine extramarital affairs may go through several marriages. Perhaps even sadder, if the innocent partner does not determine why s/he was attracted to a sex addict, the innocent partner is likely to repeat the same mistake (Becker, 2012b, p. 59).

Child in the family - trauma from abuse. A child is traumatized by physical, emotional, or sexual abuse. A young person is not emotionally prepared for adverse treatment (Ferree, 2010). For lack of a better defense mechanism, the child may bond to the deep wounds caused by trauma. The hole in the soul leads the child to develop coping behaviors. For a traumatized child, relief is an adaptive response of choice. Too often, it is sexual behavior (p. 129).

Sexual trauma confuses the psyche of a child. For example, exposure to pornography is bewildering. A child's normal existence does not involve viewing images of naked people performing sexual acts. It does not involve involuntary undressing of the child nor sexual touch. The child is traumatized by conflicting feelings. A child may be aroused by sex but, at the same time, he or she experiences trauma. A young child lacks an understanding of choice related to good and bad touch. However, the child instinctively knows that viewing pornography or sexual activity does not normally occur around the dining room table. Trauma is reinforced by the secrecy of the event or by the perpetrator's threat of harm if secrecy is broken. *If a child believes he or she consented to the abuse or if the child experienced sexual pleasure during the abuse, profound guilt and shame feelings usually follow* (Ferree, 2010, p. 129).

A child is not developmentally ready to accept the reality of the reproductive system let alone expose his or her body to the pleasure seeking of another person. Such premature awaking of sexual response is contrary to nature. The act of exposure for the child, and all children in similar circumstances, will remain a memory for a lifetime (Weiss, 1998, pp. 27-29).

While improper exposure to sex usually occurs between the ages of four and 12, it is possible for abuse to take place earlier than age four. However, a child younger than four does not have the vocabulary or mental maturity to formulate a story to which s/he can relate later in life. However, a child does experience disturbing feelings related to abuse, which occurred before age four. Abuse before age four can affect the child's emotional development (Maltz, 2001, p. 38).

Most sexual abuse is initiated by a person who is acquainted with the child. Estimates of perpetrators who knew their victim are between 80% and 95%. Confusion reigns in the mind of a child when sexually approached by a parent, stepparent, grandparent, sibling, coach, teacher, neighbor, or any trusted relative or family friend. Who can a child trust if s/he is not safe in the presence of a family member or family friend? (Steffens & Means, 2009. p. 227).

Even a teenager is a victim of age improper exposure when a differential of power is involved. For example, if the perpetrator is an older person whom the teen admires or a person from whom the teen craves attention, the youngster finds his/herself in an unbalanced relationship. In such cases, teenagers do not have the mental, emotional, and relational experience to exercise mature judgment. The perpetrator is in a power position over his or her victim (Ferree, 2010, p 128).

Humans respond favorably to attraction, attention, pleasure, touch, arousal, flattery, and even manipulation. Nature makes these conditions attractive, particularly to a young person. The human condition causes a young person, and some adults, to respond inappropriately. Subsequent to the submission to sexual activity, a victim often blames self because s/he may not realize that s/he is a victim of abuse. In this case, the victim accepts the blame, which belongs to the perpetrator (Ferree, 2010, p. 129).

Normalizing children's sexual trauma. Although parents may provide all of life's necessities: food, shelter, and clothing—dysfunctional parents are unable to nurture their child in order to form an emotionally whole and healthy son or daughter (Steffens & Means, 2009, pp. 226-228). They lack the parenting skills needed to enable their child to overcome the trauma of sexual abuse. Conversely, functional parents who are present for their abused child will enable the child to internalize that s/he was a victim of another person's immoral behavior and the child is not responsible for the abusive act. Minimizing the consequences of sexual abuse in a healthy way is called *normalization* (Becker, 2012b, pp. 34-35).

A functional relationship between a child and parents is critical to defuse the intensity of a sexual event. In normalization, the parents provide basic sex information to place what happened into context. The parents show affection and assure the child of the parents' desire to protect the child against any future event. An event normalized through parental love and understanding, is significantly diminished or even neutralized. In an ideal world, every child exposed to improper sex will have her/his event normalized.

A child needs to feels safe when telling parents about an event. Unfortunately, a child may fear adverse consequences of telling his or her parents. The child fears punishment or, at the least, made to feel guilty. In some cases, parents lack the parental skills needed to normalize the abuse. Unfortunately, normalization is the exception and does not reflect a typical parental response (Becker 2012b, pp. 34-35).

Sexual trauma and adulthood. The effect of childhood or teenage sexual trauma carries over into adult life in the form of sexual behavior. "Addiction in its various forms becomes a solution to the anxiety and stress of the trauma" (Carnes, 2003). Other behavioral consequences of exposure may include isolation, difficulty forming self-sacrificing relationships, and an unhealthy attitude toward other people's bodies (Trauma and Sex Addiction section, para 1).

The trauma history will most likely contribute to maintaining self-defeating belief systems and low self-esteem, resulting in poor decision-making and a lack of healthy relational skills. That combination, in turn, will work against their potential for recovery from anxiety and depression as well as their capacity to make healthier partner choices. (Black, 2014, para. 3)

Ferree (2010) captured the essence of sexual trauma by observing: "Like no other form of trauma, sexual abuse creates a wound in the soul. Remember, our sexuality is most akin to our spirituality, so harm in this area is especially damaging" (p. 129).

Carnes (1997b) explored trauma reactions in, *The Betrayal Bond: Breaking Free of Exploitative Relationships*. For example, he noted, "The starting point for all trauma survivors is a complete acceptance of betrayal" (p. 69).

Family history of addiction. Addiction is pervasive. "Forty million Americans ages 12 and older—or more than one in seven people have an addiction involving nicotine, alcohol or other drugs. This is more than the number of Americans with heart conditions (27 million), diabetes (26 million), or cancer (19 million)" (CASA, 2013, p.1). Parents, emotionally deprived as children, may suffer from alcoholism, drug or sex addiction, and gambling.

Carnes (2003) further reported:

[S]ex addicts tended to come from families where there were addicts of all kinds. For example, mothers (25%), fathers (38%), and siblings (46%) had significant alcohol problems. Mothers (18%), fathers (38%), and siblings (50%) had similar problems with sexual acting out. Parallel patterns existed with eating disorders, pathological gambling, and compulsive work. Only 13% of sex addicts reported coming from families with no addictions (p. 1).

Addiction is often multi-generational. Understanding the dynamics of one's family of origin is enhanced by completing a reasonably simple *genogram* (Introduction to the Genogram, 2014, p. 1). A genogram displays family relationships, hereditary patterns, and psychological factors that shape relationships. It serves to identify repetitive patterns across generational lines (Bradshaw, 1998 p. 62). Addiction affects the family's functional structure, and as one might expect, the attributes of a dysfunctional family flow from one generation to the next. Changing the family trauma response requires *interdicting* history.

Shame is also multi-generational. Shame fosters aberrant sexual behaviors and kills marriages. Further, shame-based people have a tendency to marry other shame-based people. Bradshaw (2005) expanded on shame-based couples:

As each member of a couple carries the shame from his or her own family system, their marriage will be grounded in their shame-core. Shame-based couples maintain a lack of intimacy through poor communication, nonproductive circular fighting, games, manipulation, vying for control, withdrawal, blaming, and confluence. (pp. 45-46)

All too often, an addict's children inherit the curse. The first factor is the inability of the dysfunctional adult generation to provide emotional nurturing to their children (Carnes, 2001b, p. 44). If the lack of emotional nurturing is compounded by untimely exposure to sexual behavior or material, the stage is now set for their prodigy to become sexually addicted (Campling, Corley, Katehakis, Valenti-Anderson, & Weedn, 2012, pp. 156-159).

Legal. Adverse legal consequences due to out-of-control sexual behavior include separation and divorce, child custody disputes, restraining orders, and prosecution for criminal activity (Sbraga & O'Donohue, 2003). In addition to the addiction, a therapeutic concern for mental health providers is the health of the marriage. Although marriages can survive bankruptcy or even prison, the dissolution of the marriage is a breakdown in the fundamental structure of society (pp. 13, 31).

The addict who solicits or trades child pornography is almost guaranteed to have legal consequences. Such behaviors as soliciting a child for sex or molesting a child will result in long prison terms.

Legal consequences also result when an addict engages in voyeurism, exhibitionism, or frotteurism. Sexual harassment in the workplace may result in legal or occupational difficulties (Sbraga & O'Donohue, 2003, pp. 13, 31).

Financial. Money spent on pay-for-view pornography, sex books and videos, phone sex, massage parlors, provocative clothing, prostitution, escort, stripper, possible legal fees and such, drain the family resources. An addict, blinded by the call of sex, takes financial risks beyond reason.

Susan's Story. I had a good job but I was addicted to phone sex and ran-up a debt of $158,000.00 over several years. I am an attorney and I had access to my client's accounts. I began to borrow money from trust accounts and I padded my expense account. I also cheated on my tax returns and filed false claims. Eventually I was caught and I lost my license to practice. To pay back my clients from whom I had misappropriated money, I had to sell the family home and liquidate my retirement account. My addiction cost the family my livelihood, family trust, and deprived my children of a college education at a school of their choice.

Social. Preoccupation with sex often precludes interest in a social life. The addict's focus turns inward.

Jack's story. I am a successful insurance broker and I am addicted to pornography. I spend several hours a day or evening searching the Internet for images of women who meet my concept of beauty. I would prefer to play with my computer rather than go out to dinner with friends or family. My wife knows about my addiction. She fears I would leave her if she made a big deal over my behavior. We have no social friends and we only rarely visited with either of our parents.

Occupational. Both males and females experience adverse occupational consequences but females experience economic loss earlier than males and to a greater degree (Ferree, 2010, p. 76).

An addict may garner trouble at work in several ways. One is using an employer-provided computer to search for pornography. Pornography has become a problem in the workplace. "Seventy percent of Internet pornography traffic occurs between 9:00 A.M. and 5:00 P.M. Seventy-two percent of companies that have addressed Internet misuse reported that 69 % of those cases were pornography related" (Carnes, 2003, Background section, para.1).

Today, more corporations have a zero-tolerance policy when an employee is caught using the company-provided computer for sexual behavior. Not only are the company's resources improperly depleted but also time spent searching for sexually gratifying material takes away from productivity. Leading software publishers estimated that $83 billion a year was lost in lower productivity by American companies (Carnes 2003). An employee may also be tardy or absent from work because of late night Internet searches for pornography. Because of sexual thinking and fantasy, the employee's quality of work may be adversely affected. The addict may also have strained work relationships (Background section, para.1).

Another pitfall in the workplace is related to sexual harassment or stalking.

Mike's story. I viewed pornography on my computer at work. Although I knew others had been fired because of improper use of the company-supplied computers, I thought my uncle, the owner of the company, would never fire me. I was wrong. My fellow workers felt I sexually harassed them by leaving provocative images on my computer screen when I was away from my desk. I lost a high paying position because I exposed others to porn. I also held a self-serving false belief that my uncle would not fire me.

Loss of reputation and self-respect. Mike was well known in his field. Once he lost his job, word spread through his professional community as to why. Mike found it difficult to convince other potential employers that he would be worthy of hire.

The loss of reputation can be one of the most devastating effects of sex addiction.

Bob's story. I was a respected senior-level employee at a large accounting firm. When my company discovered my porn collection on my work computer, I was excused from my position. For a year, I did not seek new employment because I feared a potential new employer would find out why I lost my prestigious job. My fear paralyzed my own self-respect and recovery.

Emotional and mental health. *Persistent Depressive Disorder, Dysthymia* is a mental health condition associated with sex addiction. Another name for Dysthymia is low-grade depressed mood (APA, 2013). Low-grade depression often begins in childhood. A child emotionally abandoned by one or both parents lacks a healthy sense of self-worth. The young person begins to use sexual stimulation to provide the feelings that an otherwise normal life would provide. As a result, the child withdraws and begins to live in his or her doldrums. As long as his or her depressed moods continue, s/he will medicate his or her adverse feelings.

For a woman, stress from hiding her sexually addictive life and falsely living the appearance of a socially responsible person, creates a propensity to become a victim of mental disorders. For a woman, depressed mood and acting out become a self-fulfilling emotional prophesy. "No one will love me or meet my needs" (Ferree, 2010, pp. 77, 149).

"Women are two or three times more likely to develop dysthymia than are men" (Campling, Corley, Ferree, & Hudson, 2012, p. 80; Duckworth, 2009, p. 1). Low-grade depressed mood is a co-existing deficiency.

Other possible co-existing deficiencies are many. They include anxiety, paranoia, loneliness, and hopelessness. The addict may also experience feelings of self-loathing, lack of self-esteem, profound shame, overwhelming stress, harmful family conflict, and possible ideation of suicide. Goodman (1998) added, "Sexual addiction can occur in the context of other psychiatric disorders including manic-depressive conditions, schizophrenia, personality disorders, and substance dependence" (p. 2).

During the recovery journey, the therapist will motivate the addict to seek uplifting activities and relationships to preclude co-existing deficiencies from adversely affecting recovery.

Physical health. Depending on the nature of the addict's sexual behaviors, health consequences can be life damaging. Common health issues include exhaustion, sleep and eating disorders, ulcers, high blood pressure, depression, high anxiety, cervical cancer, or injury due to excessive or violent sexual activity. "In fact, two-thirds of sex addicts suffer from a sleep disorder—usually insomnia and 38 % have an eating disorder" (Carnes, 2001b, p. 199).

Out-of-control sexual activity can result in pregnancy, HIV infection, genital herpes, syphilis, gonorrhea, and other sexually transmitted diseases (STDs). Excessive masturbation or intercourse can lead to penile, clitoris, or vaginal damage. Anal sex can lead to rectal tearing. Addictive sadomasochistic sex can lead to physical body damage (Ferree et al., 2012, pp. 37-38).

Spiritual heath. On a deeper level, an addict knows that aberrant behavior does not support spiritual health. During the third phase of the sex addiction cycle (See Exercise Six), typically the addict seeks forgiveness. Although the addict believes his or her promise to end acting-out behavior, his or her brain does not. Acting out is compulsive. When he or she continues to act out, the addict feels hypercritical of self and not worthy of love. The soul hardens and the addict sinks into ever-increasing layers of lies to justify the continuation of addictive behavior. Spiritual despair may be the consequence (McDaniel et al., 2012, pp. 38-39).

PART TWO: CONDITIONS WHICH FOSTER SEXUAL ADDICTION

This part presents four
models which provide examples of
how a person may become sexually addicted.

CHAPTER THREE: ROADS TO SEXUAL ADDICTION - FOUR MODELS

This chapter explores alternative roads that lead to sexual addiction. Although the route to sex addiction takes many forms, from clinical experience the featured models are the most prevalent (Becker 2012b, pp. 20-33).

Model One

Exposure to sexual behavior or material during childhood, together with family environment that lacked emotional nurturing, creates a psyche-gap that the child fills with sexual activity similar to that which the child experienced during his or her initial exposure to a sexual stimulus (Ferree, 2010, pp. 126-129).

Model Two

Absence exposure to healthy sexuality during childhood is followed by an overwhelming exposure to sexual behavior during late teen or early adult years. Once exposed the young adult compulsively seeks sexual expression.

Model Three

Multiple attempts to form a sexual relationship with another person fail. Unsuccessful advances made by the addict during late teen or early adult years are followed by an opportunity to control his or her sexual environment by paying for sex. In this model, arousal is dependent on gaining control of others. An addict shuns human attachment for fear of rejection or feelings of inadequacy.

Model Four

Mental illness, use of certain medications, substance abuse, and PTSD may trigger emotional and psychological pain that the victim soothes through sexual stimulation.

Which Model?

Model One is the primary road that leads to sexual addiction. For this reason, much of the information provided will relate to model one.

An addict often asks the question, "Why me, why did I become a sexually addicted person?" No man or woman asked to be a sex addict. Most were exposed to family of origin deficiencies and age inappropriate sex that led to sexual addiction. When a child begins to repeat sexual practices, the child does not have an understanding of the consequences nor is the child sufficiently mature to apply a moral compass to guide such behavior.

The attributes associated with model one follow. Some attributes are applicable to more than one model but presented once.

Primary Road that Leads to Sexual Addiction- Model One

Upon entering therapy, an addict has little or no knowledge as to the origin of his or her sexual addiction. However, when an addict begins to understand how early *sexual exposure* and living in a *dysfunctional family* contributed to his or her sexual addiction, the addict is empowered with an important new perspective: "I was exposed to conditions that foretold of sexual addiction at a time when I was unable to understand what was happening. Later in life, I accepted aberrant sexual behavior as our own. It is now time for me to do something about my sexual addiction?"

Human sexuality begins early in life and nature intends it to evolve as a child ages. It is normal for a young child to touch his or her genitals. It is *not normal* for a person other than a loving caregiver to touch a child and only then to keep the child clean or attend to any medical condition. A young child instinctively senses the difference between types of touch. Even so, it is prudent to teach a child the meaning of good and bad touch (Ferree, 2010, p. 129).

The majority of children engage in some form of sex play during prepubescent years. Sex play among children of the same age and with equal power in the relationship does not lead to sexual addiction. In fact, a causal exposure among peers can be therapeutic when it takes the mystery out of body parts (Bradshaw, 2005, p. 75).

Sexual abuse. Inappropriate exposure to sex may lead to sexual addiction. For example, when an older person exposes a seven-year-old to pornography, an abusive event has occurred. When a person, at least five years older, engages a child in physical sexual behavior, another abusive event has occurred. A prepubescent child is not ready for the emotions that s/he feels when exposed.

Carnes' (1998) found ...such exposure is sexual abuse. As children, addicts reported experiencing physical abuse (72%), sexual abuse (81%), and emotional abuse (97%). Furthermore, the more sexually and physically abused the respondents were as children, the more addictions they had as adults. Emotional abuse was a significant factor in addicts who abused children themselves. (p. 1)

Catalytic event. When a child is sexually stimulated for the first time, the child instinctively knows it is not *normal*. The first such stimulation is a *catalytic event* (Carnes, 1994, p. 56). A catalyst provokes or speeds a significant change. Thus, a catalytic event is a potential change agent in the child's future because, for many, it leads to sex addiction. Many children experience a catalytic event simply because of the high number of children who are sexual abused. At the time a child experiences a catalytic event, the capacity to make a choice is absent. The child is not responsible for the event. When a child is abused, it is about the abuser's distorted sexuality and not the child's.

Bradshaw (2005, p. 71) says that when sexually abused, a child has been abandoned by those in his or life who were ordained to shield the child from profound evil. Carnes (1992) includes childhood *abandonment* as a catalyst, which leads to asexual addiction (p. 77).

An abused child may mentally block a traumatic event. Due to the trauma associated with a catalytic event, the child may not initially recall the event. It may take time to put the pieces of his or her childhood sexual puzzle together. Additional memories may surface during recovery (Maltz, 2001, pp. 44-45).

A catalytic event involves a differential in power. Normally, sex play between children of the same age is not a catalytic event unless a notable difference in *maturity* exists between the children or sexual *knowledge* of one of the children is significantly advanced over that of the other children.

Those who relate to model one and two and to a lesser degree, model three likely have experienced a catalytic event. It is rare for those who relate to model four to experience such an event. However, exceptions abound to almost any concrete statement made when dealing with human beings.

Arousal. The normal consequence of sexual stimulation is *arousal* (Carnes, 2001b, pp. 244-245). Babies engage in self-stimulation. Doing so is part of normal self-discovery and learning response to touch.

A child's memory of his or her catalytic event is long lasting. One reason is *intensity*. When the acts of another person stimulate a child, the intensity of the arousal is significantly greater than normal self-stimulation. The brain encodes the intensity of the arousal feelings. The child is flooded with new feelings, often mixed. The specific sexual activity in which the addict engages as an adult often mirrors the sexual stimulus first experienced in childhood. For example, a child introduced to pornography may continue to view pornography as an adult (Becker, 2012b, pp. 34-35).

Stimulating and traumatic. A child's catalytic event is *stimulating* but also *traumatic*. The child feels guilty for engaging in an activity that should not have happened. A nearly universal response of a child is to blame self. Adverse feelings about self are reinforced if the child continues the behavior. Paradoxically, the child may engage in masturbation to calm trauma feelings associated with sexual abuse. Although masturbation can be a normal part of self-discovery, a traumatized child uses it to relieve emotional ache (Carnes, 1997b, p. 9). Trauma also influences the emotional development of a teenager. For example, trauma promotes isolation, which may become the foundation for a *loaner* or *nerd* personality traits (Ferree, et al., 2012, pp. 52-54).

A child with no understanding of consequences often replicates the sexual behavior first experienced during his or her catalytic event. If a child habitually repeats sexual stimulation, compulsivity has begun. Sex begins to dominate the maturing child's behavior. In teenage years, the child may branch-out to other forms of sexual stimulation and may engage in untimely intercourse and other sexual activities (Becker, 2012b, p. 36).

A healthy relationship rarely forms between a child and the person with whom s/he had a sexual experience. Offenders are just a means to an end.

Physical and emotional abuse. Physical and emotional abuse is traumatic in the life of a child. For example, when beatings or other pain-causing forms of punishment are frequent occurrences, fear enters the life of a child.

Black (2014) described the impact of trauma:

To live with chronic fear during the vulnerable childhood and adolescence years, when one is developing beliefs about oneself and the world at large, is traumatic to emotional, psychological and spiritual development. (Familial section, para.2)

Shame. "Addiction and obsessive disorders are symptoms of being emotionally abandoned and shamed in childhood" (Bradshaw 1988, p. 70). "The *shame* scar is not easily removed" (Hastings, 1998, pp. 15-21). In adverse circumstances, it is developmentally consistent for a young child, to believe, "*I am bad.*" Shame tells the child that s/he is *defective.* Shame tells the child that s/he does not deserve to be loved (Bradshaw, 1988, p. 10). These are horrible beliefs for anybody but particularly for a child. These feelings stay with the child and eventually become adult feelings.

Shame and guilt are not the same. A person feels guilty when s/he has done something wrong. Feelings of guilt emanate from one's conscience and can lead to changed behavior. Bradshaw (1988) stated, "Guilt says, I've made a mistake, shame says, I am a mistake. *Guilt* says, what I did was not good; shame says, I am no good. It makes a profound difference" (p. 2).

Healing from shame begins with the recognition that one is giving too much *power* to shame—it rules the life of the addict. The power needs to be exposed and mitigated. Secrets and isolation keep shame in power. Potter-Efrom, et al., (1989) addressed shame-based secrets and isolation:

Isolation is a common reaction to feelings of shame. The more deeply a person is shamed, the more she will tend to hide her thoughts, feelings, and actions from others. Shamed people keep vast areas of their lives secret because they believe that others would scorn them if others knew who they really were. Unfortunately, shame prospers in secrecy. By concealing her [or his] identity, the person who is deeply shamed only convinces herself [or his] more that she [he] is fundamentally defective. (pp. 132-133)

Disclosure pierces the veil of shame. Disclosure is part of a 12-step program, as well as group and individual therapy. Full disclosure supports rigorous honesty in healing the marriage relationship. One is freed from shame when his or her addiction secrets are exposed to the light of day (Carnes, S 2011, pp. 35-39).

Dysfunctional Family

Carnes (1991) found that the majority of sex addicts were raised in *rigid, authoritarian, and disengaged* families. These are families in which all issues and problems are black and white. Little is negotiable and only one-way to do things. Success in the family means doing what the parents want to such an extent that children give up being who they are. Normal childhood development does not happen (p. 4). A rigid family environment does not meet the child's need for affirming expressions of love, attention, and healthy touch that all children need. (Ferree, 2010, p. 116)

A sex addict who comes from dysfunctional families is more likely than a non-sex addict to have been abused (Herkov, 2006, para. 7). For the future addict a dysfunctional family has multiple contributing elements. **They are:**

Lack of attachment. The first is lack of *attachment* during pre-verbal, pre-logic *infancy*. Nature intends that intimate bonding take place between a mother and her child. Bonding occurs when an infant is held, rocked, cooed, through eye contact, and nurturing touch, and a myriad of other loving expressions that begin at the time of a child's birth and continue through the child's developmental years. If the child did not experience appropriate attachment, his or her physical and emotional development may be delayed or compromised. A child who did not experience appropriate bonding as an infant may later look to other sources for comfort, for example, by sexual touch to compensate for the lack of nurturing touch. The adult who experienced poor attachment as an infant will either seek or disdain human relationships—often to the extremes (Ferree, et al., 2012, pp. 47-49).

The lack of attachment during infancy affects the adult's deregulated system and leads to chronic depressed mood, persistent anxiety, and a numbed state. As a child, a woman who experienced a lack of attachment is prone to soothe herself with drugs, alcohol, and compulsive sex and other behaviors (Katehakis, 2012, p. 188).

Parental abandonment. Second, an element found in nearly all dysfunctional families is abandonment. It happens when parents are not attuned to their child's need for emotional nurturing. The parents are not present in a way that leads their child to express joy in his or her life. An emotionally abandoned child feels distanced from his or her parents. It is painful to the child, even more painful and damaging than physical abuse. A child finds him or herself marooned on an island of life, with no rescue in sight. "Females raised in this environment crave to be held as they would have been in a healthy family. Mother hunger is at the core for sex and love addicts" (Ferree, 2010 p. 54).

Physical abandonment can result from parental separation, divorce, military obligations, work-related assignments, or a choice to be absent from the family. Some forms of separation are laudatory, such as military service. Laudatory or not, a child may suffer angst from the lack of parental presence and emotional support (Steffens & Means, 2005, p. 228).

Sexual abandonment is often a reality. As in model two, rigid families choose not to address anything sexual. When a parent is sexually addicted, discussion of sex awakens his or her feelings of shame. As such, shame *rules out* even a healthy discussion of body-related matters. A female child may reach puberty without the remote expectation of menses. A male child may be surprised and upset by wet night clothing caused by nocturnal emission. Unfortunately, when parents do not fulfill their obligation to prepare their child for their maturing bodies, a child will seek answers elsewhere—and open themselves to wrong answers (Ferree, 2010, pp. 136-137).

Lack of emotional nurturing. Third, almost every sexually addicted adult suffered from a lack of emotional nurturing at the hands of a parent(s). A child looks to his or her parents for support including education, sustenance and shelter, emotional comfort, correction, and spiritual indoctrination, to name a few. When emotional nurturing is lacking, the child withdraws from parents, siblings, and peers and engages in behaviors hidden from other members of the family (McDaniel et al., 2012, p. 39; Ferree et al., 2012, p. 52). The child learns to respond only to conditional love. For example, parental love is conditioned on academic or athletic performance

Too often, the father in the family lacks the ability to nurturer his child. A consequence of a strained or nonexistent relationship between a child and father is toxic and plays a pivotal role in contributing to future addiction. If emotional nurturing is lacking, a state of abandonment is the result. Sex addicts are survivors of abandonment (Ferree 2010, p. 133).

Some fathers are workaholics or find reasons to spend little time at home. A rigid father rarely participates in homework exercises or other school activities except to be critical. The father's tendency to criticize his child is the norm.

When a child's father is, absent from the home due to a failed marriage or separation, the child's hole in the psyche is even more painful. The child believes, "It is my fault that my dad left our family, if only…."

Bradshaw (1988) explained:

For example, if the parents are abusive and hurt the child through physical, sexual, emotional or mental pain, the child will assume the blame, make himself bad, in order to keep the all-powerful protection against the terrors of night. For a child at this stage to realize the inadequacies of parents would produce unbearable anxiety. (p. 10)

Clinical experience suggests that the *severity* of the consequences related to the lack of attachment and/or abandonment is age related. The younger the child when s/he experiences emotional abandonment, the greater the consequences. In addition, the severity of the exposure to sexual material or conduct affects the prognosis for recovery. The greater the severity of childhood sexual trauma, the lower is the expectation for recovery.

Destructive messages. Fourth, destructive parental messages are the hallmark of dysfunctional families. It is understandable that girls or boys, subjected to ego damaging messages, are unable to talk to their parents about sexual abuse or anything intimate. In fact, destructive messages form a relationship barrier that leads a child to isolate further from his or her family. Some common messages sent by dysfunctional parents are:

- It is not safe to express your feelings.

- We will love you only if you do well in school or sports.

- You need to fix dinner and take care of your siblings—there is no time for play around here.

- You are a failure!

- You are just a girl, what do you know?

- Your opinion doesn't count in this house. I will tell you what to think!

- You need to be the man of the house.

- A "B" on your report card is not good enough. You can do better.

- You will never measure up to our expectations.

- I will give you something to cry about.

- You are bad just like your mother/father.

- You couldn't possibly amount to anything.

- Children are to be seen, not heard.

- Why can't you be like your older siblings?

Each statement is harsh and discouraging. Disapproving *messages* are toxic to both girls and boys. Girls, because of their relationship orientation, may rebel or engage in destructive attention-generating behaviors such as cutting, promiscuous sex, alcohol, and drug consumption, avoidance, and binge/purge cycles. *Anorexia* is a frequent companion of sexually addicted females (Carnes, 1997a, pp. 59-60). Males tend to disengage from their family; stay away from their homes; and use gangs, alcohol, drugs, promiscuous sex, and sports to defuse their distress (Bradshaw, 2005, p. 27).

Richard's story. Every time I brought home a report card, my father would chastise me about the C that could have been a B, and the B that could have been an A. My father never addressed the improvements I made from my last report card, only the grades that needed improvement. I concluded it was a no win game. The same scenario was repeated each report period through college. One semester I received all A's except for one B. My father focused on the B. In graduate school, I earned an all A semester. My father looked at the transcript, put it down, and walked away without saying a word.

Many years later, I talked to my adult son, Leo, about his memories of growing up. Leo said he had many good memories but he really did not like how I always focused on what could be improved in school rather than what he had achieved. I was stunned. I realized I repeated my father's message—the message that hurt me deeply.

How did it happen?

Richard's father sent several destructive messages: "Your effort is not good enough, there is always room for improvement, and I will love you more if you get all As." The messages were packed away in Richard's adult bags. His baggage from childhood was never unpacked. Unless Leo unpacks the baggage handed to him by Richard, he is likely to pass the same message, the same baggage, onto his children.

Behavior, messages, and attitudes flow from one generation to the next unless someone in the chain makes the effort to break the cycle.

Family rules. Fifth, *dysfunctional* families have rules controlling behavior. For example, an internal rule may relate to how the family regards dad when he arrives home from work. Other family rules include the content of conversation at the dinner table, mandatory attendance at church, and who gets the last piece of desert. *Rules* related to acceptable school grades, talking back to parents, or a mandatory curfew are more pointed. Rigid families harshly enforce rules related to bad behavior. Such rules are harmful to creativity and emotional development of a child (Ferree, 2010, pp. 113-114).

A primary rule is *don't talk*! For example, discussion of sex, Uncle Harry's drinking problem, politics, or religion, is taboo. The, *don't talk rule,* is toxic when a child becomes fearful of expressing his or her needs, opinions, or asking questions (Ferree, 2010, pp. 105-106).

Another toxic rule is, *don't feel.* For example, expressing hurt feelings, outward anger, or crying are unacceptable. Some rules become family traits. For example, a family may engrain habits to blame others or to gossip about relatives and neighbors. The message a child internalizes is, to feel safe "I must hide my feelings and my behavior must conform to the family norm" (Ferree, 2010, pp. 106-107).

When a family does not talk or feel it substitutes a pain avoidant way of coping. For example, when questioned, mother answers, "your father isn't grumpy when he comes home from work—it's all in your head, or Uncle Harry is not an alcoholic, he is just a heavy drinker, or teachers are always right." When parents deny reality, the child doubts what s/he knows and feels devalued (Ferree, 2010, p. 108).

An addict, raised in a rigid and disengaged family, finds it difficult even to discuss family rules. The family does not debate the merits of each rule; the dominant parent sets the family rules (Becker, 2012b, p. 69).

Demeaning parental messages form the basis for a person's rules of life. If rules taught to a child are discouraging, adult rules will likewise be discouraging. Family rules are often unarticulated. However, rules are standards by which family members and others are expected to obey. The young child may not be aware of a rule until it is broken. The child is frustrated when the offending rule is only expressed by inference.

The first rule on the family list is mom and/or dad is always right. Dysfunctional family rules serve to stifle discussion and preclude healthy parental models (Ferree, 2010, pp. 104-109.

Sean's story. I carry many rules around in my head. I believe that we must have order. I have a real thing about shopping carts left around parking lots. All shopping carts must be returned to their proper place. One day I drove into a grocery store parking lot and I observed a patron empty his cart and abandon it in the parking space to which I was heading. I stopped my truck right in the middle of the parking lot, and preceded to lambaste the poor fellow. In retrospect, I think my anger was out of proportion. He had it coming, didn't he? I wonder why this rule is so important to me.

Sean harbors many other rules including those he uses to set boundaries for his own sexual behavior. His rules are judgmental and include his prejudices. Others do not know Sean's rules but, paradoxically, he expects others to obey them. It is not difficult to see that Sean is an angry man—people constantly violate his rules. How could they not? Sean relieves his anger by masturbating—even though refraining from masturbation is one of his own rules.

A rule-based family and/or the family *religion* may impair a spiritual connection to God. When a child is taught that God is all-loving, the adult's relationship with God is based on love. However, if children view their earthly father as punishing, likely they will view God as punishing. Rule-based religions attract rule-based people (Becker, 2012b, pp. 111-114).

Isolation in the family. A feeling of not belonging is a consequence of growing up in a family structure in which a child is not valued for being him or herself. When a child shares self, needs, feelings, dreams, and non-conforming thoughts, and is ridiculed, or even worse, ignored, the child learns to withdraw to avoid humiliation or verbal abuse. At the time of one's greatest need, the child does not inform his or her parents about a disturbing instance, such as, fondling by a babysitter. The survival mode quickly becomes isolation and loneliness (Becker, 2012b, pp. 34-35).

Carnes (2003) noted:

> Most sex addicts, however, come from families in which members are 'disengaged' from one another—there is little sharing or intimacy. Children develop few skills about sharing, being vulnerable, or risking anything about themselves. As a result, they learn to trust no one but themselves in such families. The further result is that self-delusion is then hard to break, and secrets become more potent than reality. The worst effect is that the children are unable to ask for help. (Characteristics section, para. 3)

Intimacy challenged. Addiction preludes a close marital relationship. It causes a man or woman to feel alone in their marriage (Becker, 2012b, p. 41). In the case of the male addict, his focus rarely includes meeting his partner's desire for intimacy. He associates intimacy with sex and is blind to the concept of non-sexual intimacy. Examples of non-sexual intimacy are taking a walk together and holding hands, watching a movie together, engaging in a loving discussion, going to the gym together, and sharing a pizza and (root) beer (See Exercise 23). A female addict withdraws from normal family activities as well as from intimacy with her partner, both sexually and non-sexually (Sbraga & O'Donohue, 2003, pp. 185-196).

Dual Images. A model one addict internalizes the concept of dual images. On one hand, the addict projects a positive image to the world: Look at me; "*I am a good person and an upstanding member of the community.*" The second image, carefully hidden says, "*I am a flawed person, a sex addict.*" The addict fears discovery of the second image and then the world would know. In reality, neither image is accurate. The good person image is too positive and the hidden image is too negative. The addict needs to seek congruency, that is, reconcile a person's public and private self, in the presentation of his or her personas. The congruent image says, "I am not bad; I am dealing with a bad problem. Bear with me while I work on my problem" (Becker 2010, pp. 40-41).

Congruent images defuse shame. The first step in a 12-step program addresses congruency by encouraging addicts to *tell it like it is*. In other words, *become vulnerable*. Doing so dispels shame by exposing embarrassing secrets to the light of day. Telling one's story also awakens long-hidden feelings. Recognizing feelings are new for addicts, comprise an essential component of recovery (Sbraga & O'Donohue, 2003, pp. 137-138; Weiss, 2000, pp. 7-20).

Ralph's story. My thinking is not always logical. When someone cuts me off in traffic, I hear in my head, 'You are not important and less worthy of the space on the road.' I just fume when I feel I am devalued.

Ralph's anger is not in proportion to the importance of the event. It is triggered by his childhood perception of being flawed. Becoming aware of his anger triggers, may enable Ralph to understand he has the choice to change his distorted thinking and perception of himself. He talked about his two faces. He said, "My first step in healing my *two faces* is to acknowledge that, in reality, my bad self is a fraud. Like other sincere people, I am on a journey. Bad is part of life, it is not who I am."

I was less angry this past week. I did not verbalize my anger but I was still angry. It will take time for me to become aware in the present moment of my underlying feelings of inadequacy before I react in anger.

Ralph's syllogism if grounded in positive thinking can help him to reject thinking based on childhood experiences.

Late Teen or Early Adulthood Onset - Model Two

Not every potential addict experienced age-inappropriate sex. For about 10 to 15 % (experience-based estimate) aberrant sexual behavior began during late teens or in early adulthood. In this scenario, the child resides in a home where anything sexual is never part of the family dialog. Parents shun sex education—as if sex did not exist. As such, the child enters the adult world with little or no understanding of reproduction or sex in general. Usually friends introduce the young adult to sex. The new discovery is like removing a cork from a vacuum bottle. The young adult inhales everything sexual and begins to make up for lost time. Frequently the teen or young adult begins to binge on sexual practices, which lead to addiction.

Rejection - Model Three

A young person may be shy or so socially inexperienced that any attempt to date during high school or early adulthood met with rejection. Anger and self-deprecation followed. To minimize feelings of rejection, the young person turns to paid sex where s/he is in control of the environment. Sexual activity may include living in a world of deviant sexual fantasy, exhibitionism, voyeurism, pornography, or cybersex. "A deviant sexual fantasy is anything imagined that, if acted out, could harm another person" (Sbraga & O'Donohue, 2003, p. 169).

In this model, the addict shuns normal human sexual contact for fear of rejection or feeling inadequate. Model three includes women who seek a relationship without commitment.

Impact of Mental Illness or Substance Abuse - Model Four

A small percentage of people become addicted because of a mental illness or a personality deficiency.

Aberrant sexual behavior can be a symptom of a brain lesion, a side effect of medication or a symptom of endocrine abnormality or sexual obsessions and compulsions. A syndrome that meets the diagnostic criteria for addiction can occur in the context of other psychiatric disorders, including manic-depressive conditions, schizophrenia, personality disorders, and substance dependence (Goodman, 1998, p. 2).

Sexual compulsivity may be a factor in bipolar or borderline conditions, as well as with alcohol and drug use (Carnes, 2000). Other co-addictions may include eating and sleep disorders, gambling, gastrointestinal stress (somatic symptoms), Post-Traumatic Stress

Disorder (*PTSD*), and anxiety. Co-existing disorders are addressed at the time of assessment for sexual addiction. A characteristic of PTSD is engaging in high-risk behavior (p. 11).

Dave's story. At age 20, I joined the Marines and assigned to combat duty in Afghanistan. I watched as my best friend's body was blown apart after he stepped on an IED. The place where he stepped was near where I had just stepped. I felt guilty and sad I survived but my friend did not. I experienced other traumatic events that plagued my mind.

After a year, I returned home. I found I could not sleep. I frequently awoke in a panic, needed to change my soaked nightwear, and lost considerable weight. The military diagnosed my symptoms as acute PTSD.

Before serving in the military, Dave occasionally viewed adult heterosexual pornography but he said his desire was not compelling and occurred infrequently. Upon returning home, to relieve his PTSD symptoms, Dave found himself surfing the net for provocative sexual images. He stumbled onto teenage sensual images and his viewing of online pornography became a multi-hour daily event. He now faces court charges for having downloaded and sharing child pornography. Without having experienced trauma leading to PTSD, Dave would not have become sexually addicted.

PART THREE: THE ADDICT'S BOND TO SEXUAL ADDICTION

Includes three chapters
that present conditions that
attach a person to sexual addiction.

CHAPTER FOUR: CONDITIONS WHICH BOND AN ADDICT TO SEXUAL ADDICTION

Life of the Sex Addict

Depression, anxiety, anger, brain indoctrination, sexual thinking and fantasy, denial, and shame, bind an addict to sexual addiction. Each condition warrants attention in a clinical setting.

Depression

Depressed mood is both a consequence of and contributes to sexual addiction. Treating depressed mood as a consequence of sexual addiction is part of ending aberrant sexual behavior (Becker, 2012b, pp. 73-77). Symptoms of depressed mood span a continuum from mild to severe. They are:

Bad hair day. A day when a healthy person feels mildly depressed. For most, feeling mildly depressed passes quickly.

Low grade depressed mood. DSM-V labels chronic low-grade depressed mood as Dysthymic Disorder (APA, 2013). To diagnose a person with *Dysthymia*, the depressed mood must exist for at least two years, during which the person experiences at least two of the following: poor appetite or overeating, insomnia, low energy or fatigue, low self-esteem, poor concentration, difficulty making decisions, or a feeling of hopelessness. Although the person is able to function, life rarely includes joy. In fact, because of the length of time an addict has lived in low-grade depressed mood, most cannot describe what it would be like to feel normal. The majority of sex addicts function consistently in *low-grade depressed mood* (pp. 168-169). See APPENDIX C for a DSM-V description of Dysthymic Disorder.

Full scale depressed mood. A person who suffers from full-scale depression barely functions. He or she has difficulty concentrating, eating, sleeping, and relating to others. Clinical experience posits that a sex addict is a survivor and rarely sinks to this level. Exceptions arises from stress-induced depressed mood due to divorce, legal actions, and discovery of transgressions, job loss, or child custody proceedings.

Day to day life for a sex addict does not include a gregarious outlook. Alternatively, the addict chooses sexual behavior to raise his or her mood above the level of low-grade depressed mood. Because the addict is chronically depressed, acting out is also chronic.

The addict, when contemplating acting out, rationalizes:

- I need this!

- My spouse and I live on separate planets.

- I cannot live without my fix.

- Life is a bear. I deserve to be happy occasionally.

- Who will know?

- I have tried to stop but I keep going back.

- I earned it!

- Oh, the hell with it, I am going for it!

When an addict no longer lives in low-level depressed mood, the propensity to act out diminishes (See Exercise Eight and 23).

Anxiety

Anxiety is a state of emotional discomfort, one in which a person finds it difficult to cope. An anxious person may be fearful that something bad is going to happen. A pervasive feeling of uneasiness, restlessness, difficulty concentrating, difficulty controlling worry, or apprehension is the norm (APA, 2013, p. 276).

The relationship between anxiety and unwanted sexual behavior is strong, as the narrative below will show.

A woman who forms superficial relationships with little or no attachment is prone to chronic anxiety. Such people live with a tenuous connection to reality.

Sexual anxiety. Visual stimulation may create significant sexual tension. Once an addict sees an attractive person or pornographic image, a response is triggered. It is different from just being aroused. A person who experiences sexual anxiety often has great difficulty concentrating, feels restless, and cannot perform normal daily functions. The anxiety affects work performance, family, and other life responsibilities. For the male, the most compelling symptom is tension in the genital area that does not initially include an erection. The tension is highly disturbing. It remains despite efforts to change thinking or activity (Becker, 2012b, p. 70).

Barry's story. During the warm months, co-eds dress, you know, very casually. Even in class, uncovered flesh distracts me. It is hard for me to concentrate. Heaven knows I want to stop, but I often come back to my room in a state of sexual tension. My whole body aches. I feel as if my genital muscles are spring loaded. I feel tense and ready to respond. I hate to fight the battle—to act out or not. It just seems I am unable to focus on other activities until I relieve these feelings.

Situational anxiety. A sexually addicted person often reacts to his or her environment. A particular situation will trigger a longing to act out, for example, a desire to make contact with a potential partner. S/he becomes tense, irritable, unable to think clearly, and obsessed with relieving his or her situational anxiety (Becker, 2012b, p. 71). Procrastination and situational anxiety are often linked.

Todd's story. My father was a doctor and my mother taught chemistry at the university. I was always exposed to books and our dinner table conversation was like a seminar—very high level conversation. By the time I was five, I had read several of Dad's *Hardy Boys* books. So that I could attend the best high school in town, my preschool, kindergarten, and elementary schools were picked by my parents based on academic excellence. They said going to the best schools would improve my chances of attending Harvard or Yale. From my earliest days, I knew anything less than a top performance in school was unacceptable.

I inherited my parents' intellect but I was prone to procrastination. In grade school and high school, procrastination never hurt me. I earned excellent grades. When I went to a top Ivy League school, I found I was competing with the cream of the crop—others who were equally bright. Unfortunately, I brought along my propensity to procrastinate. Consequently, I feared I might not complete my studies and fail to get top honors.

When I sat down to study each night, usually around midnight, my anxiety was intense. I found I could dispel my anxiety by relieving myself. After I masturbated, I could concentrate. If I did not act out, I was miserable. I never felt the desire to masturbate unless my anxiety was at its peak.

Todd habitually reacted to the situation created by procrastination. He taught his body to demand a physical release. As long as Todd continues to procrastinate, his masturbation will continue. To end his sexual behavior, Todd first has to understand why he procrastinates.

Chronic anxiety. Anxiety may become a way of life; some sufferers live in a constant state of unrest, uneasiness or feel apprehensive. Surviving each day is a formidable task (Becker, 2012b, p. 72).

Mack's story. My nickname, Mack, was a curse. I never felt like macho Mack. My dad began to call me Mack when I was young. He would say, 'where is my Mack truck?' I was not a Mack truck. I was Matthew! I grew up feeling as if life was going to hand me a bad deal. I constantly felt uneasy and apprehensive. I was sure, given the opportunity to succeed; I could pluck defeat out of the jaws of victory. Dad thought so too. He constantly told me how I disappointed him.

Benjamin, my brother, sexually abused me. The abuse continued throughout my grade school years. I lived in fear of Benjamin who told me I had the body and face of a pretty girl. Moreover, they called me Mack. I felt sad and angry. Why did I have fine features? Was it my fault Benjamin always found me when no one else was around? I was afraid to tell mom or dad. I was sure dad would tan my hide. To top it all, I began to stutter. Stuttering just seemed to make matters worse. School kids taunted me, 'Pretty boy—talk like a girl.' I felt ashamed and no good.

Life became even worse for me. Around age 10, I began to wet my bed at night. Dad really yelled at me when he learned I wet my bed. He called me a sissy. I had to hide my problem from him. I found a piece of plastic to cover my bed sheets. I awoke when I felt wet and my bed-wetting ended.

My problems continued in high school. I was a loner and would masturbate frequently, the way Benjamin had taught me. I dropped out of college after my first year. I found a job in a video store. I lost that job because I could not concentrate and was irritable. I came to work late because I had difficulty sleeping. Masturbation was the only fun I had.

Mack was diagnosed with a generalized anxiety disorder (APA, 2013). His unfortunate life experiences taught him not to trust himself or anyone else. He was very isolated in his anxiety. He would first have to address his childhood experiences and internalize that he was not a bad person—others had betrayed him. He had no choice in the events that shaped him. He would benefit from the guidance of a therapist to rethink his life perspective and to understand he is a person of worth who could make new choices as an adult. Both his anxiety and masturbation are chronic. Only after Mack is able to see outside the wall he built to protect himself from pain will he defuse his chronic anxiety (pp. 222-226).

Carnes (1991) described the effect of sexual abuse and the resulting anxiety:

Abuse and neglect deepen this distrust of others and further distort reality. Neglected children conclude they are not valuable. In addition, they live with a high level of anxiety because no one teaches them common life skills or provides for their basic needs. Children find ways to deaden the anxiety they inevitably feel, and they do so compulsively. For sex addicts, compulsive masturbation is a good example of an anxiety-reduction strategy. Parents can control food and alcohol, but it is difficult to stop a young person from masturbating. (p. 7)

Barry, Todd, and Mack all suffer from anxiety related to their sexual behavior. Sexual behavior as well as anxiety is addressed in therapy (See Exercise Nine).

Anger

Anger is beneficial or destructive based on how and why it is expressed. Anger at injustice is creditable. Anger expressed as a corrective tool, can encourage a child to understand the seriousness of poor behavior. A child may express anger as part of learning to express emotions. Anger used inappropriately can express contempt, disrespect, self-centeredness, or even cruelty.

Destructive anger often accompanies sexual addiction. Anger from childhood betrayals and abuse are expressed sexually in adulthood. Anger, an expression of power, restores or protects a sense of self. An addict compensates for low-ego strength by expressing anger through sexualized rage (Carnes 2001b, pp. 220-221).

> Anger adds intensity to the sexual experience and becomes a neurochemical escalator, just as fear does... [A]nger often lies at the core scenarios, stories, and beliefs embedded in the arousal template. Therefore, current sexual behavior can draw enormous energy from past wounds and experience. (Carnes, 2001b, p. 218)

An addict is angry with self for abusing sex; at parents who s/he perceived failed to provide emotional nurturing, at family members who were not present in times of stress or need, and at God for not answering prayers to *cure* his or her the addictive behavior.

Anger is a dominant trait for some female addicts (Ferree, 2010, p. 153). While angry at life and everyone in it, women are blind to the addiction nexus. Life's downside, relational dysfunction, lies, destructive core beliefs, failed trust, and relapse all have adverse connotations for the addict (Sbraga & O'Donohue, 2003). Each adverse condition may set the stage for bonding anger with eroticism. Sexual behavior compounded by anger is often irrational and may be expressed as rape (pp. 187-188).

The actualization of a woman's anger response is manifested in her over-reaction to daily events. Her anger usually masks deeper feelings of loneliness, emotional turmoil, and in particular, *fears*. A woman, more than a man, fears what will happen to her when she is unable to manage her out-of-control behavior. Fear expressed as anger strikes at the core of the female being (Ferree, 2010, p. 153). Her emotional stability is in jeopardy.

Anger and sex addiction relate to a man's damaged ego. When he makes irrational demands on his family, takes umbrage with others or, reacts with physical force, suggests his ego is challenged and his emotional balance is in crisis. Such behavior is common for a male sex addict. A man also expresses anger in a passive aggressive way. For example, when an ego damaged man fears he will not win an argument, he withdraws from the exchange. He reverts to criticism, belittling, bullying, foul language, and blaming others to control the outcome of an argument. His expression of anger is intended to win an argument without addressing the issue (Becker, 2012b, pp. 66-68).

Defective Self

Children raised in a rigid family believe that parents expect flawless behavior. As such, the child understands that parents place a high value on performance and the way to earn their love is to meet their expectations of perfection. The child is in a quandary because perfection is an impossible goal. As an adult, s/he wants the world to believe s/he is perfect but the wounded self knows perfect is just a front—inside, because of addiction; s/he knows s/he is defective. When the mask of perfection is pierced, s/he fears that the defective self will be exposed for all to see. S/he fears being devalued (Sbraga & O'Donohue, 2004, pp. 34-35).

When the addict thinks that another person may expose his or her defective self, the natural reaction is fear.

Mary's story. Let's face it, I am not likely to walk up to each new person I meet and say, 'Hi I'm Mary, I have sex every chance I get.' In fact, I will likely call my problem by any socially acceptable name—stress, anxiety, depression, anger, not being loved, a relationship problem—anything but sexual behavior. I have a difficult time admitting, I can't control my sexual behavior, even though I have tried many times. If I share with my family, or friends, that sexual activity has a grasp on my life, I expect they will reject or abandon me. I fear my world may collapse if I am exposed. I go to great length to display my good self.

Mary's feeling of being a defective human began after a neighbor boy molested her. She felt it was her fault because she let him do it. She believed she was a bad person because she enjoyed his stimulating touch. Mary's reaction was to isolate her bad self and to build a mental barricade behind which she hid. She never told her parents about the sexual abuse she experienced because she feared their response. She internalizes her fear as anger.

In therapy, Mary learned that her thinking was distorted. It was not her fault she was abused nor was she bad. A critical recovery task is to explore and discard inaccurate judgments. She was far from flawed. She was pleasantly surprised that her friends applauded her choice to enter therapy.

Denial

A common expression of denial is to believe no problem exists. When the stakes are high, it is not easy to accept reality. Doing so means the addict has to accept that sexual behavior is not providing an acceptable life style. It often takes a significant event such as discovery, an arrest, losing a job, or a marital separation before the addict begins to comprehend reality (Carnes, 2001a, p. 17).

In a group program, Josh said to David, "Pornography doesn't hurt anyone." David replied, "Do you really believe that? Do you really believe that sex with yourself doesn't harm the marriage relationship?" Yet, just a few sessions back, David had tried to convince the group that masturbation was okay because every man does it. Denial has many faces.

An addict may deny the need to end acting-out behavior. In therapy, his or her response is some form of, "How can I have my cake and eat it too?" (Carnes, 2001a, pp. 15-16). An addict has an incredible ability to create myths and lies to justify sexual behavior. Perhaps, the greatest reflection of denial is the addict's failure to comprehend the pain that aberrant sexual behavior causes not only to self, but also to family, and, if applicable, his or her victims (Becker, 2012b, p. 8).

For the most part, a man or woman in denial will believe:

- I can handle this.

- It is not so bad.

- I can stop it whenever I want—just not right now.

- No therapist will understand my problems.

- If I thought, I was hurting somebody I would do something about it.

Society exploits sex in the movies, on television, Internet, and even at the Super Bowl. Yet, when a man or woman admits to an out-of-control sexual appetite, that same society castigates him or her. Society seems to say, it is okay for a man or woman to go into a candy store but if we catch them eating any of the goodies they will be ostracized, sued, or incarcerated. In this environment, it is reasonable for a man or woman to deny their weakness.

Because denial is common early in treatment, the recovery journey begins with exposing lies and rationalizations to the light of day. Twelve-step programs and group therapy encourage the addict to come to terms with reality. In the fourth step of the 12-step program, the addict develops a *searching and fearless moral inventory*, that is, a complete list of traits and behaviors that betrayed the addict's moral values. Participants are encouraged to apply *rigorous honesty* to compiling a sexual inventory. If done in the spirit of the program, stripping denial of its power is therapeutic.

Shame

Shame fuels a compulsive lifestyle. It contributes to low-ego strength. To feel better, acting out sexually is a form of self-medication. Unfortunately, sexual good feelings are quickly followed by the return of shame (Carnes, 2001, pp. 28-33). Bradshaw (1988) said it this way:

Shame is like a hole in the cup of our soul. Shame fuels compulsivity, and compulsivity is the black plague of our time. We are driven. We want more money, more sex, more food, more booze, more drugs, more adrenalin rushes, more entertainment, more possessions, and more ecstasy. Like an unending pregnancy, we never reach fruition. (pp. 4-5)

A man in a group program said he prayed for 25 years for relief from his addiction. Because of his shame, he did nothing other than pray. He expected God to work a miracle, while he sat back and waited. He said, "It never seemed that God was listening." Then one day, quite contrary to his expectation, God's answer to his prayer was, he was caught. The potential consequence, although always possible, was now clear, and the addict was too late to avoid it. He now has to face his shame.

Addicts believe other addictions cause less shame than sexual addiction. They feel alcoholism, gambling, or drug addictions are far less shameful. During their recovery journey, they realize that a thorn in the side is painful, regardless of its name. Once the addict achieves a high-level commitment, shame seems to dissipate.

Habit

Multi-tasking is a byword in our society. News media show people talking on cell phones, eating, and even reading a book while driving. Why do people think they can do at least two things at once? Multi-tasking people etch driving skills into their brains and they are no longer think about responses to road situations.

When new behaviors become automatic, they become a habit. It is a basic form of learning, in which the person, after repeated exposure, stops thinking about how to respond to a stimulus. Addicts etch sexual behavior into their brains too. Sexual behavior becomes habitual. For example, if a man awakes in a state of arousal each morning and masturbates, he has formed a sexual habit. Old habits are hard to change because habitual behavior is imprinted on his neuropathways. Conversely, it is possible to form new habits through repetition of healthy behavior (Becker, 2012b, p. 38).

Sexual habits are insidious because the addict engages in sexual behavior without making a conscious choice. When an addict admits s/he has a problem, s/he is saying, my most pleasurable activity is causing me more pain than pleasure (Becker, 2012b, p. 35).

Sexual Fantasies and Thinking

Sexual arousal results when the brain processes pleasurable thoughts or fantasies. For example, an addict will see an attractive person, store the image in the brain's sexual file cabinet, and later construct a sexual fantasy around the image. The addict may also use pornography to stimulate a sexual fantasy as a launching pad for sexual activity (Becker, 2012b, p. 39).

Those in therapy talk about engaging a fantasy to produce a state of calm in anticipation of sleep. Fantasy reduces stress and is a coping mechanism for dealing with life's problems. Fantasy also medicates depressed mood.

A child uses non-sexual fantasies as a defense mechanism—to ward off feelings and memories of emotional, physical, or sex abuse. When traumatized by sexual abuse, the mind of a child may disassociate from reality. When the mind disassociates, it compartmentalizes what is happening in the present time and substitutes a mental sequence of another time and place or a fantasy absent the pain of the present moment. The child uses disassociation to survive the trauma of abuse. Later in life, dissociation or sexual fantasy may be used to deal with stress and depressed mood (Carnes, 2001b, pp. 2, 44, 202).

Complete recovery from sexual addiction requires an ending to sexual thinking and fantasy. Eliminating the mental component of acting out begins with *awareness* that a fantasy is forming in the addict's head. The addict has a few seconds at the beginning of an episode to choose to change the usual response. Some of the strategies include:

Verbalize a mantra. Verbally express commitment to not to go there! Repeat the mantra until the temptation is neutralized. The mantra distracts mental processing of sexual thinking or fantasy.

Humanize the object. Recognize and verbalize that the object of a fantasy could be someone's mother, daughter, or sister. Adding personality makes a fantasy less attractive.

Substitute an alternative fantasy. Evoke an alternative healthy fantasy to replace a sexual one. For example, playing a fantasy round of golf is distracting and pleasurable.

Sexual Dreams

Dreams with a sexual content may have a positive value. They provide a window into the addict's mind and often mirror the behavioral and emotional components of the addict's original catalytic event. Dream analysis can help an addict understand the underlying meaning of his or her sexual behavior. The dream may lead the addict to confront the root cause of his or her addictive behavior. (Maltz, 2001, p. 49). For example, Joe's dream was to attack physically a prostitute. With the assistance of a therapist, Joe realized that the pain of his father's beatings was reflected in his dreams. He realized he needed to address his anger as a part of his recovery journey.

The Brain Rules Sexual Addiction

The brain is a magnificent creation. It would take a book to list each specific brain part and how each functions in relation to other parts of the brain or body. Humans attribute sexuality to genitalia. Arousal is obvious when a man has an erection but the physiology of arousal is the product of many complex operations in the brain and body.

Although researchers could always observe human behavior, they now can observe how the brain reacts in real time to chemical flows and stimulation. Understanding how the various brain chemicals react to promote sexual behavior, clarifies many recovery concepts.

The following is a synopsis of how seven classes of brain chemicals function. They cause the brain to crave chronic viewing of pornography and engaging in masturbation.

Testosterone. Testosterone is a steroid hormone that is responsible for the development and maintenance of masculine characteristics such as deepening of the voice, muscle growth, facial and body hair, and penis size. Testosterone in the adult also relates to social behaviors. For example, social experiences such as competition cause testosterone levels to rise or fall.

Testosterone flows into the blood stream in response to sexual stimulation, that is, it prepares the body and brain for sexual intimacy. External stimulus (pornography) or internal stimulus (sexual fantasy or a memory of a sexual encounter) increase the flow of testosterone and raise sexual desire. (Struthers, 2009, p. 100). If the stimulus is chronic (frequent exposure to pornography), the heightened sexual desire takes the brain to a higher level of craving for sexual activity and any signal is a trigger to act out

Men in healthy marriages have lower levels of testosterone and thus are less prone to react to sexual temptation outside the marriage—providing they have not been living a dual sexual life (Burnham et al., 2003). Paradoxically, irritability and anger are promoted by low testosterone (Abstract section, para.1).

Testosterone is also a sex-related hormone for women and plays a role in a woman's reproductive cycle. It contributes to female arousal or the physical part of sex—the tingling feeling that lets a woman know her body is ready for sexual intimacy (Marshall 2012, p. 1).

Dopamine. Dopamine is a neurotransmitter, that is, a chemical released by nerve cells that sends signals to other nerve cells. It regulates the brain's *reward and pleasure center.* Dopamine enables the human to perceive a reward and to take action to move toward sexual intimacy. For example, dopamine triggers feelings of ecstasy, exhilaration, sexy mood, and a craving for sexual intimacy (Kastleman, 2007, p. 40).

Dopamine involves many different neuropathways. Marital relations promote neuropathways that reinforce intimacy, that is, it is analogous to *glue* which strengthens the marriage relationship. Conversely, persistent sexual activity outside the marriage form pathways that distort a man's concept of women. For example, viewing naked women daily creates a neuropathway by which a man's normal attraction to sexual stimuli is distorted. His aberrant pathways, with time, may become permanent. All women become objects including those fully dressed. Therefore, the effort to reverse sexual addiction becomes a significant challenge. The brain becomes distorted and the demand for orgasm becomes accentuated. The addict navigates a sexual ship caught in a whirlpool—with no rescue in sight.

Dopamine activity begins in the limbic system, the most primitive part of the brain. Aberrant sexual behavior increases dopamine in the nucleus accumbens of the brain. The nucleus accumbens houses nerve cells, positioned right below the cerebral cortex, called the *brain's pleasure center.* An addict describes a spike in dopamine as *motivation* or *pleasure* (Struthers 2009, p. 101). More accurately, dopamine signals feedback for predicted rewards. It increases sexual sensitivity and makes the addict long for a sexual partner. If a man perceives an attractive woman, his dopamine level will increase as his brain predicts a reward. When men and woman are sexually aroused by close contact, dopamine levels rise. At orgasm, the brain of a woman is flooded with dopamine and it acts like powerful mind bending drug.

Norepinephrine. "Norepinephrine is both a hormone and neurotransmitter. It increases sexual arousal and sexual memory. The effects are excitement and autonomic arousal that occur throughout the body in preparation for sexual activity" (Struthers, 2009, pp. 101-102). It influences the reward system; it makes sex enticing for both men and women.

Norepinephrine is also responsible for stored emotional stimuli. For example, it sears into the brain images of the environment and sexual activity associated with a child's first exposure to sex. Often a child will remember his or her first encounter with sexual stimuli for a lifetime. It plays a role in impregnating stimulating pornographic images into a sex addict's memory. It also explains why partners in love can remember in detail each other's physical characteristic as well as past sexual encounters (Struthers, 2009, p. 103).

Serotonin. Serotonin is a neurotransmitter that contributes to feelings of well-being and satisfaction. It is released after climax and it engenders a deep feeling of calmness and a release from stress (Kastleman, 2007). Serotonin also reduces appetite, improves mood, and suppresses pain perception. High levels of serotonin elevate mood but decreases sexual response in men. Low levels of serotonin in women cause depressed mood (p. 42).

Endogenous opiates. These opiates, produced in the body, include endorphins, enkephalins, dynorphins, and endomorphins. The rush, feeling of euphoria, or release experienced during sexual orgasm relates to the infusion of endogenous opiates; that is, when semen is released, it occurs along with opiate activation. Endorphins work as *natural pain relievers*. Repeated activation of endogenous opiates results in tolerance in the form of diminished euphoria. When viewing of pornography is linked to masturbation, the craving for more stimulation increases (Struthers, 2009, p. 104-105).

Oxytocin. It is a hormone that acts primarily as a neuromodulator in the brain. Oxytocin is released during orgasmic climax and acts as a natural tranquilizer, lowers blood pressure, reduces susceptibility to pain, promotes feelings of attachment, and induces sleep (Kastleman, 2007, p.42). If testosterone fosters sexual desire, oxytocin binds a man to a woman. As such, Oxytocin is called the *joyful brain chemical* (Kastleman, 2007, p. 41-42). As levels rise, couples hold hands, hug, and watch a romantic movie. While released slowly during sexual activity, larger quantities are released after orgasm—and result in sexual satisfaction and higher levels of trust (Struthers, 2009, p. 105). "When humans experience skin-to skin contact, that touch releases oxytocin into the brain, which is associated with feelings of well-being, pleasure and attachment" (Ferree, 2010, p. 51).

"If an addict repeatedly views pornography, s/he will bond to an image and not to a person" (Struthers, 2009, p. 105). As such, a habitual viewer of pornography finds greater sexual satisfaction in visual images than in marital relations.

Delta-FosB. Delta-FosB, in conjunction with Dopamine, is generated when a man or woman use an addictive stimulus such as cocaine or pornography. All addictive stimuli cause an increase in Delta-FosB. In non-technical terms, Delta-FosB sponsors a change, a rewiring of the brain, which causes men and women to seek the pleasurable feelings that accompany drug or pornography use.

Delta-FosB increases' craving that traps the addict into escalating use. Researchers characterize the search as a quest for *unending novelty* (Wilson, 2009). In addition, Delta-FosB makes the addict prone to relapse. These consequences explain why it is so difficult for the addict to end addictive behavior. The altered brain fights to continue its addictive state (Enth, 2001, p. 2).

Over time, the addict must view more stimulating pornography to get the same effect. This adaptation, perversely, dampens the pleasurable effects of sexual behavior. On the other hand, Delta-FosB increases sexual urges and corrals the addict into a destructive spiral of increasing use. The human brain facilitates the formation of an addictive state by the constant supply of powerful brain chemicals. Men and women are able to generate euphoric feelings solely by activating their own brain chemicals—without any outward sexual activity.

Delta-FosB has extended consequences for the addict. It is endurable, that is, the feeling of sexual cravings remains active for weeks to months and for some even much longer. The continuing feeling of sexual desire makes the addict subject to prolonged withdrawal (Nestler, Barrot, & Self, 2001, p.1). Enth (2001) addressed withdrawal. The brain "promotes the continuation of addictive behavior because of the discomfort the addict feels when s/he stops acting out" (p. 2). For example, "women report feeling anxious, moody, depressed, sad, angry when they pursue sobriety" (Ferree, 2010, p. 52).

Benefits of Neurological Research

Although the brain's chemicals keep a person addicted, current research may support the development of new drugs to counter adverse consequences of escalation and withdrawal. In the meantime, researchers have provided new insights into the working of the brain and its chemical flows. Their work has explained many of the sex addiction characteristics observed by sex addiction specialists.

Sex addiction therapists understand that men continually seek new and more tantalizing pornographic images. That is, they seek the perfect sexual image—a goal they never achieve. Sex addiction therapists now know that the action of Delta-FosB increases craving that traps the addict into progressive use. Therapists now have a scientific explanation to confirm their observations (Struthers, 2009, pp. 86-87).

A second example is tolerance. Sex addiction therapists long ago observed that an addict increases his or her intake of pornography to maintain the same level of pleasure. Scans now show that the desensitization of the neuron (Cdk5) to dopamine explains the tolerance characteristic of addiction. In addition, repeated activation of endogenous opiates results in tolerance in the form of diminished euphoria (Struthers, 2009, p. 105).

A third example relates to the effect an addict experiences when bingeing on pornographic images. The build-up of the brain chemical, Delta-FosB promotes a cycle of craving and bingeing. Chronic use of pornography alters the brain. When the flow of testosterone becomes chronic due to frequent exposure to pornography, the heightened sexual desire elevates the demand for sexual activity and any signal is a trigger to act out. The result is a repeated bingeing and craving. Sex addiction therapists call this obsessive and compulsive behavior (Enth, 2001, p. 2).

Fourth, brain changes make the user hyper-reactive to porn (sensitization). The effects of norepinephrine are excitement and autonomic arousal that occur throughout the body in preparation for sexual activity. Due to exhaustion of arousal chemicals, the addict's life becomes boring but porn energizes the addict's reward circuit. Ultimately, brain changes cause the addict's will power to falter. This state is called powerlessness (Becker 2012b, p. 4).

In addition to understanding an evolutionary underpinning—man's necessity to replenish the human race—researchers have used brain scans to trace how Delta-FosB, dopamine and glutamate receptors act to keep an addict clicking away at each new and novel pornographic image. Because of current Internet technology, an addict views vast amounts of pornographic sexual material. Today's addict reaches a greater level of addiction intensity than past generations (Wilson, 2012).

Is it all hopeless? Actually, no. Long-term recovery calls the addict to make a high-level commitment to end acting out (Carnes, 2001, p. 137). An addict can achieve sexual sobriety through traditional therapy and 12-step programs. Contrary to expectations, other forces are at work to change adverse sexual behavior. Researchers found that the damaging effects of Delta-FosB and related brain chemicals are subject to exhaustion. For most, with time and sexual sobriety, the damaged brain will heal.

CHAPTER FIVE: PORNOGRAPHY

This chapter presents the connection between pornography and sexually addiction.

Definition of Pornography

A universally accepted definition of pornography is nearly impossible. The US Attorney General's 1986 Commission on Pornography defined pornographic material as *predominantly sexually explicit and intended for the purpose of sexual arousal*, and hard-core pornography as *sexually explicit in the extreme and devoid of any other apparent content or purpose* (Attorney General's Commission on Pornography, 1986 pp. 323-347).

Although married couples may use sexually stimulating material, even such use falls within this definition when the focus is more on the stimulating images than engaging a partner. Some find it hard to believe that pornography of any type is healthy within the marriage. Why does a man or a woman require external materials to facilitate sexual arousal? In such cases, other issues are at work, which precludes marital intimacy.

Some consider any erotic material used for sexual stimulation as pornographic. For example, Bob found lingerie ads in newspapers and catalogs to be his form of pornography. David found images of large-breasted women to be tantalizing and he never went further than his everyday TV shows. Ann found men with a muscular build stimulating. Her subway ride back and forth to work was her pornography studio. Alice found men's underwear advertising stimulating. In the final analysis, pornography is what each person finds sexually stimulating. What stimulates one may not stimulate another and vice versa.

The subject content of marketed pornography varies. "The US Attorney General's 1986 Commission on Pornography (1986) evaluated multiple types: a) Sexually violent; b) Nonviolent that depicts degradation, domination, subordination, or humiliation; c) Nonviolent and non-degrading; d) Nudity; and e) Child pornography. The first two portray pornography that adversely affects behavior. The third is reasonably benign and fourth is morally objectionable according to the Commissioners. The last, child pornography, exploit's children and is not tolerated by today's society" (pp. 323-347). In recent years, law enforcement agencies at the Federal, state and local levels have become more active in prosecuting purveyors and users of child pornography. Sex offenders (rapists, incest offenders, and child molesters) may use pornography to arouse themselves before and during their assaults.

Classification of Pornography

Although more classifications of pornography exist, it is usually found in the following mediums: literature, photos, hand held devices, Internet, sculptures, drawings, paintings, animation, sound recordings, movies, TV, films, DVDs, Blu-ray, pay-for-view, videos, or video games. Dial-a-Porn and violent representations are growing in availability. A few of these are listed below:

Literature and photos. The spicy novel with sexually stimulating stories and scenes has been around for ages. In the past century, magazines such as *Playboy* and *Penthouse* became popular and served as the source of initiation into the world of sex for many boys.

On line exchange of pornography. Email and posting to social media provide a new means of sharing provocative sexual images. Newspapers frequently feature articles about teens who use cell phone cameras to video and share their sexual exploits. Voluntary sharing has become a popular activity among the younger generation.

Film, DVD, and video. Early during the previous century, pornography came off the printed page onto film and presented an even more explicit sexual enactment. Adult bookstores look forward to visiting conventioneers who find a trip away from home is an opportunistic time to purchase future pleasure. Today intelligent phones, computers, and cable TV are the delivery modes of choice.

TV and pay-for-view. In recent years, the home which subscribes to a full range of cable or satellite TV channels has available more pornography than one could ever digest. The only difficulty is finding a time to view X-rated material and not get caught. One addict set the alarm clock for a predawn hour to watch stimulating material before going to work. An addict who travels frequently may find hotel pay-for-view movies a downfall.

Movies. Going to a movie theater without being exposed to explicit sex scenes and nudity is a challenge. Although acceptable in today's society, they can cause addicts and patrons in general, to retain images and mentally process them later. However, sexually explicit movies are more toxic to sex addicts as a whole.

Immodest dress. Both women and men dress for attention. Clothing, and how it is worn, can be revealing, and sexually alluring. Young people seem not to recognize that the way they dress will cause other people to experience sexual arousal. Provocatively dressed individuals are more toxic to sex addicts as a whole. One man remarked, "I need blinders when I drive across a college campus. Some young women wear less clothing than they would in a doctor's exam room."

Internet and smart phones. The Internet and smart phones provide the ultimate presentation of pornography. Although many web sites entice an addict to pay more money for explicit images, plenty of material is available free. If depression was analogous to the common cold of the last century, online pornography is the pneumonia of this century. Of greater concern is the number of young people and teenagers who have unfettered access to sexually stimulating material.

Cybersex. Cybersex has as its common elements: the use of a computer, Internet access, expected anonymity, and provocative material to stimulate arousal followed by masturbation. Multiple cybersex venues exist such as dial-a-porn, synchronous live chat rooms and live video streams, instant messaging, visual images of real or graphically generated persons, and interactive sex through a web cam.

Technology enabled sharing of pornography is the primary venue sought by a sex addict. Isolation and desire for secrecy are common characteristics of an addict who hides behind the fantasy world of pornographic images. All pornographic material has an element of objectification, which is a core principle of sexual addiction. A sex addict will obsess over pornography and lose his or her freedom to distinguish between fantasy and reality.

Online pornography. Ewald (2003) commented on the toxicity of the Internet.

The internet has become the newest, most rapidly growing form of sexual acting out for many sexual addicts today. They spend increasingly amounts of time surfing the net. The Internet just happens to provide many of the things sex addicts seek all in one place; isolation, secrecy, fantasy material, endless varieties, around the clock availability, and instant accessibility. (para. 5)

Pornography is a millstone around the neck of both men and woman. As much as half the male population viewed pornography during any given week (Family Safe Media, 2012), and 30 % of women regularly view pornography (Lee, 2014, para. 1). Carnes (2010) found that over 40 % of women engage in problematic cybersex. In recent years, interest in pornography is narrowing the difference between the characteristics of male and female sexual addiction (slides 3, 6).

Women frequent chat rooms twice as often as do men (Ferree, 2010, p. 63). Introduction to pornography for women often begins in adolescence, just as with men. A 2006 study of 563 college students found that "62 % of female respondents had seen online pornography before age 18. Most girls were first exposed between the ages of 13 and 16" (Weiss, 2012, para. 1).

Compulsive viewing of pornography is a primary acting-out behavior. Online voyeurs mistakenly believe they can enjoy their own secret world and never be caught. Contrary to their expectation, online voyeurs do enter therapy because they have been caught!.

Bart's story. I believed viewing online pornography did not affect my marriage. I was an upwardly mobile young executive and I often took work home. I had an agreement with my wife that I would not do office work while she and the children were awake. After she retired for the evening, I went online. I spent an hour or two attending to office work, but then I would succumbed to the temptation to view pornographic material. I felt I deserved to reward myself, for I was an outstanding breadwinner and my wife did not seem to desire sexual intimacy as much as I did. I looked forward to viewing pornography and subsequent masturbation.

My wife was a sound sleeper and never disturbed my late night computer sessions. That was, until one night when she walked in and saw the sick images on my computer. Not only did she see the pornographic images but also I was masturbating.

Bart's wife was traumatized by her husband's behavior. She told him to seek help or move out. Bart was devastated. Although Bart entered therapy, he found the road to sexual sobriety more difficult than he expected. After a year of therapy, Bart continued to attend several 12-step program a week to keep him straight. He also found that a physical exercise program encouraged him to maintain a better mental disposition. "Discovery was initially the worst thing that could have happened to me," Bart said. He now realizes it was the opportunity for life changing choices and a far better relationship with his wife.

A man also goes online from his computer at work and believes he will not be caught.

Mario's story. I work for a state government and I am an IT professional. I know I can defeat any filter or tracking tools used by our IT shop.

It was not the control software that caused me to lose my dream position. One Friday afternoon I was called to my supervisor's office and told to pack my things. I was no longer an employee. My supervisor explained that a coworker filed a sexual harassment complaint after she saw me masturbating as she passed by my work cubicle after hours. I was devastated and my wife was outraged.

My family was in crisis. We were without medical insurance to care for our disabled son. I obtained freelance work but barely kept the family afloat. I paid a high price for the lure of sexual stimulation.

Barbara's story. My company made it clear that anyone caught viewing pornography at the work site would be fired. I am a highly skilled graphic artist and I thought, no matter what I did, I would never be fired. My company needed my award winning talent. I viewed online pornography after my coworkers left for the day. I was caught and told by my boss that I had one more chance.

Barbara failed to heed the warning. She was subsequently fired for improper use of her company computer. Barbara entered therapy to convince her boss she was serious about changing her behavior. She learned it was not her boss who she needed to satisfy, but herself. She made good progress and is employed by another company.

Impact of Pornography on the Viewer

Addiction to pornography is objectifying self. It is a form of idolizing sexual stimulation to the point of compulsive self-worship. Because the object of love is self, it is a total loss of loving intimacy. The addict has alienated his or her normal feelings in deference to the predominance of arousal feelings.

The mind has the capacity to retain viewed images. Just as the traveler's memory of the Grand Canyon is long lasting, visions of stimulating pictures or video sequences may last a long time. Norepinephrine imprints stimulating images to the addict's memory. Both men and women complain they cannot maintain arousal during marital intercourse without mentally processing past sexual events or pornography. In these cases, is the addict having relations with his or her partner or with a chemically generated image in the head?

Impact of Pornography on Marriage

Frequent exposure to pornography greatly harms the marriage relationship. It is impossible to see one's partner as an intimate friend when porn and self-sex fulfill the addict's craving. Intimacy with self or other people precludes loving intimacy in a marriage (Struthers 2009, p. 55). Once pornography becomes ingrained, the marriage bed is shared with strangers from the film studio. Pornographic stored images are in competition with reality (Struthers 2009, pp. 83-84).

An addict may view *adventurous* practices online and try to manipulate his or her partner into mimicking such practices. In this case, marital relations become an exercise in gymnastics rather than shared love and tenderness. As noted, an addict sees bodies as objects for pleasure and fulfillment. An addict who views violent or degrading pornography adopts the mental attitude portrayed by the actors and may look to his or her partner to emulate the violence or degradation. Marital relations are taken over by perversion (Carnes, 2001, p. 202). The purveyor of visual sexual stimulation will never be satisfied. Tolerance of violence or degradation becomes further out-of-touch with reality. It is reasonable to conclude that pornography will cause conflict, pain, and suffering in any marriage (Struthers, 2009, pp. 84-85).

Impact of Pornography on Young People

Pornography corrupts the minds of young people. At a time gone by, a boy's first exposure to pornography was in middle school or high school when he discovered a porn magazine in the trash or at a friend's house. Now a child in grade school has access to images formerly available only in an adult bookstore. At one time, these images were inaccessible to youth; now they are merely a mouse click away. "The average age of first exposure to Internet pornography is 11 and the largest consumers of Internet pornography are in the 12-17 age group" (Family Safe Media, 2012).

Prolong use of the Internet affects young people more than older counterparts. The reason, brain placidity, is a characteristic of young people's brains. As such, young people experience an outcome formerly seen because of aging or illness—Erectile Dysfunction (ED). Young men who looked for answers to ED were diagnosed with depression, anxiety, memory impairment, ADHD, to name a few. They tried medications like Viagra, Effexor, Ritalin, Prozac, and Xanax, all to no avail.

For a group of young men, their mental light bulb became a beacon to illuminate a novel answer, at least in our society. They were tired and embarrassed by their inability to perform. They reasoned, if they stopped viewing pornography and masturbating, their sexual relationships with women may improve. Their supposition was right! In time, their ED symptoms disappeared. It took about three to six months for the consequences of viewing pornography to reverse and allow them to return to normal sexual interest. Word spread rapidly through social media. A new trend in society is for young men to end their acting-out behavior in favor of marital type behavior (Wilson, 2012, video, 13:51-15:44).

Pornography and the Brain

Wilson (2012) in a You Tube video, *The Great Porn Experiment*, explained the relationship between certain brain chemicals and pornography addiction. As the addict begins to view pornography, daily responsibilities are ignored, regardless of the consequences. When the brain begins to release endogenous chemicals, the viewer feels highly aroused. Elevated levels of dopamine cause the viewer to focus intensely on sexual images. Chronic viewing of pornography causes an excess of Dopamine to accumulate in the brain's reward center. Extreme concentrations of Dopamine in the brain's reward center trigger a molecular switch called Delta-FosB. The build-up of the brain chemical, Delta-FosB, in turn, promotes a cycle of craving and bingeing on pornography. To the addict each new and exciting image becomes an unending novelty or a genetic opportunity. Over time, Delta-FosB changes the brain's structure. High levels of Delta-FosB cause the addict to experience a numbed pleasure response, that is, former daily pleasures no longer satiate. Everything in an addict's life becomes boring except super exciting porn. Finally, changes in the frontal cortex frustrate the addict's ability to say no. With a loss of will power, the addict is captured by addiction and an unending attraction to pornography (video, 7:21-8:41).

Kastleman (2007) summarized how other brain chemicals affect a pornography viewer. Although the physical and chemical processes are virtually identical to those in marital sexual intimacy, radical differences abound.

- Norepinephrine induces feelings of exhilaration and increased energy by giving the body a shot of natural adrenaline. Norepinephrine also increases memory capacity, which explains why an addict can recall viewed images with vivid clarity years later.

- Pornography triggers the release of testosterone, which, in turn, increases the desire for more pornography.

- After sexual relations, oxytocin in conjunction with the release of serotonin, invokes a deep feeling of calmness. The addict seeks the flow of oxytocin to cope with the stress and pressure of life, as well as an antidote to feeling lonely and isolated. Oxytocin calms and soothes but only for a very short time and then the addict returns to feeling even more lonely and isolated.

A lot more is happening here than viewing pornography. If sexual arousal is discounted, similarities to intimacy in a healthy marriage cease. While taking steps to act out, a tidal wave of conflicting messages wash over the viewer—shock, arousal, anger, lust, guilt, attraction, and fear of being caught. Many of these emotions are contrary to those intended to accompany a loving exchange of intimacy. Pornography has one critical difference—it lacks a human heart—it is heartless. Pornography is *"me-me, mine-mine, more-more"* and the climax is nothing more than bringing to fruition a stimulus-driven chemical reaction in the brain. Neuropsychologists refer to pornography as *"visual crack cocaine."*

When the arousal chemicals are exhausted, the addict emerges from his or her acting-out trance. Rational thinking returns and the hopeless dialogue begins: "What have I done? What was I thinking? I was not thinking; that was the problem" (pp. 40-55).

Statistics on Pornography

Multiple sources of pornography are available to most human beings in American society. With the advent of videos and DVD's, the addictive nature of pornography has grown. With motion, nothing is left to the imagination. Internet pornography is pervasive. "A viewer in the United States has access to more than 500 million pages of pornography and the number is growing. Every 36 minutes a new pornographic video is being produced" (Family Safe Media, 2012).

The market for Internet pornography is huge and growing. Unfortunately, children exposed to pornography become potential victims for sexual addiction. The following tables give insight into how insidious just one form of sexual stimulation has become—Internet pornography.

United States Pornography Revenues
Revenue from pornography is more than $97 billion a year. The pornography industry has larger revenues than the revenues of the top technology companies **combined:** Microsoft, Google, Amazon, eBay, Yahoo, Apple, and Netflix. Revenue from pornography in the United States exceeds the combined revenues of ABC, CBS, and NBC

Pornography Time Statistics
Every second - $3,075.64 is spent on pornography
Every second - 28,258 Internet users are viewing pornography
Every 39 minutes: a new pornographic video is created in the United States

Internet Pornography Statistics	
Pornographic web sites	4.2 million (12% of total web sites)
Pornographic pages	**420 million**
Daily pornographic search engine requests	68 million (25% of search engine requests)
Daily Gnutella child pornography requests	116,000
Web sites offering illegal child pornography	**100,000**
Youths who received sexual solicitation	one in seven

Children Internet Pornography Statistics	
Average age of first Internet exposure to pornography	**11 years-of-age**
15-17 year olds who have multiple hard-core exposures	80%
8-16 year olds who have viewed porn online	**90% (most while doing homework)**

Adult Internet Pornography Statistics	
Percentage of Internet users who view pornography	42.7%
Men admitting to accessing pornography at work	20%
US adults who regularly visit Internet pornography web sites	40 million
Promise Keeper men who viewed pornography in the last week	**53%**
Christians who said pornography is a major problem in the home	**47%**

(Family Safe Media, 2012)

The problems that pornography causes are staggering and growing. If, while at church last Sunday, you looked left and right, one of those two people could say pornography is a problem in their home. Laaser (2008) reported, "The evangelical community struggles with sexual addiction particularly with the Internet, in large percentages— no fewer than 50 % and possibly as high as 66 %. Christian women struggle with pornography, somewhere between 25-33 % as well" (Prevalence section, para 2). If "53 % of Promise Keepers view pornography," other men have a lot of company (Family Safe Media, 2012).

According to Laaser (2002):

We are experiencing an epidemic today of people who are trapped in pornography. One recent survey revealed that as many as two-thirds of Christian men have struggled with it. Another recent survey claims that one-third of all pastors are involved with pornography. Some believe we are living in the most sexually saturated time in history. It is hard to go any place today and not confronted with pornography. Even a trip to the grocery store checkout lane will bombard the shopper with sexual images and messages. Our youngest children who are computer literate can accidentally click into the worst of images on pornographic web sites. (para. 1-2)

Perverted Internet pornography. When one thinks of viewing Internet pornography, it is reasonable to think of a man or woman viewing humans in some form of normal sexual activity. In reality, the Internet provides both normal sex as well as a large menu of perverted sex. Briefly, examples of perverted sex include bestiality, sadomasochism (S & M), sexual violence including rape, exploitation of children, sadism; and sex with corpses, excessive focus on parts of the body such as feet; and excessive focus related to body functions such as feces, enemas, and urine and other perversions. These forms of pornography are not available to the average person without the Internet.

A therapist asked Glen to disclose the nature of the material he viewed online. The purpose of asking him to disclose Internet pornography images of choice was to explore a connection between his current acting out behavior and a disturbing event that occurred during childhood.

Glenn's story. I was a city boy. Around age 10, I went to my uncle's farm for the summer. To my cousin Jim, a farm boy, animal copulation is part of everyday business. My cousin Jim realized I never saw animals mate. He took me to the pasture one day when the veterinarian was breeding a stallion with a prized mare. I was not ready for what I saw. I was sexually stimulated and confused when I saw the animals mate. I remember dreaming about what I saw over the next several years. In fact, I became fascinated with human copulation as well.

Glenn, as an adult, found an Internet site that featured bestiality, that is, sex with animals. He returned to that site and others like it for several years. He never understood why this perverted act stimulated him. While in therapy, he was able to see the connection between what happened at age 10 and his fixation as an adult.

Progressive. Online pornography, in contrast to magazines, is many times more insidious. An addict who seeks sexual stimulation from online sources often begins with just looking for images and then progresses to viewing bodies in movement. As the addict progresses to more stimulating material, he or she may begin to exchange email or files with provocative images, web cam sexual scenarios, and videos, newsgroups, social networks, social media, and home pages.

Ewald (2003) explained the progressive nature of Internet pornography:

Sex addicts on the internet often experience a rapid progression of their addiction. They eventually move to more extreme behavior by taking greater risks, and even being caught more frequently. (para. 5)

Internet secrecy. Those in therapy confirm that internet secrecy is a myth. Internet providers keep electronic records of all Internet activity. Law authorities can access usage data when cause has been determined. The computer, unless otherwise modified, records Internet web sites accessed and images are downloaded to temporary files. The so-called temporary files remain until the system is set to delete or the user deletes them. Even after images are erased, forensic computer experts have the technology to restore erased files. Their own computer is a virtual living conscience. Internet searches on a workplace computer are also subject to discovery. IT staff has programs to identify high volume users or users who frequent high profile web sites. An addict may lose his or her employment by engaging in behaviors s/he thought would not be discovered.

Marvin's Story. I came to counseling because of my addiction to pornography. My therapist asked me to describe the nature of the porn I seek. I told him I sought young adults in various sexual scenarios. I only search for pornography where the ages of the participants are 18 or over. He asked how I knew the ages of participants. I was shocked when I realized I did not know. I admitted that the participants could possibly have been under the age of 18. I realized I could be accused of viewing child pornography.

Five-step Pattern in Pornographic Addiction

Psychologists identified a multi-step pattern in pornographic addiction:

Exposure. The first step is exposure to improper sexual behavior or material during childhood.

Addiction. In the second step, early exposure is both stimulating and traumatic, but with chronic viewing, the urge to go back for more overcomes any reservation one may have. Repeated exposure leads to a habit, which forms the basis for sexual addiction. Addiction rules the addict's life.

Escalation or progression. In the third step, the addict seeks ever increasing provocative stimulation. The sexual images that yielded last week's high no longer work this week.

Desensitization. In the fourth step, what was previously degrading is now passé. The addict continues to look for greater stimulation but never finds it. However, the search takes him or her deeper into depravity. Notwithstanding depravity, the viewer convinces self that pornography is normal—everybody does it.

Acting-out fantasies. In the fifth step, the addict who fantasized about sex is no longer satiated with fantasy but wants the real thing. The man or woman who flirts in a chat room now seeks person-to-person contact. Not every addict proceeds to step five, but the risk is real. (Hughes, 1998, p.1)

In summary, the addict fails to understand that online pornography is unrealistic—in most cases performed by actors to maximize arousal. As such, normal sexual activity in the marriage bed becomes boring and unfulfilling. The addict, who hides his or her lack of sexual enjoyment, may be betrayed by his or her inability to perform. The addict does not understand the meaning of love, if s/he ever did in the first place. An addict may find self-sex more fulfilling than marital relations. Love is self-sacrificing; addictive behavior is not. The marriage relationship suffers! Both partners are lonely and isolated because a *10-ton elephant is in the room called sex addiction.*

CHAPTER SIX: MARRIAGE AND ADDICTION

This chapter examines disclosure-based trauma and the role of codependency in the marriage relationship.

Obstacles to Recovery

Many marriages, where one of the parties is sexually addicted, end in divorce. Although divorce may be the answer for some, another solution is to live through recovery. However, the obstacles need to be exposed and faced—not to discourage but to forewarn of the hazards that must to be addressed (Becker, 2012a, pp. 1-8, 56-67).

The sexually addicted male. Before marriage, sexual stimulation defined a sex addict's need. For example, he likely manipulated his future spouse into an early sexual encounter during courtship. After he succeeded the first time, successive encounters were intended to replicate the first experience. Once sex entered the relationship, all normal friendship development ceased. Once he sexually exploited his future partner, he may even seek to exploit other women.

A sexually addicted man cannot provide uncompromising love to his partner. Even if he is sexually addicted to his partner, his sexual demands meet his needs first. (Some signs that a man is sexually addicted to his partner include unreasonable and frequent demand for sex, lack of foreplay, harsh criticism of performance, and no verbal communication during sex.) A sexually addicted man tries to straddle the gap between addiction and marriage—one foot in addiction and the other in the marriage.

The sexually addicted female. Ferree (2010) found that sexually addicted women present multiple conditions:

Dysthymic disorder. A female sex addict experiences low-grade depressed mood because of her out-of-control life. Women generally do not exhibit symptoms of full depression, although for a few, feelings of hopelessness may lead to suicidal ideation. The underlying problem is the genesis of her sexual addiction.

Marital or relationship issues. Sex addiction is an intimacy disorder and no marriage is healthy where self-sex or infidelities violate the marriage bond. A woman may blame her partner, which may create separation between the partners. It is common for the male to have his own addiction issues. Women often have attachment issues, which contribute to an abnormal desire for attention, validation, and reassurance. Sexually addicted women often present with sex and love addiction symptoms.

Substance abuse. A woman may be diagnosed as a co-addict, that is, both partners have their own addictions. She may be addicted to alcohol or drugs and he is addicted to sex.

Eating disorders. Addicted women often struggle with anorexia, bulimia, or binge eating. Reducing food intake prepares a woman to engage in the *hunt* while bingeing satiates a failed relationship.

Anxiety disorders. Chronic anxiety is a common consequence of lack of infant attachment, childhood abuse, or adult rape. Anxiety plays a role in keeping a relationship unstable. Chronic or situational anxiety reflects a cry for help.

Bipolar disorder. Promiscuous behavior is a symptom of the manic phase of a bipolar disorder. Medication is usually required to control bipolar induced mood swings.

Personality disorders. Such disorders present as a pervasive pattern of relating to others in a dysfunctional way. A diagnostic criterion for Borderline Personality Disorder is acting out sexually. A diagnosis of a personality disorder will often explain a propensity for destructive relationships or dysfunctional behavior.

Each of these factors, in addition to behavior associated with sexual addiction, will affect diagnosis and treatment of women. (pp. 89-93)

Personality Difference

A sexually addicted man often looks for a partner who, in his mind, is morally superior. He reasons that a morally superior woman will motivate him to end his addiction. However, after he is married and his partner begins to act like a morally superior person and tries to fix him, he no longer appreciates her effort. Because he cannot stop his addictive behavior, he no longer wants to be fixed. Instead, he wants his partner to participate in his behavior. He wants her to join him in offbeat sexual practices, be available frequently, and let him be himself (Becker, 2012a, pp. 3-5).

A perceived morally superior woman often scores as a value-oriented person on the Myers-Briggs Type Indicator (MBTI). The sex addict often scores as a logic oriented person. While opposites may have a compatible relationship, it is more usual for them to differ and disagree.

Briefly, the Myers-Briggs Type Indicator (MBTI) measures psychological preferences in how people perceive the world and make decisions. These preferences are extrapolated from theories proposed by Carl Jung. Jung's types are similar to left or right-handedness: Individuals are born with, or develop certain preferred ways of perceiving and deciding. The MBTI sorts these psychological differences into four opposite pairs, or dichotomies, with a resulting 16 possible psychological types. *None of the types is better or worse than any other type.* Briggs and Myers theorized that individuals naturally prefer one overall combination of type differences (Keirsey, 1978, pp. 2-4, 13-14).

The third of the four dichotomies measure preference for *feeling* (value-orientation) or *thinking* (logic-orientation). In this scenario, the non-addicted woman makes her decisions based on her value orientation (feeling) whereas the sex addict makes his decisions based on his logic orientation (thinking). As such, the partners are opposites in how they make decisions. Neither understands where the partner is coming from and often attributes the difference to meanness. For example, a couple agreed to leave at 8:00 A.M to visit relatives. The sex addict was in his driver's seat at 8:00 A.M. At 8:15 A.M., his value-orientated partner was still in the house. He found her doing dishes. When questioned, she replied, "If something happened and someone came into my house and found my dishes undone they would judge me as a lax housekeeper." Neither could understand why the other was upset (Keirsey, 1978, pp. 2-4, 13-14).

Where one of the partners is sexually addicted, decision-making is often polarized. Personality preference when explored during therapy assists the partners to have a better understanding of how nature contributes to the challenge of marriage.

Codependency - Sex Addiction Induced-Trauma (SAI-T)

Another consideration, which affects the marriage, is codependency. In this context, codependency occurs when each partner expects the other partner to cause his or her happiness. For example, the female partner expects her spouse to engage in behavior that will make her happy. Of course, if he is sexually addicted, his behavior will not make her happy. She is unable to make herself happy.

Some in the mental health community have begun to substitute the concept of *sex addiction induced-trauma (SAI-T)* for codependency.

Sex addiction induced-trauma (SAI-T). Proponents of sex addiction induced-trauma believe that disclosure of aberrant sexual behavior induces a profound traumatic experience for the *innocent* partner. To emphasize any other relationship phenomena such as the implications of co-behavior does a great disservice to the innocent partner. As such, justice demands that full attention be given to the impact of trauma and to discount co-responsibility (Steffens & Means 1997, pp. 28-39).

In his book, *Out of the Shadows* (2001), Carnes introduced codependency as it is related to sexually addictive behavior in a marriage. Recently, Minwalla, (2012) noted that Carnes' traditional treatment model was developed and organized around the diagnosis of co-addiction, which views the partner as having her own disease termed co-addiction or co-dependence. He suggests that the codependency model casts the partner into a diagnosis rather than emphasizing the profound marital betrayal (para 3).

The innocent partner experiences clinically significant sex addiction induced-trauma (SAI-Trauma).

Trauma results from disclosure and the associated chronic patterns of sexually acting out, relational perpetration, emotional abuse, deception, betrayal, psychological manipulation, and compartmentalization. Sex addiction induced-trauma is particularly acute where the innocent party learns about his or her partner's deception and relational violations (Minwalla, 2012, para. 7).

Steffens and Means (1997) framed the impact of addiction induced-trauma:

We view the partner as a person in a relationship with a sex addict; someone with human reactions and behaviors in *response* to discovering that his or her most intimate relationship is not what it originally seemed. With the passing of one moment in life, security is replaced with betrayal and death of life-long dreams. At that point, the partner knows that the person, with whom he or she lives, sleeps and invests time and feelings...participates in hidden sexual behaviors that jeopardize his or her finances, safety, health, and even her life, not to mention their children.

Prior to this discovery, the person believed his or her partner loved only him or her and remained faithful. Suddenly, their relationship holds dangers and dark secrets. Discovering that much of one's life is built on lies proves traumatizing and destroys their sense of safety and security. (p. 30)

Codependency. Substitution of addiction induced-trauma for all semblance of codependency may not be warranted. If trauma is the only focus, codependency symptoms are ignored but the symptoms remain a challenge within the parameters of marriage.

Those who believe that codependency still needs to be addressed hold that any marriage, where sexual addiction is a factor, will experience intimacy and other relationship issues—in addition to trauma. Codependency simply depicts the relationship as it is. The marriage, by definition is broken. Sexually addicted partners tend to marry at the same level of *brokenness*. As such, most innocent partners have issues they ought to address. Although the innocent party did *not* cause her partner's sexual addiction, living with a *diseased* partner likely created isolation, self-esteem, and intimacy issues. Both partners will benefit from therapy. He needs to address his sexual addiction and she will benefit from addressing trauma as well as codependent issues (Bradshaw, 2005 pp. 34, 236-237 - Ferree, 2010, pp. 234-235).

For the purposes of the following discourse, the term *codependency* is used, not because it suggests that the female spouse is responsible in a pathological way for co-addiction, but because of the addict's behavior, the innocent party may be codependent in ways that affect both partners. The following scenarios and analysis originate in Becker *Recovery from Sexual Addiction: A Man's Guide* (2012b, pp. 55-65).

Again, sex addiction induced-trauma is a recognized outcome of profound betrayal and must be addressed in therapy.

To begin, a few thoughts may add clarity:

The Alcoholic Anonymous community first coined the term codependency. Melody Beattie (1987), a well-known author in the field of codependency defined it, as "A codependent person is one who has let another person's behavior affect him or her, and who is obsessed with controlling that person's behavior" (p. 31). Brawand (1991) defined a "codependent person as one who depends on satisfying the needs of others to feel his or her own value" (p. 121). In each of these definitions, happiness lies outside of the ability of the husband or wife to make themselves happy.

For the sexually addicted, a clear road map to codependency begins with parents. His or her parents were likely codependent. Codependency is also a sign of childhood abandonment. More often than not, one unconsciously finds a partner who also experienced dysfunction in his or her family of origin. Odds are both partners grew up in similar circumstances.

Bradshaw (1988) clarified:

Co-dependence is the most common family illness because it is what happens to anyone in any kind of the dysfunctional family. In every dysfunctional family, there is a primary stressor. This could be dad's drinking or work addiction; mom's hysterical control of everyone's feelings; dad or mom's physical or verbal violence; a family member's actual sickness or hypochondriasis; dad or mom's early death; their divorce; dad or mom's moral/religious righteousness; dad or mom's sexual abuse. Anyone, who becomes controlling in the family to the point of being perceived as a threat by the other members, initiates the dysfunction. (p. 164)

Note: The following scenarios assign the role of sex addict to the male. The genders roles could be reversed.

Codependency in a marriage. Clinical experience has shown that a sexually addicted man often marries into a codependent relationship. That is, he looks to his spouse as having the power to *cure* his addiction. Conversely, she looks to him as a source of her happiness. Her desire for the husband of her dreams is at odds with her fear of abandonment because of his sexual needs. As such, her husband failed as a source of her happiness.

Codependency will affect the marriage and may affect the addict's recovery. Both partners may find it beneficial to examine their role in the marriage. Although the following scenarios are not a universal characterization of the marriage relationships among all sexually addicted men and their spouses, it is reality for many.

"Often, we pick addictive partners that somehow replicate our abuse, and we form a trauma bond that is extraordinarily difficult to break. Sometime we return to the relationship time and again before we break free" (Ferree, 2010, p. 170).

The man's wife often plays the role of a mother who feels responsible for fixing her child (husband)—a way of dealing with her own insecurity by making herself feel indispensable. An addict, raised in a dysfunctional family, lacks good social skills. His deficiencies, including his addiction, give his partner plenty of reasons to chastise him.

The addicted man plays the role of the damaged child who needs someone to parent him. His wife takes the superior position in the marriage and the addicted man takes the subordinate position. The marriage is unbalanced. Mutual respect and acceptance of one another based on equality is absent. The unbalanced marriage fosters resentment, feelings of inadequacy, and keeps the man addicted (Bradshaw, 1988 p. 164).

Interestingly, in this scenario the addict's wife does not see herself in a superior position. She sees herself in the victim position. She sees herself as the recipient of her partner's broken promises to do better, his inability to show affection other than through sex, and his inability to communicate except through anger. She sees the man whom she thought she loved and married fail miserably. She keeps trying to guide (or fix) him because she craves the husband of her dreams (Beattie, 1987, pp. 35-36).

Neither partner is getting what they expect or want from the marriage. The addict's isolation grows and he uses his addiction to medicate his dissatisfaction with married life. Her intended effort to motivate (or fix) him has the exact opposite effect and she grows more frustrated with his failures.

Who is to blame? The purpose is not to assess blame. The characterization merely conveys the reality of marriages where the husband is sexually addicted. If a man and woman believe they are in a codependent relationship, through therapy, they can address what is not working in their relationship.

To explore how codependency affects marriages, two stories follow. The stories include many of the characteristics found in codependent relationships. The stories could be written in either the male or the female voice. The stories also describe how sex addiction affects a couple's marriage.

Codependency - Characteristics Are Often Evident Before Marriage

Jim and Barbara's story. Jim dated while he was in high school for social conformity. Because he had not witnessed respectful and loving interactions between his parents, his relationship skills were also lacking. He did not know what it meant to know and appreciate a person of the opposite sex. Outside of school dances and similar functions, his social contact focused primarily on *making out*. Although making out never progressed beyond heavy petting, it was not for a lack of desire.

Barbara also dated in high school. The man she dated was several years older and was in the Peace Corps. For her, the relationship was safe because of the distance and infrequency of face-to-face contact. Having experienced a dysfunctional family environment, she too lacked understanding of a healthy relationship. She had a sense of loneliness because she often disagreed with her parents.

Jim and Barbara's parents were alike in many ways. Neither set of parents showed much affection. Jim's father was an alcoholic. Barbara and Jim felt their parents loved them, but external signs of affection were rare. When Jim left for college, he perceived that anything short of a high-level performance was unacceptable. Barbara's motivation was grounded in an internal perception that her parents would be disappointed if she did not succeed in her academic pursuits.

Barbara and Jim met at a college-sponsored mixer for incoming freshman where upperclassmen attended. Jim felt an immediate attraction to Barbara. To him, she had all the physical attributes that met his criteria for an attractive girl. He felt she was a bit naive, but thought it was cute. Conversely, although she thought Jim was reasonably attractive, she was not interested in dating him. She had not planned to get involved with a college man because her studies were more important to her.

Jim invited Barbara to several campus social affairs and fraternity parties. The first several times she turned him down. She finally agreed to go to a fraternity mixer. By this time, Jim was sexually attracted to Barbara. Jim began to plot ways to manipulate Barbara into a sexual relationship to satisfy his needs. Several months after their initial encounter, their relationship turned sexual. Once sexual activity entered into their relationship, neither seemed to place a priority on developing a strong non-sexual friendship. The glue that held the relationship together was physical and emotional dependency on each other.

Jim and Barbara dated for several years before they married. During this time, Jim's sexual needs continued to grow while Barbara tried to satisfy her desire for love by giving into Jim's needs.

Codependency - Characteristics Flourish in Marriage

Jim and Barbara married and began a family. A year or so into the marriage, it became apparent to Barbara that Jim was very self-centered and manipulative. His needs always seemed to come first. Joint decisions were often the result of Jim's persuasion. While he was a good economic provider, as a loving companion he was far from ideal. Barbara felt very alone in the marriage. She directed her energy to raising their children. She tried numerous times to talk to him about her needs and her perception of a loving marriage. He repeatedly made promises to do better but did not do so. His perception was, as long as he provided a good living for the family, he fulfilled his end of the bargain. Because he felt that Barbara constantly suggested ways in which he needed to improve, he shied away from give and take discussions because he feared he would see himself as a failure. Jim and Barbara grew apart in their marriage. He did not believe that Barbara loved him.

More than a decade into their marriage, Barbara learned that Jim had been unfaithful. Jim had marital affairs with several women at work and was addicted to pornography. In one long evening, he confessed all of his transgressions and begged for Barbara's forgiveness. Jim insisted he would become a new man. Jim initially felt relieved that his greatest and most shameful secrets were exposed. The stress of leading a secret, dual life had become almost intolerable.

His promise to become a new man was short lived. He kept a secret stash of pornographic material for his periodic fix. In the deep recesses of his mind, he reasoned that he, as he had done in the past, could manipulate Barbara into accepting his promise to change his ways—and move on. Not this time! Barbara now recognized his manipulative behavior and was not satisfied with his explanations, or his promises. Barbara was angry and decided she was not going to let Jim get away with what he had done to her and their family. She formed a plan to hold him accountable to his promise to change his behavior.

Jim wondered if the cure was worse than the disease. He considered leaving Barbara but was terrified with the thought of being alone and separated from his children. He hoped that Barbara's fury would abate with time, but he was wrong.

Barbara also wondered whether she wanted to stay in the marriage. Was it worth it, she asked herself. She contemplated leaving Jim, but was confounded by the thought of financial insecurity and raising their children by herself. She convinced herself to stay until the children were in college. She made plans to get a job so she could grow financially independent. She saw Jim as a selfish bastard who was out to get his sexual needs met notwithstanding the total disregard for the marriage covenant. Although she did not call it *punishment*, she felt he had it coming when she monitored his every move. She had given up hope of ever trusting him again. Yet, deep down she felt she needed him and the security that he provided. She saw Jim as a pathetic sex monger and herself as the victim of his total selfishness.

Jim and Barbara's marriage had hit rock bottom. Both were very angry people living under the same roof and incapable of seeing a way out of their dysfunctional relationship.

Epilogue. Jim and Barbara lived in a codependent destructive world. Both lived under false premises. Jim thought his future happiness lay in Barbara agreeing to love him for whom he was without her trying to change him. Barbara saw her future happiness as a product of a reinvented Jim, and she was going to take charge of his reinvention.

Barbara would not be successful in changing Jim. Only Jim could change Jim. Sex could no longer be his greatest necessity. Jim's good friend suggested he consider seeking counseling. On his own volition, Jim entered sex addiction counseling and participated in an accompanying 12-step program. Jim's recovery would take time and he would have to grieve for the damage he had done to Barbara and their children, himself, and to all those around him. Barbara entered therapy to address her pain due to her spouse's sex addiction induced-trauma

Marital therapy will be necessary to establish trust, friendship, and a spiritual connection in the marriage. The restoration journey will take years. If Jim and Barbara do not fully invest in the therapy program, they are doomed to repeat the same failures in any subsequent relationship or marriage. Ultimately, with therapy and commitment they have a chance to heal their marriage.

Codependency - Characteristics in Jim and Barbara's Marriage

The following are characteristics of codependency found in Jim and Barbara's story. The principles set forth mirror the experiences of many couples where the male is sexually addicted.

Characteristic # one: The origin of codependency is found in a child's dysfunctional family. Parents of codependent children are often codependent themselves, as were Jim and Barbara's parents. The traits are handed down, that is, taught to each succeeding generation. The parents of the codependent children are ill equipped to provide emotional nurturing to their children. Instead, dysfunctional families abound in addiction, narcissism, and the inability to show love to their children. When parents are internally focused on their own problems, they are ill equipped to build healthy relationships with their children. They cannot give what they do not have.

Jim's father was an alcoholic. As such, he was not aware of the developmental needs of his son. Jim learned from his father how to be self-centered. He learned that earning his father's love was dependent on his performance. His father looked to Jim to succeed where he had failed. Jim's mother was a codependent enabler of her husband's alcoholism; that is, she continued to purchase alcohol for her husband. Jim could not get his emotional needs met from his family of origin. Although he was unable to codify it as a child, as an adult, he recognized that his parents emotionally abandoned him. His emotional deficiency led him to satisfy his needs without regard to the needs of those around him.

From his parents, Jim also learned to manipulate others into meeting his needs. He used his ability to dominate others to control normal interactions in his relationships. He was unable to be a friend and have empathy for others.

As a child, an older sibling sexually abused Jim. As he grew older, he turned to sexual stimulation for feelings of well-being. He substituted sexual satisfaction for friendship and respect in his relationships.

Barbara's father was emotionally distant from his family. His work and weekend golf took precedence over his family. If he had a choice, he chose to be absent from his wife and children. When Barbara was a teenager, her mother often talked about wanting to leave her husband, but never did so. Barbara now recognizes that her parents were in a codependent relationship. Barbara did not experience a sense of well-being from her parents. She felt she had to earn parental love. Among her siblings, she was the caretaker and the responsible child.

Both Jim and Barbara had all the classic traits of people who enter into a codependent marriage.

Characteristic # Two: Children of codependent dysfunctional families have ill-formed or incomplete personalities. Adult behavior, either intentionally or not, builds on the dysfunctional personality traits learned in the family of origin.

Jim often felt deficient in his social skills and questioned his self-worth. Because of his low self-esteem, he often wondered if anyone really could love him. Nevertheless, his distorted thinking led him to equate sex with love. Through his previous experience with sexual stimulation, he sought mood escalation by repeated attempts to manipulate his high school and college girlfriends. It never occurred to Jim that much more was available in a healthy relationship than sex. After all, he reasoned, if a girl would participate in sexual activity with him, surely, they loved each other.

Barbara's hole in the soul was her desire for love. In response to the attention she received from Jim, she was manipulated into an early sexual relationship. From time to time, she felt sex occupied far too much of their relationship. Several times, she attempted to establish more healthy boundaries. She was no match for Jim's manipulative skills.

Attractive body parts attracted Jim to Barbara. He lacked the insight needed to consider her personality and her personhood. He felt that the essence of their relationship was to have Barbara depend on him. Although Barbara frequently felt uneasy, she also lacked the skills to evaluate objectively their relationship. She bought into depending on him for an active college environment. After all, he was a fraternity man and she wore his pin.

Characteristic # Three: In marriage, codependency fosters pain and negativity. Once married, Jim's eyes began to wander. He needed the thrill of pursuing a new conquest. He began to repeat the cycle he began with Barbara. Jim's pursuits outside of the marriage further distanced him from providing the emotional nurturing Barbara so dearly needed.

Barbara substituted her desire for marital happiness by raising their children. Her friends saw her as an outstanding and dedicated mother. She tried to meet her children's every need. Barbara transferred her dependence on Jim to dependence on her children for her emotional well-being. She tried to fill the hole in her soul by forming a loving relationship with her children. However, children are unable to return love, as would a healthy adult.

Jim continued to insist on sex with Barbara. She feared saying no because of Jim's anger. Barbara felt disconnected from Jim. She gave him what he wanted but she felt she was paying dues.

Characteristic # Four: Fear, anger, and depressed mood are all companions of codependency. Jim continued to live in two worlds—one foot in his sexual fantasy world and one foot inside the marriage. Although he believed he was clever enough to avoid discovery, he realized that his life was out of control, and getting worse. He was ashamed and lived in a low-grade depressed mood. He knew that his relationship with Barbara had gone from good to bad but he had no idea how to change it. He did not intend to give up his best friend, sex. After all, as many sexually addictive men reason, a man needs some pleasure in life.

When Barbara learned of Jim's closely held secrets, she felt conflicting emotions. On the one hand, she was relieved that her suspicions were real and she was not crazy. On the other, she was outraged and felt great anger. She was also dominated by fear. She was fearful she would be alone in life; what would become of her and the children? How could anyone understand the intense feeling of betrayal she felt? She was so depressed that getting out of bed each day, eating, and caring for the children seemed like monumental tasks.

Characteristic # five: Old behaviors continue. For Jim and Barbara, codependency was an integral part of their marriage. Jim used his ability to manipulate Barbara so he could continue to get his needs met. Barbara used her anger to respond to Jim's betrayal of their marriage contract.

Neither would be successful.

Both would benefit from counseling. Jim needed to address his addictive behavior. Barbara may seek counseling to heal the consequences of her marital relationship and the trauma she experienced from Jim's betrayal. They both must deal with the present crisis and support the family.

Joe and Alice's story. Joe, a mid-level executive, had multiple affairs during his 20 years of marriage to Alice. It was usual for Joe to have more than one affair going at the same time. Although his marriage to Alice provided him with two wonderful children, he continued his liaisons. He said, "I do not feel particularly close to Alice. She does her thing, and I do mine."

Joe password protected his computer and email account. One evening he inadvertently left his email account open. Alice stumbled onto Joe's email exchanges with his ladies. Pandemonium ensued.

Alice demanded full disclosure. Joe complied but refused to give sufficient details to satisfy Alice. Joe reasoned he did not want to cause her more pain than he had already caused. He also talked about his fear that Alice would leave him if she knew the details. Alice wanted a full accounting of all his transgressions and she wanted him to keep her abreast of his behavior and thinking daily. She was angry and terrified. She felt betrayed, and was concerned about the future of their marriage and the raising of their children. She was suffering from sex addiction induced-trauma.

Neither Joe nor Alice wanted a divorce but the bond between them was fractured. Joe said that for years he wanted to let Alice know his most guarded secrets of infidelity, but feared she would try to fix him or leave him. In fact, his fears became a reality. Alice, in her despondency, did everything she could to hold Joe accountable to her perception of a good marriage. In her zeal to monitor Joe, she obtained his credit card and telephone records for as many years as she could. Continually she questioned any call that was not readily recognizable. She constantly accused him of going back to being unfaithful. She obtained the phone number for each of the women with whom he had been unfaithful. She called every one of them to make it clear that Joe was no longer available. She embarrassed him by talking about what a rotten person he was to anyone who would listen—at his work, church, and community.

Alice continued to demand more information and frequently asked questions about one or more of his affairs. Periodically Joe would provide the detail of an affair after which Alice berated him for the content of the detail. After each disclosure, she yelled that she could not trust him because she did not know how much more he had not told her.

Codependency is a challenging condition in any marriage.

If we remember that a codependent woman is more like a child living in a woman's body, trying desperately to hide from the terrible emptiness at her core, her behavior becomes more understandable. Clinging to an abusive relationship feels preferable to letting go and falling into a terrible abyss. (Kasl, 1990, p. 39)

They discussed their behavior in a joint marital therapy session. Alice and Joe made promises to change, but they did not. Their marriage therapist speculated that Alice had experienced sexual abuse as a child. In other words, she had her own shame. Unless they deal with the roots of their dysfunction from childhood, it is unlikely the marriage will survive.

The other side of the coin. Perhaps other couples experienced the same steps that Alice took to reclaim her husband. What is wrong with her taking positive action? Why should she not demand accountability? Why should she not demand that Joe confess his transgressions in real time so she could monitor his promise to change? After all, she is the victim of his profound selfishness—putting his needs ahead of everything dear and sacred to the marriage contract.

Alice is justified in her anger. However, if Joe is not committed to hold himself accountable to changing his behavior, Alice's efforts are headed for frustration and divorce. Joe has to see that placing his sexual needs ahead of all else has a dim future.

Alice's efforts to hold Joe accountable add to Joe's shame. Although hardly an excuse to justify acting-out behavior, shame and feelings of worthlessness often contribute to acting out. A sexually addicted man often self-medicates negative feelings.

A visual picture of Joe and Alice's codependency relationship. Picture two elevators standing side by side. Joe occupies one and Alice the other. When Alice's elevator is at the tenth floor, Joe's elevator is in the basement. When Joe's elevator is in the basement, he sees himself as the errant child, looks up, and sees a scornful mother. Joe gives Alice the power to chastise for he believes he deserves it, but he intensely resents her for doing so. Alice takes the power given to her and dutifully scolds and punishes. She is no longer the partner but has taken the role of Joe's dysfunctional mother.

They ride their elevators to the opposite levels. Alice's elevator is now in the basement and Joe's is at the tenth floor. Alice sees herself as the victim of Joe's self-centeredness. She sees his behavior as willful, destructive to the marriage, and selfish. She sees him in a superior position—doing his own thing without regard to the consequences, particularly to the marriage. Joe supports her vision by continuing to put his sexual needs first.

Joe and Alice continue to ride their respective elevators, alternating between the basement and tenth floor. As they ride, their anger intensifies and each blames the other for their predicament.

What needs to change? In simplistic terms, both Joe and Alice would do well to ride their elevators to the fifth floor, get off, and face one another.

Ideally, Joe admits he is powerless to stop his behavior—it has become unmanageable. Joe needs to expose his sense of shame to the light of day—take positive steps to come out of isolation and adopt new behaviors to enable him to forgo living in low-grade depression. Perhaps one could argue that Joe deserves to feel guilty but doing so will not support Joe's recovery journey.

Alice rejects the role of Joe's mother. Alice tells Joe, "It is not my job to change you. That is your challenge." If so inclined, she can tell him, "I will pray for you. If you would like a friendly ear while you are in therapy, I may agree to listen, but I am not willing to be your accountability partner or make suggestions."

Joe's fifth floor position is to thank Alice and to commit to counseling. His therapist will likely recommend he attend 12-step programs in addition to individual or group therapy.

While Joe works his recovery program, Alice, with the assistance of a therapist, needs to explore how to set loving boundaries without taking responsibility for Joe's recovery. She is suffering from sex addiction induced-trauma and needs guidance to address her trauma. Alice may also choose to deal with the origins of her codependent behavior in therapy.

Codependency addressed. In a healthy marriage, partners see themselves neither in a superior position nor as the victim, but as equals. Each takes individual responsibility to grow in wisdom. The addict's goal is to accept he has a problem, which he commits to address. The wife's goal is to accept she is the victim of his sex addiction induced-trauma. The two support each other in a quest to become whole and shun the paralyzing effects of shame.

In a codependent relationship, each partner's identity lies outside of the self. Each expects the other to provide wholeness. Neither partner is independent in the relationship. For example, if the intent of the woman is to change her partner's behavior, she is saying, for me, happiness lies in how my partner can change, not how I can function independently. In a codependent relationship, both parties want to be in charge but neither party feels that they are, and yet, each party feels the other is in charge.

If the marriage ends. Not all relationships weather sexual addiction and codependency. For some marriages, the history of dysfunction spans years or even decades. By the time, the partners face the demon it is too late. Often one of the partners agrees to counseling, not to restore the marriage, but to give the spouse a soft landing. In such a case, the partner has already decided to exit the relationship. Means (2003) discussed what happens next. Grief and more grief will prevail "during the transition period that separates the past from the future. The ache you feel will eventually ease, but for now, your pain may be almost unbearable" (p. 166). She advises to allow time for grieving and to seek support from their community—spiritual, friends, or counseling.

PART IV: RECOVERY

This part addresses recovery and modifying
aberrant sexual behavior. It is a guide for the mental
health community to assist sex addicts achieve long-term sexual sobriety.

CHAPTER SEVEN: THERAPY PLATFORM

Five Stages of Enlightenment

The *Five Stages of Enlightenment* is the foundation of the recovery program presented in this book. The Five Stages address the *understanding* and *treatment* of male and female sexual addiction. The program provides a conceptual framework for the presentation of *36 therapeutic exercises*. The exercises form a logically ordered therapy program. The exercises, as part of a *treatment mosaic*, are designed to bring about long-term sexual sobriety. (Refer to the book's *Table of Contents* for a listing of the exercises.)

The presentation of each exercise is preceded by a précis written to introduce a topic to the therapist. The précis, followed by a clinical note, provides guidance to administer the exercise. Clinical notes also target areas of emphasis and clinical objectives.

Each précis is followed by an exercise designed for use by the addict and administered by the therapist. The introductory narrative found in each exercise is educational and delineates the purpose of the exercise and therapy goal.

The *exercises* are applicable for use with individuals or in group therapy. The outline of *Five Stages of Enlightenment* program by chapter follows:

Chapter Eight - *Stage I - Expose Addictive Behavior, Denial, and Shame to the Light of Day.* Recovery depends on a greater self-awareness, an understanding of how and why addictive sexual behavior became ingrained, and why addiction continues despite adverse consequences.

Chapter Nine - *Stage II - Address Factors that Bind an Addict to Sexual Addiction.* Multiple factors keep an addict steeped in sexual addiction. They include sexual thinking and fantasy, acting-out cycle and rituals, depressed mood and anxiety, anger, habit, isolation, loneliness, and pornography.

Chapter 10 - *Stage III - Recovery—Modifying Behavior.* The core of recovery is eliminating addictive behavior.

Chapter 11 - *Stage IV - Live a Healthy Life Style.* The gateway to changing the addiction torment is living a healthy life style.

Chapter 12 - *Stage V - Relapse Prevention.* Continuing sexual sobriety depends on planning for inevitable future temptations.

The *Five Stages of Enlightenment* program is adapted from Carnes' sexual addiction research and concepts. The stages frame a paradigm for presenting a logical progression of therapy.

The *Five Stages of Enlightenment* program differs from Carnes' 30 task-model for recovery in presentation but not in philosophy.

Carnes' (2000, pp. 8-13) research postulates a six stage regimen as part of a five year recovery program. From his research, he divides treatment into three phases: strategies, initial treatment, and extended therapy. Most of Carnes' (2000) treatment goals are addressed in the *Five Stages of Enlightenment* recovery program (pp. 8-11).

The presentation timing of some components has changed. For example, a dysfunctional family of origin is one of the principle factors that contribute to becoming addicted. The Five Stages introduces childhood environment early in recovery whereas Carnes addresses childhood environment later in his program.

Carnes' 30 task-model for recovery is supported by research and years of clinical testing. APPENDIX D presents Carnes' task-model. The program takes up to five years to complete (Carnes 2000, p. 7). Although numerous addicts need a five-year recovery program, some cannot commit to a five-year program. The task-model provides for 18 months of individual therapy. Although an addict benefits from long-term individual therapy, cost considerations make it difficult for some clients to remain in individual therapy for 18 months. The Five Stages recovery program shortens the time an addict participates in therapy and, as does Carnes, advocates long term attendance in 12-step programs to maintain sobriety.

According to Ferree (2010), Carnes' task-model is largely based on the cognitive behavioral modality and is more apt for working with men. Because women, in general, are relational, a Rogerian type relationship is a more important factor than a task oriented therapy (p. 248).

Treatment Goals

The *Five Stages of Enlightenment* program serves as a catalyst whereby addicts become aware of the origin of their addiction and the conditions that keep them addicted. They gain understanding of the adverse consequences, learn how they can internalize a choice to make a *high-level commitment* to change behavior, and make lifestyle changes to reinforce *long-term sexual sobriety*.

Carnes (1994) framed sex addiction treatment goals in terms of actions needed. The Five Stages program endorses these actions.

- Allow the addict to hear the faulty beliefs of other addicts.

- Break through the addict's myths and rules through assignments and permission giving.

- Expand the addict's options for nurturing, handling anxiety, and developing a lifestyle congruent with personal values.

- Challenge the addict's family roles and rules.

- Provide information about healthy sexuality.

- Uncover multi-generational patterns.

- Give spiritual assistance. (p. 234)

Assessment

At the beginning of therapy, the client is introduced to assessment and diagnosis. The client is asked to sign the therapist's informed consent and HIPA statements and confidentiality boundaries are discussed. The therapist needs to probe for suicidal tendencies and thinking as well as any intention to hurt self or others. The therapist is also required to assess whether the client is engaged in abusive behavior with a child or elder adult. Such behavior may be reportable to the police and Child Protective Service (CPS).

Assessment includes structured testing and open-ended questions. The book, *Making Advances: A Comprehensive Guide for Treating Female Sex and Love Addicts* includes a guide to assessment instruments (Campling, et al., 2012, pp. 72-74). This guide is included as APPENDIX E. Another recognized assessment instrument is the *Minnesota Multiphasic Personality Inventory* (MMPI). The MMPI is a psychological test that assesses personality traits and psychopathology. It is primarily intended to test people who may have mental health or other clinical issues (Framingham, 2011, para 1).

APPENDIX A, provides Carnes' *Sexual Addiction Screening Test* (SAST) (Carnes, 2012). As an evaluation tool, the instrument is a standard in the field of sexual addiction. The test is self-scored and a scale follows to inform the client of the degree to which s/he is sexually addicted (ITAP).

APPENDIX B provides an evaluation-screening test for women. The Women's *Self-Test for Sexual/Relationship Addiction* (Carnes & O'Hare [n.d.]), is found in Appendix B. Once scored, the results inform the client of the degree to which she or he is or are not sexually addicted.

In addition, a question and narrative answer version of the Sexual Addiction Screening Test (SAST) is presented in Exercise Four. The narrative version is a second level application that is used after the results of the test instruments indicate that the client is sexually addicted. The narrative version is a source of greater insight into the addict's sexually addictive behavior.

Diagnosis

As with any client, the therapist will provide a *clinical diagnosis*. Because the DSM-V does not have a diagnosis specifically for sexual addiction, alternative diagnoses, if relevant, may relate to alcoholism, dysthymic disorder, anxiety, OCD, PTSD, adjustment disorder, or paraphilia disorders as well as any other co-addiction or conditions relevant to the client.

Clinical Exercise Three provides the client with an opportunity to record his or her sexual history. It has the same purpose as does step-one of the 12-Step program but it is structured to reveal the characteristics of behavior rather than present an iteration of sexual transgressions.

In addition, a host of medical, substance, and mental disorders need consideration. APPENDIX E (Diagnostic Considerations) delineates co-existing conditions that need to be ruled out for each client.

Treatment Plan

A sex addiction treatment plan is a road map that tracks therapy through individual or group therapy and post therapy follow-up. Because relapse is always a possibility, follow-up visits ought to be scheduled for at least two years after sex addiction therapy is completed. The addict will benefit from attendance at 12-step programs at least until s/he has completed the 12-steps and, ideally, has served as a sponsor. Once the addict changes from a *taker* to a *giver,* the potential for relapse is significantly diminished.

In therapy, treatment needs to address all dysfunctional behaviors, both sexual and other addictions as well as any mental health disorders (See APPENDIX E - Diagnostic Considerations). Therapy requires a level playing field. For example, if the addict continues to get high each day, none of the addictions can be addressed. The behavior that causes the greatest dysfunction is addressed first. For example, if behavior results in legal consequences, that behavior needs to be addressed immediately. The sex addiction therapist may or may not address all conditions. For example, medical issues are usually referred to a physician.

A treatment plan is prepared by the therapist whereas the relapse plan is prepared by the addict and reviewed by the therapist. The content of the relapse plan will include many of the elements from a treatment plan but in greater detail.

Although each client is unique, treatment still follows core principles. Treatment as delineated in the *Five Stages of Enlightenment* and accompanying exercises is a good place to start. For some, Carnes' 30 task-centered treatment plan is a better alternative.

Treatment Alternatives. Carnes (2000) assessed the effectiveness of treatment components by asking 190 men in recovery which components they found to be most and least useful. The results of his research are informative and may guide the therapist's selection of treatment options (p. 9-10).

Below are the most effective *treatment options* selected by at least half of the participants. They are listed in hierarchical order:

- Higher power (87%). (See Exercise 30 for an explanation of the term Higher Power.)

- Twelve-step groups for sexual addiction (85%). (See Exercise 31 for an explanation of the term Twelve-step.)

- Friends' support (69%).

- Individual therapy (65%).

- Period of celibacy (64%) (See Exercise 16).

- Sponsor (61%).

- Exercise/Nutrition (58%).

- Twelve-step programs for other than sexual addiction (55%) (See Exercise 31).

Treatment choices selected by less than 30 % of participants are:

- Outpatient group (27%).

- Couples' therapy (21%).

- Family therapy (11%).

- Aftercare (Hospital) (9%). (Carnes, 2000, p. 10)

Outpatient group therapy is often a mandatory form of treatment for sex offenders, whereas group therapy conducted in a less structured setting is usually voluntary. The rigors of mandatory attendance may explain why Carnes' research found a low regard for outpatient group therapy.

The *Five Stages of Enlightenment* treatment program is effective in *group* counseling. In a group program, the addict learns from fellow travelers as an adjunct to individual therapy or written materials. Hearing a group member's addiction story often motivates other members to break through their own denial barriers.

Treatment Modality. Treatment modalities for counseling the sexually addicted vary. Cognitive-Behavioral therapy disrupts cognitive distortions and dysfunctional beliefs. For example, when introduced to cognitive-behavioral principles, the addict is empowered to identify dysfunctional thinking and feelings that precede his or her sex addiction cycle (See Exercise Six). Thus, a cognitive key is to become *aware* of mental triggers and to interdict them before *tunnel vision* takes the addict down his or her acting-out ritual (See Exercise Seven).

Other modalities, tested in a clinical setting, are effective. For example, Gestalt techniques work well. The empty chair or role reversal techniques inspire the addict to recognize distorted beliefs. Person-Centered therapy helps the addict to internalize unconditional love as opposed to feeling devalued because of addictive behaviors.

Hayden (2012) clarified:

Treatment for sex addiction, then, is most likely to be effective when it emerges from an integrated approach that brings together various treatment methods, is individually tailored to the addict's personality and evolves as he/she progresses. (The Problem of Sex Addiction section, para. 7

Recovery Journey

By analogy, recovery is like a journey. Early in the journey a man and woman will fall into one *acting-out pothole* after another. As time goes by, addicts may see a pothole ahead but fall in just the same. In time, they gain strength and are able to pull themselves to the top. To climb out of a pothole requires the support of a 12-step program, a sponsor or accountability partner, and therapist. Well down the road, the journey becomes easier. The man or woman see the acting-out potholes in advance and are able to jump over or walk around them. However, the journey is life long and no possible outcome includes *cured*. Sexual urges or temptations are a lifetime companion for the recovering sex addict. Once sexual sobriety becomes a reality, the addict must continue to refine his or her relapse prevention plan to preclude a return to addictive behavior.

Recovery is not linear. During recovery, the addict repeatedly searches for insight into the meaning of a *high-level commitment* as a way to change his or her addiction dance.

Early in therapy, an addict may accept as noise such behavior as masturbation or sexual fantasy. The addict's denial is often phrased as; "I am not hurting anybody," or some other rationale. In Chapter Four, denial is presented as a factor that bonds an addict to sexual addiction. Mitigating denial is a factor in each successive purging of sexual behavior.

The recovery journey includes many facets. They are presented below:

Twelve-step programs. According to Carnes (2000), attendance in a 12-step program is a recovery requirement. An addict needs the support of those who face the same issues. A 12-step program includes *working the steps* and meeting regularly with a sponsor. Weekly attendance (or more frequent) at 12-step meetings continues long after formal therapy ends (p. 11). (See Exercises 31 and 34).

Exercise/Nutrition. Healthy living, that is, a regular exercise program, healthy diet and weight control, and proper nutrition reduce the urge to act out. Group program participants reported physical exercise as one key to their sexual sobriety. If the therapist has doubts about the client's health habits, a referral to a medical physician is in order.

Abstinence contract. At the beginning of therapy, an addict is encouraged to undertake a *period of sexual celibacy*. One of the objectives of celibacy is to reduce the power of brain chemicals to foster sexual behavior. Another is to change the focus from fighting temptation to freeing the addict to concentrate on elements of recovery, such as therapy and attendance at 12-step meetings. An abstinence contract is a written agreement between the addict, the addict's spouse, and the therapist. Ideally, the contract excludes sexual contact, flirting, objectification, seduction, pornography, masturbation, relational sex and love affairs, and all forms of marital sex. It also addresses curtailing sexual thinking and fantasy (Carnes, 2001, p. 202). Even sexual thinking and fantasy keep the brain's neuropathways contaminated. The period of abstinence lasts for two to three months.

The abstinence contract includes specific *content*. It begins with a list of sexual practices from which the addict pledges to refrain during the duration of the contract. Second is a list of strategies (See Exercise 20) the addict will employ when tempted to engage in sexual activity. The third is a plan to solicit the addict's accountability partner or sponsor to support the addict and his or her abstinence pledge. Finally, the contract incorporates a goal statement, which reflects the addict's long-term expectation of what a high-level commitment will look like in post recovery (Carnes, 2000, pp. 9-12). Ultimate recovery includes a high-level commitment to sexual sobriety (Carnes, 2001, p. 137).

Recovery requires an assessment of what constitutes healthy sexual behavior. The period of celibacy is an ideal time to discuss what the addict's future sexuality will look like. Implementing an abstinence plan is addressed in Exercise 16.

Feelings. The restoration triad includes behavior modification, normalizing shame, and reconnecting addicts to normal feelings. While living in a dysfunctional home, the future sex addict (child) learned that expressing *feelings was unsafe*. The child learned to *repress* his or her feelings. Since it was not safe to express feelings as a child, the addict forms a belief that sharing feelings as an adult is not safe either (Carnes, 2001, pp. 216-218).

During recovery, addicts are encouraged to rediscover their normal feelings. For a sex addict, reintroduction of feelings is primarily experiential. Therapists can assist addicts to become aware of their feelings in the present moment by asking them to name a feeling when their body language depicts stress, discomfort, levity, consternation, shame, guilt, or any physically depicted emotion to which a feeling is naturally attached. *Rediscovered feelings* are owned when addicts begin to name their feelings without being prompted.

Spirituality. At the time sex addicts enter therapy they may be spiritually empty. By analogy, their inability to control behavior may promote spiritual floundering. Addicts are often drifting upon a sea of shame, from one failed relationship to another, from one sexual experience to the next, and with little hope of seeing land. The addicts' spiritual boat is burdened by heavy weights, which make it difficult to steer. The heavy weights are distorted core beliefs and impaired thinking. Steering currents may keep them at sea. Addicts need to call upon their Higher Power to assist them to navigate the currents, off load heavy weights, and shift the winds in order to reach shore (Weiss, 1998, pp. 77-81). (See Exercise 30).

Sexual addiction is a self-centered illness. Recovery is enhanced when the addict's priorities change to *serve others*. For example, a powerful therapeutic experience is serving as a sponsor in a 12-step program. At the proper time, the addict serves other addicts while developing more insight into his or her own behavior. It takes time before the addict is ready and able to change from being a *taker* to a *giver*. The change is an opportunity to embrace the tenets of the 12-step and, for many, an important concept in spiritually (Weiss, 1998, p. 78).

Disclosure. Disclosure of past sexual behavior is a component of the 12-step program and sex addiction therapy. *Disclosure* promotes *marital honesty* (See Exercise 29) as well as supporting relapse prevention (See Exercises 32-36). Most addicts disclose sexual secrets or practices only after being discovered (Corley & Schneider, 2002a, p. 8). At some level, the addict realizes that *addiction depends on secrets*. Unburdening secrets diminishes denial (Corley & Schneider, 2002a, p. 53-73). Disclosure also provides relief from shame.

Although the addict feels a sense of liberation after disclosure, the addict's partner may not feel the same. Hearing about the addict's profound betrayal may cause the innocent partner to experience significant disclosure-related trauma and even PTSD (Corley, Ferree, & McDaniel, 2012 p. 220). In addition to distress, the innocent partner simply lacks knowledge of the nature of sexual addiction. What can s/he do about the person s/he thought s/he knew intimately, but did not? What should s/he do with all the new information? *Disclosure* is best made in a counseling session with the assistance of a therapist who can guide the disclosure, set boundaries, and enable the innocent partner to manage the effects of trauma (Schneider, Corley, & Irons, 1998, pp. 189-217).

When the partner of a sex addict suffers from PTSD, situations that bring back memories of the original betrayal may cause panic, fleeing, weeping, and disassociation (Steffens & Means, 2009, p. 93).

It is likely that the addict will want to share more memories in due time. Some partners are equipped to handle additional disclosure, but for many, it is another painful experience. The couple needs to understand the difference between disclosure that heals a relationship and disclosure that merely allows the addict to unburden his or her conscience. A therapist guides the process of setting disclosure boundaries. Subsequent disclosures also take place in the presence of a therapist (Becker, 2012b, p. 102).

Medication. An addict may benefit from a regimen of antidepressant medication (*SSRI or SNRI's*) to address attributes of sexual addiction: low-grade depression, anxiety, sexual urges, and behavior.

A number of studies have indicated that antidepressant medications, particularly the SSRIs, can reduce the frequency of addictive sexual behavior and the intensity of urges to engage in addictive sexual behavior, even when the patient does not have major depression. (Goodman, 2009, Psychiatric Pharmacotherapy section, para. 2)

As appropriate, the addict should be referred to a psychiatrist for an evaluation. The addict may also benefit from a physical health evaluation.

Treatment for Women. Even thinking about changing behavior is a challenge for an addicted woman. An empathic relationship between a woman and her therapist is the most powerful healing intervention possible—particularly for those who experienced an attachment deficit as a child. Only by conveying, a sense of a *genuine caring* will encourage a woman to move forward in her recovery.

According to Ferree (2010), "the therapeutic relationship is critical because of the extraordinary shame women carry. Female addicts are emotionally fragile and require more therapeutic nurturing" (p. 248). It is essential for therapists to create a safe environment for their clients to heal. Therapy may move at a slower pace to allow trust to develop. "You must endure their countertransference with patience and grace" (Ferree, 2010, p. 248). "Carnes' task-centered treatment modality is not as effective with women as it is with men, and sometimes counterproductive" (Ferree, 2010, p. 248).

Some women relate better to a male therapist. On the other hand, most females readily connect with a woman. A female therapist, instinctively relational, conveys the message, "*You are loved here.*" The woman reacts with optimism when she feels her therapist is her recovery cheerleader. She responds to knowing she is not alone; she is with someone who understands and does not judge her (Ferree, 2010, p. 247-249).

Generally, a woman enters therapy at the time of a *crisis*—discovery, loss of work, threatened divorce, venereal disease, or pregnancy. The therapist begins therapy by conveying a sense of connection that allows the woman to feel secure. The early phase of therapy encourages the woman to deescalate her sexual behavior, manage her crisis, and break through denial. A functional support system will be necessary. The therapist, initially, may fill the support gap through phone calls or other means of communicating (McDaniel et al., 2012, p. 27).

When ready, the woman begins to explore the *elephant* (Sexual Addiction) in the room. It begins by examining the consequences that were derived from a lack of attachment and/ or abandonment by her family of origin. It is a shock for her to realize that *parental love* was likely compromised. Another early step is to realize how her acting-out rituals and cycle kept her addiction alive. She also needs to grasp how relational sexual behaviors have failed her. She is encouraged to feel empathy for her child within and compassion for those who hurt her and those she hurt.

Sessions with the spouse of the addict. Given that sexual addiction contributes to a dysfunctional marriage, the marital relationship needs support. One or more sessions with the addict's partner can yield several benefits.

- If the innocent partner lacks knowledge about sexual addiction, answer questions about sexual addiction, therapy, and the 12-step program. Alternatively, introduce the book, *Why is My Partner Sexually Addicted? Insight Women Need* (Becker, 2012a). (See Exercise 28).

- Discuss the beginning of addiction; often long before the couple formed a relationship or even met. Unless the partner was an enabler, the partner did nothing to contribute to the spouse's addiction.

- Ask the partner to let therapy be the catalyst for the addict's recovery. Actions by the innocent partner will not cure the addict's addiction.

- Ask the innocent partner to support the spouse's recovery by engaging in healthy non-sexual activities (See Exercise 23).

- Explain the benefits of proper disclosure of addictive behavior.

- Explain how a sexual abstinence contract promotes sexual sobriety.

- Encourage the innocent partner to set loving boundaries.

Recovery from Sexual Addiction. Every addict's psyche is unique and what works for one may not work for another. Change does not occur until the addict internalizes that the pain of addiction exceeds the pleasure of acting out. The *Five Stages of Enlightenment* treatment program includes compelling reasons in support of change in addictive behavior and a relapse strategy to prevent future aberrant behavior. Together with the guidance of a competent therapist, the program assists the addict to make a choice to travel the recovery road (Ferree, 2010, p. 192).

The term, *recovery*, means the addict has participated in therapy and has achieved long-term sexual sobriety. The statement is short and simple because exceptions to any definition of recovery could fill several chapters. Notwithstanding all the possible exceptions to the above statement, the final determination is an assessment between the client and therapist.

The time needed for *recovery is not predictable with any confidence.* However, a very broad estimate derived from clinical experience posits a year to 18 months of therapy, on average, particularly for group participants. The time does not include post-therapy attendance at a 12-step program(s) and check-up sessions. Others benefited by longer-term therapy. Some never achieve total sexual sobriety.

For the therapist it is always heartening to witness when the client's mental *light bulb* becomes a beacon and shines with understanding. For an addict to realize fully that his or her behaviors hurt family members, friends, partner, self and spiritual relationship, is an early therapeutic step.

For the addict in recovery another view is possible. Ewald (2003) said it this way:

Addiction can be a positive factor in their life, if we realize that it may be the one thing that enables one to endure the worst situations and go on to live a life that can later be full and rewarding. The addict must learn the value of his or her self as a whole person, rather than as a sexual object. By doing this, the addict will understand that recovery is not possible without abstaining from it and they are able to develop a new sense of themselves. They begin to appreciate their sense of strength and purpose. Then a new way of looking at life emerges. (para. 7)

Therapeutic Treatment Exercises

The following exercises are intended to inspire. Each was constructed to stimulate addicts to consider all the various factors that influence their addictive behavior. At some point, most addicts break through denial and choose to make a high-level commitment to end their sexual addiction.

An addict's mental *light bulb* may illuminate from an unexpected source of energy. At times, the source seems to be Divine intervention or, at least a keen intuition! The therapeutic relationship between the client and therapist also fosters healing and recovery. In addition, the interaction and cross talk within a sex addiction group is a significant source of enlightenment.

The format of the exercises varies. Multiple exercises are presented in a question, answer, and discussion design. Some are open-ended surveys and several require the addict to research an answer.

At times, subject matter first presented in PART THREE, supplements the exercises. For example, the presentation on codependency in PART THREE complements the text included in the codependency exercise.

Finally, this book's comprehensive educational content and exercises serve as a platform for the addict to participate in a 12-step program.

Chapters Eight through 12 present the *Five Stages of Enlightenment* as a framework for the *36 therapeutic exercises.*

CHAPTER EIGHT: STAGE I - EXPOSING ADDICTIVE BEHAVIOR, DENIAL AND SHAME TO THE LIGHT OF DAY

At the beginning of therapy, clients frequently lack perception as to why they became sexually addicted. This book, together with therapy, exposes the addict to a new way of thinking about one's addictive behavior. To choose new thinking patterns, simply stated, requires a compelling reason why one ought to change thinking. Recovery first depends on enlightenment, that is, gaining a greater awareness of self, how and why sexual behavior became ingrained, and why one continues to engage in it. In time, recovery involves making a choice to end aberrant sexual behavior.

Awareness Leads to Choice

Before clients can choose to change aberrant sexual behavior, they require insight into their disease. They benefit by *awareness* of:

- Their distorted or magical thinking.

- Lies and myths they believe.

- Family structure and rules that set the stage for addiction.

- Understanding how multi-generational patterns affected an addictive life.

- Spirituality, is it dead or alive?

- Their dysfunctional core beliefs.

- Their sexual thinking and fantasies.

- Their aberrant sexual behavior.

- The impact of low-grade depressed mood.

- The consequences of anger and anxiety.

- The role of isolation that influences sexual behavior.

These behaviors confound the ability of the addict to see reality. Therapy and participation in a 12-step program raise the client's awareness of the nature of sexual addiction. Awareness and knowledge lead to choices, which, in turn, lead to the opportunity to change one's life.

Therapist introduction to Exercise One:
Roots of Sexual Addiction

Childhood sexual behavior begins before the child understands what is happening. Exercise One provides several vignettes that describe the conditions of early exposure to sexual behavior. Several dominate themes play out in these vignettes.

They are:

- Exposure to unsuitable sexual material or stimulation occurred during prepubescent years.

- The child's relationship with his or her parents, particularly the father, was distant or lacking.

- Parental involvement in the life of their child lacked emotional nurturing and affirmation. Their love was conditional and the child learned s/he had to perform well in school, sports, arts, etc., in order to be loved and to behave according to rigid parental expectations.

- Parents were not told about their son or daughter's exposure to sex, not by the child or anyone else.

- The child feared or anticipated bad consequences if his or her parents learned about his or her exposure to sex.

- Each child was confused, that is, felt both pleasure and guilt when introduced to sex.

- Following the introduction to sex, sexual behavior was repeated and, for some, it becomes a habit.

- Sexual behavior, learned as a child, was likely repeated as an adult.

An adult addict does not function well because of the burden of shame. Believing self is bad because of early exposure to sex or parental abandonment is a primary source of shame. An early step is to dispel shame rooted in the child's belief that s/he was responsible for engaging in sexual behavior.

Assist the addict to recall early exposure to sex and explain, *"Sexual addiction roots lie in the behavior of other people, not in his or her behavior."* This is not to excuse adult aberrant sexual behavior. It is intended to dispel shame, that is, the addict's belief that s/he is a bad person or damaged goods. S/he is not a bad person or damaged goods; s/he is dealing with a bad problem that initially was not of his or her making.

Clinical notes. In Exercise One, the addict will explore early age exposure to sexual material or abuse. Following the reading of several child abuse stories, the addict is invited to explore his/her own catalytic event (first exposure to abusive sex) and the characteristics surrounding his/her own exposure to sex.

Two caveats, first, some clients are not in touch with their catalytic event at the beginning of therapy. Second, the roots of sexual addiction did not begin in prepubescent years for all. A client may have experienced a catalytic event during teen or later years (Chapter Three).

At the end of Exercise One is an alternative story. It is a story by a man who experienced conditions found in models two, three, or four. Below are the four models.

Model One. Exposure to sexual behavior or material during childhood, together with a lack of a nurturing family environment, creates a psyche-gap that the child fills with sexual activity similar to that, which the child experienced during his or her initial exposure to a sexual stimulus (Ferree, 2010, pp. 126-129).

Model Two. Absence exposure to healthy sexuality during childhood is followed by an overwhelming exposure to perverse sexual material or behavior during late teen or early adult years. Once exposed, the young adult compulsively seeks sexual expression.

Model Three. Multiple attempts to develop a sexual relationship with another person fail. Failed advances, made during late teen or early adult years, are followed by the opportunity to control their sexual environment by paying for sex. In this model, the arousal is based on gaining control of others. The addict shuns human attachment for fear of rejection or feelings of inadequacy.

Model Four. Mental illness, use of certain medications, substance abuse, and PTSD may trigger emotional and psychological pain that the victim soothes through sexual stimulation.

The objectives of this section are:

- To explore the conditions that fostered sexual addiction.

- To bring to light the catalytic event s/he experienced.

- To reduce shame by proving that the sexually addicted person did not freely choose to be a sex addict.

Exercise 1: Roots of Sexual Addiction

Childhood exposure to sex begins before a child can comprehend the consequences. One of the more devastating consequences of early introduction to sex is shame. Early initiation to sex and parental abandonment are primary sources of shame-based addiction. The child's believe that s/he was responsible for allowing sexual behavior to occur is rooted in shame. It gives birth to the belief that self is bad.

The child, and later the addict, must come to understand that the roots of *sexual addiction lie in the behavior of other people, not in his or her own behavior.* This change in perception dispels shame and the child's belief that s/he is a damaged human being. The addict is not a bad person but s/he is dealing with a bad problem that initially was not of his or her making. This is not to excuse adult aberrant sexual behavior.

The following vignettes present the characteristics generally found in the roots of sexual addiction. They are presented in detail to relate how destructive untimely exposure to sexual material and behavior can be. At times, the descriptions are graphic—unfortunately, the acts of abuse are graphic. Children live through these events and some are affected for life. Each child in these vignettes was introduced to sexuality at a time in life when human development does not allow the child to make informed decisions. The vignettes show common themes about the beginning of sexual addiction illustrative of Model One above.

While the vignettes are presented in the male voice, a female child is more likely to be exposed to sex than a male child is.

Jack's story. From my earliest memory, I recall my mother tying me to a chair whenever I was in her way, which was often. I remember my mother constantly yelling at me—telling me how I could do better. It was nearly impossible for me to satisfy her expectations. She was a perfectionist. I was the older of two boys.

Dad was not around much. He often worked away from home for months at a time and, when he was home, he did not have time for us. I have no memory of a pleasant conversation with him. I do not remember him taking time to teach us about sports or anything meaningful. I do remember his pornographic magazines. Around age 10, I found his collection. What impressed me were pictures of women with large breasts. When I stared at the pictures, I felt strange—what I now know as arousal. My arousal feelings would turn to guilt. My mother also had large breasts. As a child, I scanned the daily newspapers as I looked for images of women with large breasts. As a teenager, when I was home alone, I would look at Dad's magazines and fantasize about having sex with one of the women pictured while I masturbated.

I have a very vivid memory of a shameful encounter with his father. Around age 12, my father caught me looking at one of his porn magazines. My enraged father stripped me naked in front of our home and beat me. Other children, including several neighborhood girls around my age watched. I remember a profound sense of humiliation. Later I sought out one of the girls who had watched. I left her naked. I hated her and my father.

As an adult, I thought it was all right to masturbate. All men do it, I reasoned. I continued to masturbate with the aid of pornographic pictures. As time went by, I sought human contact to stimulate me. I began to visit massage parlors, at times, several times a week. I spent at least a thousand dollars a month on sex. I also found much better pornographic material on the Internet. I estimate that I spent at least 20 percent of my week thinking about sexual images or masturbating.

Ted's story. I have a vivid memory of my first sex play. A neighbor boy, Chris, who was five years older, fondled me when I was six years old. I remember a titillating feeling when Chris touched my '*Willy*.' I felt very confused but I liked his attention.

I liked the new feeling but I knew it was not right. We always had to hide in the garage. Chris told me not to tell anyone. I wondered why Chris chose me—many other boys lived in the neighborhood. Could something be wrong with me? Did I cause it to happen? Was I bad? Why did I feel guilty when we had sex play? I wanted to tell my parents but thought Chris would beat me if I told. I also thought my parents would punish me if they knew what I did.

While I was in early grade-school years, several neighborhood boys engaged in sex play (I was the youngest). A few years later, I introduced a neighborhood boy to sex play. Sex play continued into my early teenage years.

As a child, and particularly as a teen, I did not have many friends. Often teased because of my size, I made friends with a football player. I was devastated when he punched me in the face for what seemed to be no reason at all. I often cried myself to sleep. Today, I recognize that I lived in depressed mood. I was not close to either of my parents. I did not have a happy childhood. I did well academically because my parents told me I had get good grades. However, no matter how hard I tried, it seemed that my parents thought I could do better. My father wanted me to play baseball but I was not good enough to make the team. Dad had a continuing problem with alcohol. My mother was busy with her social life.

I married Ann and joined the military. After a few years, I thought Ann used sex as a weapon to control me. I was sure she did not love me. When children came along, I took overseas assignments that kept me away from them. When I was away, I used alcohol and masturbation to medicate my loneliness.

Ted's thoughts turned to sex with men. He eventually made contact with others who considered sex among separated married men a reasonable thing to do. Ted had an eighteen-month affair with a man who was about five years older. Ted thought this man was a potential companion and deep male friend—the male friendship he wanted all of his life. He subsequently learned that his male partner was only interested in sex.

Hank's story. Both of my parents brought home sex partners, particularly when they were drunk. My father did nothing to conceal his sexual encounters from his children. Although I knew well who my parents were supposed to be, I regarded my older brother and sister as my real parents.

I was angry, repulsed, and ashamed by my parents' behavior. I did not understand why my older brothers were not as repulsed as I was. As my brothers grew older, they brought home pornography and eventually sex partners. I wanted to escape my environment but did not know how. Eventually, father disappeared from the family and because of lack of money, my mother, brothers, and sister moved to a government-subsidized housing project. When I was about fourteen years old, an older woman, who lived on a floor above, asked me to help her. I helped her but it became clear that she wanted help with something else. She wanted sex. The word spread and soon I was the new young stud in the project.

In my late teens, I vowed to escape. I moved to a town several hundred miles away. Unfortunately, I did not escape. I began to have affairs with several women simultaneously. I married one of the women with whom I had an affair. She wanted me to give up all of my women. I found it very difficult to limit my sexual life to one woman.

Art's story. As a boy of four or five, I remember being dressed in white tights and a frilly dress and hearing how cute I looked. I often wondered if my parents would have preferred a daughter.

Early in my life, my grandmother cared for me. My mother worked and traveled frequently as part of her job. She would come home from business trips very tired and say she needed time to herself. I do not remember my mother as affectionate. I am sure I was held and hugged but I cannot remember it happening. My father was not affectionate either; he was busy with his business, which required most of his waking hours. In grade school the message I remember was, 'We will love you even more if you get excellent grades in school.' I strived hard to get excellent grades but it did not make much difference in how my parents treated me.

During my grade school years, when my parents were not home, I went to my mother's bedroom and dressed in her clothing. I particularly liked to dress in her white pantyhose. Around 12 years of age, my mother caught me dressed in her clothing. She immediately took me to my father for punishment. Both my parents shamed me by telling me how greatly I had disappointed them. I felt guilty for wanting to dress in my mother's clothing but did not know what to do about it. As a teen, I became aroused when I dressed in female clothing and I looked forward to masturbating while viewing myself in the mirror.

I thought I came from a loving family, but during therapy, I began to question my thinking. Although I can talk to my parents, I believe their love is conditioned on how well I do in graduate school and how much money I will earn.

As a young adult, I periodically bought women's clothing and engaged in sex bingeing until I became disgusted with himself. I then trashed the clothing and tried to reform my ways. However, when I saw a woman dressed attractively, I formed a fantasy of wearing her clothes and masturbated while fantasizing. I then bought more clothes.

Simon's story. Around age five, I played unattended with neighborhood children up and down the street. One summer afternoon, two older neighborhood girls told me they wanted to play doctor with me. We went to one of the girl's back yard and made a tent with blankets. Once inside the tent, the girls undressed and touched me. They said it was *tickling*. I felt confused for this never happened before and I was not sure I liked the new feeling.

Time passed quickly and I realized I was late for dinner. I was supposed to be home before the six o'clock fire whistle sounded. Upon hearing the whistle, I ran home. When I entered the kitchen, my clothes were a mess. My shirt was out, my pants were unbuttoned, and I was missing a sock. I was frightened and was sure my mother would question me. I really wanted to tell her what the girls had done with me. Instead, she yelled at me for being late. Why didn't she ask me about my clothes? Did she know what I had been doing? I felt even more confused.

Several weeks later, one of the girls returned and took me into the woods across from where I lived. This time there were no blankets under which to hide. A neighborhood child told my father what was happening in the woods. He told me I was a bad boy. As I grew, my interest in sex play with neighborhood children grew. I wondered what was wrong with me. Why did I seem to be the one interested in sex play?

I felt isolated in my marriage. My wife's frequent criticism confirmed I was the bad person I knew I had been all my life. Several years after our wedding, an opportunity to *tickle* a child sexually presented itself. I could not resist. My feelings of guilt and shame were overwhelming. I became very depressed. I was subsequently prosecuted.

Jimmy's story. My family belonged to a prestigious country club with all the amenities of golf, tennis, swimming, and social events. My parents worked during the day. In the summer, they dropped me off at the country club on their way to work. My schedule was filled with golf and tennis lessons. Sometimes in the afternoon, I went swimming with other 11-year-old boys like myself.

I liked tennis because, Steve the tennis pro, paid a lot of attention to me. I took to spending afternoon hours in the tennis shack with Steve. Steve taught me how to re-string a racket and other useful skills. One day while spending time with Steve, I told him I wanted to join my friends and to go swimming. Unfortunately, I had forgotten to bring my swim trunks that day. Steve said he had a pair in the lost and found that probably would fit me. He told me to check the fit of the trunks while I was at the tennis shack. As I changed, Steve watched. He said that for a young boy I had a large '*Willy.*' He asked if I ever make it hard. He asked me to show him how I did it. I felt very *weird* but I did not want to disappoint my friend Steve.

As the summer went by, Steve found opportunities to fondle me. I liked the attention Steve showed to me. I felt that perhaps our secret behavior was Steve's way of teaching me to be a man—at least that was what Steve said. I never told my parents. It seemed that a time when my parents were open to listening just never happened. I knew something was wrong with what was happening. I was confused between the good feelings I experienced and the secrets Steve made me keep.

After the summer, I no longer saw Steve. He moved to a warmer climate. I continued to masturbate whenever I felt I wanted to repeat the good feelings I first experienced with Steve. As a teenager, I masturbated more frequently.

I entered therapy in my early thirties to deal with compulsive masturbation and pornography. I am committed to shed my victimhood.

Ron's story. I remember my teenaged brother, Todd, touching me when I was about seven-years-old. It happened one evening when Todd was babysitting me. We were in his bedroom sitting on his bed. It was a treat to be in Todd's bedroom because normally Todd did not allow me in his room. To this day, I remember that Todd's bedspread and curtains had matching red and green plaid patterns.

Todd had several magazines hidden in a drawer. He showed me one of the magazines. I felt very strange…I didn't know what to make of the pictures. Why would anyone let a picture be taken of their bare bottom?

Todd told me he wanted to show me something that felt good. Todd pulled my pants down and touched me. I didn't like it and I wanted Todd to stop. It didn't seem right that Todd would touch me there. Mom told me about good and bad touch and I felt this was bad touch. I began to cry and Todd stopped.

Our parents came home early and Todd told me not to tell our parents. I wanted to tell dad but I was afraid of him. Our dad often yelled at us, particularly after he had been drinking, which was often.

A few years later, I found a magazine similar to the one Todd had showed me. I still couldn't understand why anyone would allow pictures to be taken of their bare bottoms.

Common Elements Found in the Roots of Sexual Addiction

To identify the common elements found in these vignettes, answer the following questions:

Approximately, at what age was each child introduced to sexual activity, material, or promiscuity?

_____
_____
_____
_____

What type of relationship did each child have with his parents (close, neutral, distant)?

_____
_____
_____
_____

How did they feel about their parents' involvement in their lives? What did the parents expect from them?

_____
_____
_____
_____

To whom did each child tell about his exposure to sex? Why?

_____
_____
_____
_____

What parental response did each anticipate if they told about their exposure to sex?

_____
_____
_____
_____

What feelings did each child express when they were introduced to sex? (Find at least four expressions of feelings.)

_____
_____
_____
_____
_____
_____
_____
_____

Was the introduction to sex a one-time happening? What happened as each progressed in age?

_____
_____
_____
_____
_____

What happened to each in his adulthood?

_____
_____
_____
_____
_____

As an adult, did any of the men repeat the sexual behavior they learned as a child? If yes, indicate how.

_____
_____
_____
_____

As men, are any of them sexually addicted? Why?

_____
_____
_____
_____

Your story. Your catalytic story may not be as clear. It may take time for you to remember. For others, the experience is as fresh as what happened yesterday. Some remember their primary catalytic story later during therapy. You may find the memory of your catalytic story embarrassing. You may blame yourself for something you perceived was wrong or bad, particularly if you experienced erotic pleasure or you believe you cooperated in the event.

Finally, you may have difficulty recalling your catalytic story because you perceived what happened was normal. A family member who you believed was not doing anything wrong may have perpetrated the event. For example, Johnny's mother bathed him each evening until age 12. His mother took particular care to wash his genitals. At times Johnny was aroused. Johnny had no model of life to tell him that his mother's behavior was not normal.

Answer the following questions. Be patient with yourself as you recall your catalytic story.

At what age were you first introduced to sexual material or behavior?

_____
_____
_____
_____

How clearly do you remember the surroundings? Take a few minutes and record the surroundings. Where did it happen? What are the images and sounds you remember? Who else was there? What was your breathing like? What smells can you remember? Was there an atmosphere of secrecy?

_____
_____
_____
_____
_____
_____
_____
_____
_____
_____

How old was the person who introduced you to sexual material or behavior? What was your relationship to that person?

_____
_____
_____
_____

Was that person who introduced you to sex an age-appropriate companion for you? What power did that person have over you? Did that person's power make a difference? What would have happened differently if the person did not have power over you?

_____

_____

_____

_____

_____

_____

What kind of a relationship did you have with your father? Were you emotionally connected to your father?

_____

_____

_____

_____

What kind of a relationship did you have with your mother? Were you emotionally connected to your mother?

_____

_____

_____

_____

Did you feel comfortable in telling your parents what happened? Why? Did you tell anyone else?

_____

_____

_____

_____

What feelings do you remember from your first exposure to sexual material or behavior? Were you excited, afraid, curious, embarrassed? Did you have mixed feelings?

_____

_____

_____

_____

Did you have feelings of arousal? Was your body's response physical or mental or both?

_____
_____
_____
_____

Do you remember having feelings of being bad or ashamed? Describe each.

_____
_____
_____
_____

What are you feeling at this moment as you remember your catalytic event? For example, do you feel fear, shame, guilt, arousal, sadness, curiosity, confusion, embarrassment, numbness?

_____
_____
_____
_____
_____
_____

Why do you think you are having these feelings as you remember your catalytic event?

_____
_____
_____
_____

Did you repeat your catalytic event? How soon did you repeat your catalytic event? Describe your behavior.

_____
_____
_____
_____
_____

What sexual behavior(s) do you engage as an adult that mirrored the behavior that began when you were a child?

_____
_____
_____
_____
_____
_____

The story that follows is a prototype of stories associated with model two.

Joshua's story - an alternative story. I was raised in a highly disciplined family. From an early age, I knew I was to be seen and not heard. My brothers and sisters were very obedient to our parent's wishes. All members of the family had chores to begin and end each day. Although the family dined together, a common theme at the family table was father's commentary on what was wrong with the world, the government, and the neighbors. The only discussion allowed by father was a supporting story or agreement.

I felt my family was special; they knew right from wrong. However, I felt our family didn't fit in at church. We often came home right after church rather than attend church functions. Outside of members of our family, we had few friends. We were not allowed to associate with neighborhood children who were not home schooled as we were. The family watched only educational TV channels. No discussion of anything sexual was permitted. I had no knowledge of the human reproductive system until I was 15. I found it hard to believe what a neighbor boy told me. I could not believe my parents would do that.

I believe I was raised in a loving environment. I knew our parents loved us, otherwise, why would they beat us when we were in error?

I joined the military when I was eighteen. I was stationed overseas. My new friends thought it was funny when I told them I had never dated or kissed a girl. They helped me make up for lost time. I went wild with my new feelings. Sex became my primary requirement.

Your story. If your introduction to sexual addiction was similar to that described in models two, three, and four, please complete your story.

To which model do you relate? Explain in detail.

_____
_____
_____
_____
_____
_____
_____
_____
_____

If the roots of your sexual addition were not formed in childhood, relate how you first began to act out in a sexual way.

_____
_____
_____
_____
_____
_____

Did you repeat your sexual behavior? Describe that behavior.

_____
_____
_____
_____
_____
_____

What conditions fostered your acting out sexually? Explain.

_____
_____
_____
_____
_____
_____

Therapist introduction to Exercise Two:
Dysfunctional Family Environment

While completing Exercise One the addict may realize that exposure to sex occurred at the same time the child looked to parents for emotional nurturing but did not receive it. The combination of early exposure to sex and the family environment are causal factors of sexual addiction. For both men and women, the lack of a nurturing relationship with their father is a defining factor in their future addiction. In therapy, an addict rarely paints his or her father in a nurturing relationship.

Clinical notes. Exercise Two, Parts One and Two, provides a greater insight into the addict's experience with his or her family of origin. The first exercise is a question and answer survey and the second exercise is an interview. The interview option is particularly valuable in group therapy since group members, as they hear each other's stories; begin to recognize they are not alone in their experience.

The objective is to connect to the reality that parents contributed to the addict's sexual addiction. A man in therapy, when asked, whether he grew up in a loving home, answered emphatically that he did. "They wouldn't have yelled at me so much if they didn't love me!" Initially, it is difficult for him to face reality—sexual addiction was not his. The child, as an adult, no longer needs to consider self as defective and can now exercise free to change the future.

Exercise 2, Part One: Your Family of Origin

Note: The addict completes Exercise Two, Part One. Exercise Two, Part Two is in an interview format and is administered by a therapist.

As a child, did you feel isolated and detached from your parents? Did your parents conditionally love you? A child loved conditionally, knows s/he may not be able to trust his or her parents in time of need. Did you trust your parents with sexual information? For example, when exposed to sexual experiences during childhood, did you tell your parents, confident that they would continue to love you? A child is often taught that sex is bad. Did you fear your parents' reaction if they learned what happened to you?

You may realize that exposure to sex occurred about the same time you looked to your parents for emotional nurturing but you did not receive it. As such, the combination of early exposure to sex and a non-nurturing family environment are causal factors of sexual addiction. For both men and women, the lack of a paternal-nurturing relationship is a defining factor in their future addiction. In therapy, addicts rarely paint a gregarious and nurturing relationship picture with his or her father.

It is essential for you to hear that exposure to sex was not your fault. As a child, you could not be responsible. If it happened to you, it was normal for you to react to sexual stimulation.

Describe your family environment. As a child, were you emotionally nurtured?

_____
_____
_____
_____

Your family relationships formed your outlook on life. Did you thrive because of the love you received or flounder because of being starved for affirmation, support, and love.

What kind of person was your mother?

_____
_____
_____
_____

How would you describe your relationship with your mother?

_____
_____
_____
_____

Was your mother continually present in your life while you were growing up? Were her conversations with you generally pleasant, unpleasant, or too rare to remember? Did she assist with your homework?

_____

_____

_____

_____

Did your mother isolate herself from the family? Did she have time-consuming interests outside the home? Was she addicted to anger, drugs, alcohol, or sex?

_____

_____

_____

_____

Was your mother abusive physically, sexually, or emotionally?

_____

_____

_____

_____

If, as a child, you had a distant relationship with your mother, what story did you tell yourself to explain your mother's lack of attention or concern for you?

_____

_____

_____

_____

If you had a distant relationship with your mother, how do you describe the love between the two of you?

_____

_____

_____

_____

At what age do you remember your mother saying, "I love you?"

_____

_____

Can you remember examples of feeling abandoned by your mother?

_____
_____
_____
_____

How would you describe the relationship between your mother and your father?

_____
_____
_____
_____

Did you witness daily expressions of love and respect between your parents? Why do you think that was so?

_____
_____
_____
_____

What kind of man was your father?

_____
_____
_____
_____

How would you describe your relationship with your father?

_____
_____
_____
_____

Was your father continually present in your life while you were growing up? Were his conversations with you generally pleasant, unpleasant, or too rare to remember? Did he assist with your homework?

_____
_____
_____
_____

Was your father a workaholic? Did he isolate himself from the family? Did he have time-consuming interests outside the home? Did he have a hobby or workshop in which he spent much time alone?

Was your father addicted to anger, drugs, alcohol, or sex?

Was your father abusive physically, sexually, or emotionally?

If, as a child, you had a distant relationship with your father, what story did you tell yourself to explain your father's lack of attention or concern for you?

If you had a distant relationship with your father, how do you describe the love between the two of you?

At what age do you remember your father saying, "I love you?"

Can you remember examples of feeling abandoned by your father?

_____

_____

_____

_____

Would you describe your family structure as functional, loving, dysfunctional, or selfish?

_____

_____

_____

_____

Exercise 2, Part Two: Family Interview

Note: The addict completes Exercise Two, Part One. Exercise Two, Part Two is in an interview format and is administered by a therapist.

- What it was like for you growing up? Where were you born? Where did you live? Where did you go to school? How did you do in school? What did you do for fun?

- In school, when a teacher reported that you misbehaved, did your parents listen and consider your side of the story or was the teacher always right?

- Talk about your family. How many brothers and sisters do you have? Where were you in the family birth order?

- Which sibling did you get along with best and least? Why?

- Talk about family problems with health, employment, anger, alcohol, drugs, or sex in your family.

- Talk about your parents. Was the relationship between your father and mother close or distant? Did they model a healthy marital relationship?

- How did your parents discipline you and your siblings? Who was the disciplinarian in your family? How did they administer punishment?

- Do you feel that you were often justly punished or often unjustly punished?

- Did your parents emotionally nurture you? How? Did you feel isolated or close to your parents?

- Recall a tender moment with your mother—with your father. How often did it happen?

- Do you remember your parents playing a board game with you? Do you remember times of joy and laughter? Talk about life during summer vacation and during the winter holidays.

- Tell me about your mother. Was your mother continually present in your life while you were growing up? How did your mother support or fail you?

- Was the relationship with your mother close or distant? Did she favor you or one of your siblings?

- Did your mother spend time with you? What performance messages did you receive from her? Did you feel conditionally or unconditionally loved?

- How did your mother show her love for you and your siblings?

- Was your mother present in the home or away from the home a lot? Did you feel that you could tell her about something you did wrong? Why? Did you ever tell her about your exposure to age inappropriate sexual material or behavior? Why?

- Tell me about your father. Was your father continually present in your life while you were growing up? How did your father support or fail you? Was the relationship with your father, close or distant? Did he favor you or one of your siblings?

- Did your father spend time with you? What performance messages did you receive from him? Did you feel conditionally or unconditionally loved?

- How did your father show his love for you and your siblings?

- Was your father present in the home or away from the home a lot?

- Did you feel that you could tell your father about something you did wrong? Why? Did you ever tell him about your exposure to sex? Why?

- Were your parents in a codependent relationship? How do you know?

- How would you have changed your parents during your childhood years?

- Were you happy, sad, and lonely or a child that simply existed? Why?

- Talk about a fond memory from childhood. Why is it a positive memory?

- Talk about a sad memory from childhood. Why is it a sad memory?

- What is your relationship with your parents today?

- As a child, were you sexually abused or introduced to improper sexual material? How did it affect you?

Therapist Introduction to Exercise Three:
Sexual Practices

Secrecy and shame have a reciprocal relationship. The greater the secrecy; the greater is the shame. Conversely, shame fosters more secrecy. A key element in early treatment is to expose sexual practices to the light of day. Once a therapeutic relationship is established, or members of a sexual addiction therapy group have entered the trust stage, it is time to challenge the addict to take a careful inventory of present and past sexual practices.

After full disclosure, the addict needs to feel loved, not judged, or rejected. Sexual behaviors are perhaps the most intimate activities in which humans engage. Men and women rarely allow another human to enter the intimate parts of their life. It is probable that certain sexual behaviors, if disclosed, are embarrassing. Take it slow but encourage the client to share his or her full sexual history.

In group therapy, make clear that participants do *not* divulge details of sexual practices that might cause another member arousal or shameful memories. Even a therapist may not want specific details. For example, knowing that an addict engages in bestiality (sex with animals) is sufficient without hearing the how, when, or where.

Clinical notes. Exercise Three assist's the man or woman to acknowledge their sexual behaviors. Once the addict has completed the written part of the exercise, ask her/him to share verbally what s/he wrote. Doing so will relieve feelings of shame, guilt, and denial. The addict may feel a sense of relief once s/he has completed this exercise. In a group therapy program, it is common for some group members to disclose more behavior after they hear the stories of others.

The objective is to assure the addict s/he is not a defective human being but dealing with the serious problem.

The vignettes in this exercise are in the male voice but apply equally to both genders.

Both sexual thinking/fantasies and pornography are addressed in the next chapter.

Exercise 3: Do I Need to Do Something About My Sexual Behavior.

Inventorying your sexual practices exposes your most guarded secrets to the light of day. Embarrassment is a function of shame. It is not easy for you to face your sexual world; in fact, you would even like to deny that you engage in aberrant sexual behaviors. To reveal your secrets you must overcome fear that you will be adversely judged, shunned, and abandoned. You may fear that your therapist or group members will confirm what you believe, "I am a bad person." Be assured that you are not alone. Addressing the behavior that began when you were not capable of choice is necessary to normalize the shame and secrecy you have carried for many years. Once your secrets are exposed, there is nothing left to shame you. In fact, telling your story is very therapeutic. It reduces denial and shame. So tell your story, over and over. Your efforts are courageous.

Both sexual thinking/fantasies and pornography are addressed in the next chapter.

Are you struggling with the question, do I need to do something about my sexual behavior? Several men addressed the same question.

Andre's story. I believed men and women enjoy viewing Internet pornography. I felt nothing was really wrong with my viewing porn and masturbating. After all, I reasoned, who will know? I really like it. I went on the Internet at work a couple times a week, particularly after a long day. I looked forward to viewing stimulating images because I felt I deserved a little bit of enjoyment after having worked so hard. The IT department and my boss disagreed. I was fired.

Neil's story. I am married to Lisa. Although I believe we have an active sex life, I still feel drawn to self-stimulation. Lisa's job begins earlier in the morning than does mine. I told Lisa that I use the quiet time after she leaves to plan my day. However, part of my plan involves searching the Internet for stimulating material as a precursor to masturbation. I believe my private life does not affect my marriage and my arrangement works. I am having a difficult time understanding why Lisa was so upset when she found me masturbating to sexually stimulating material one morning. She insisted I seek counseling.

David's story. I am a respected counselor but I was caught with a significant number of pornographic images on my laptop. Although I feel relieved that my secret life was exposed, I fear others will find I have feet of clay.

Mike's story. I look forward to going to work each day. I ride the subway and I continually scan the car for attractive women. At times, I engage a woman in conversation in hopes it will lead to an encounter. Other times, particularly when the subway is crowded, I stand close to s woman in order to facilitate body contact. My early morning rituals have led to affairs and my last encounter left me with a case of venereal disease.

Kerry's story. I have a stressful job. Since my youth, I have experienced high levels of anxiety. I fear I will not meet other people's performance expectations. By masturbating a couple of times a day, I lessen my anxiety. I am not looking for sexual pleasure, just a decrease in my anxiety. I do it as fast as possible.

Tony's story. In college, I had a long distance relationship with Susan. We saw each other only a couple of times a year. However, we talked frequently by phone and one of our fun things to do was to talk dirty to each other. While our relationship did not survive the long distance, phone sex became part of my life.

George's story. My first marriage ended in divorce. When Margie and I began to date, sexual activity was quickly introduced into our relationship. I now realize we never became good friend; Margie was simply my sexual outlet. Today, I find myself preoccupied with sex. I visit massage parlors, striptease bars, and I use any form of sexual stimulation I can find. I feel lonely and isolated from my family. I want to know why.

James' story. As a child, I lived in my head. I was a whiz at video games and other computer challenges. I frequently find myself bored and I turn to sexual fantasy to relieve my boredom. I wonder what it would be like to live a life free of sexual fantasy and thinking.

How about you? Do you identify with an addict in any of these stories? Which one? Are you surprised to find you are not alone? Share your thoughts.

_____
_____
_____
_____
_____
_____
_____
_____
_____

Perhaps your story is different. The following questions enable you to explore your story. The questions are relevant to most addicts. However, if the questions do not relate to you, at the end of the exercise you will have the opportunity to record your alternative story.

Pornography is addressed in Exercise 14.

Masturbation

As an adult, do you masturbate?

_____
_____
_____
_____

How frequently do you masturbate? Why?

_____
_____
_____
_____

What is the typical time lapse between your masturbation events? Why?

_____
_____
_____
_____

Do you have a favorite time of the day during which you masturbate? Why?

_____
_____
_____
_____

What stimulus do you use to masturbate? Do you use pornography, sexual fantasy, sex toys, or other aids to enhance arousal? Which one(s)?

_____
_____
_____
_____

Do you find you are never satisfied after having engaged in masturbation and you seek more or better experiences?

_____
_____
_____
_____

Have you hurt someone in your life by engaging in masturbation? Who? How has it affected your relationship with that person(s)?

_____
_____
_____
_____

When did your attraction to masturbation begin?

_____
_____
_____
_____

When did your attraction to masturbation become a concern to you?

_____
_____
_____
_____

Do you experience guilt after masturbating? Describe.

_____
_____
_____
_____

Have you tried to stop masturbating? What did you do to stop?

_____
_____
_____
_____

Have you been successful? If yes, why? If not, why not?

_____
_____
_____
_____

Do you find you are able to stop for a while but eventually find yourself going back?

_____
_____
_____
_____

Has your masturbation become obsessive and compulsive? Do you want to end this behavior?

_____
_____
_____
_____

Do you masturbate to escape loneliness or isolation? Explain.

_____
_____
_____
_____

How would your behavior change if you resolved loneliness or isolation in your life?

_____
_____
_____
_____

Has masturbation affected your spiritual life?

_____
_____
_____
_____

Sexual Encounters

Do you engage in sexual encounters outside of your marriage (or committed relationship)? For a non-married individual the question is, have you had multiple relationships that frequently result in sexual encounters or are your encounters mostly fantasy?

_____
_____
_____
_____

What are your sexual encounters? How frequently do you engage in sexual encounters outside of your marriage (or committed relationship)?

_____
_____

What is the typical time lapse between sexual encounters outside of your marriage (or committed relationship)? Why?

_____
_____
_____
_____

Do you lead a double life? Do you hide behind secrecy to engage in encounters?

_____
_____
_____
_____

Who knows about your double life? How do they know?

_____
_____
_____
_____

Do you fear being caught?

_____
_____
_____
_____

What are the likely consequences of being caught?

_____
_____
_____
_____

If you have been caught, what were the consequences?

_____
_____
_____
_____

Do you find you are never satisfied with the current affair and you want someone new and exciting? Do you engage in the hunt but once you tag your victim, are you off to the next hunt? Share your thoughts as to why.

_____
_____
_____
_____
_____
_____
_____
_____
_____
_____
_____
_____
_____

Have you hurt someone in your life by sexual encounters outside of your marriage (or committed relationship)? Who? How has it affected your relationship with that person(s)?

_____
_____
_____
_____

Do you experience guilt after you engage in an affair? Describe.

_____
_____
_____
_____

Have you tried to stop having affairs? Has your sexual behavior become obsessive and compulsive?

_____
_____
_____
_____

Have you been successful in stopping? If yes, why? If not, why not?

_____
_____
_____
_____

Do you find you are able to stop for a while but you find yourself going back?

_____
_____
_____
_____

Have sexual affairs affected your spiritual life?

_____
_____
_____
_____

Do you want to end this behavior? Why?

_____
_____
_____
_____

Other Sexual Activities

Do you engage in phone sex, chat rooms, fantasy sex, web cam, or video sharing? Do you go to massage parlors, seek prostitution, seek same sex encounters, and engage in exhibitionism, voyeurism, or other sexual activities? If so, which behaviors?

_____
_____
_____
_____

When did your attraction to these activities begin?

_____
_____
_____
_____

When did your attraction to these activities become a concern to you?

_____
_____
_____
_____

How frequently do you engage in one or more of these activities? Why?

_____

_____

_____

_____

What is the typical time lapse between engaging in one or more of these activities? Why?

_____

_____

_____

_____

Do you lead a double life?

_____

_____

_____

_____

Who knows about your double life? How do they know?

_____

_____

_____

_____

Do you fear being caught?

_____

_____

_____

_____

What are the likely consequences of being caught?

_____

_____

_____

_____

If you have been caught, what were the consequences?

_____
_____
_____
_____

Do you find you are never satisfied and you want a better experience?

_____
_____
_____
_____

Have you hurt someone in your life by engaging in one or more of these activities? Who? How has it affected your relationship with that person(s)?

_____
_____
_____
_____

Do you experience guilt or shame after engaging in one or more of these activities? Describe.

_____
_____
_____
_____

Have you tried to stop this behavior? Has your sexual behavior become obsessive and compulsive?

_____
_____
_____
_____

Have you been successful in stopping? If yes, why? If not, why not?

_____
_____
_____
_____

Do you find you are able to stop for a while but you find yourself going back?

_____
_____
_____
_____

Do you want to end this behavior? Why?

_____
_____
_____
_____

Has one or more of these activities affected your spiritual life?

_____
_____
_____
_____

Legality/Job Jeopardy

Does society consider any of your sexual behaviors illegal?

_____
_____
_____
_____

When did your attraction to these activities begin?

_____
_____
_____
_____

When did your attraction to these activities become a concern to you?

_____
_____
_____
_____

Do you engage in Internet pornography or masturbation at your work site?

_____
_____
_____
_____

Do you fear being caught? Has your sexual behavior become compulsive?

_____
_____
_____
_____

What are the likely consequences of being caught?

_____
_____
_____
_____

If you have been caught, what were the consequences?

_____
_____
_____
_____

Your story. If the above questions are not relevant, in the space below, tell your story in your own words. Both sexual thinking/fantasies and pornography are addressed in the next chapter.

_____
_____
_____
_____
_____
_____
_____
_____
_____
_____
_____
_____

What are the specific sexual behaviors that concern you?

_____
_____
_____
_____

When did these sexual behaviors begin?

_____
_____
_____
_____

When did they become a concern to you?

_____
_____
_____
_____

How frequently do you engage in these behaviors? Why?

_____
_____
_____
_____

What is the typical time lapse between these behaviors? Why?

_____
_____
_____
_____

Do you lead a double life?

_____
_____
_____
_____

Who knows about your double life? How do they know?

_____
_____

_____

_____

Do you fear being caught?

_____
_____
_____
_____

What are the likely consequences of being caught?

_____
_____
_____
_____

If you have been caught, what were the consequences?

_____
_____
_____
_____

Do you find you are never satisfied and you want more or better experiences?

_____
_____
_____
_____

Have you hurt someone in your life by these behaviors? Who? How has it affected your relationship with that person(s)?

_____
_____
_____
_____

Do you experience guilt after engaging in these behaviors? Describe.

_____
_____
_____
_____

Have you tried to stop these behaviors? Has your sexual behavior become obsessive/compulsive?

_____
_____
_____
_____

Have you been successful in stopping? If yes, why? If not, why not?

_____
_____
_____
_____

Do you find you are able to stop for a while but you find yourself going back to these behaviors?

_____
_____
_____
_____

Do you want to end these behaviors? Why?

_____
_____
_____
_____

Have these behaviors affected your spiritual life?

_____
_____
_____
_____

Therapist introduction to Exercise Four:
Attributes of Sexual Addiction

The dynamics of sexual addiction are often layered like the rings of an onion—each layer is nearer to the underlying issue that causes addiction—the core of truth. This exercise peels multiple layers so the addict gains a grasp of the underlying factors that play a significant role in the practice of sexual behavior or sexual addiction.

Clinical notes. The following material is a derivative of Carnes' Sexual Addiction Screening Test (SAST). This test was adapted to provide a forum for a discussion of underlying factors leading to the practice of unwanted sexual behaviors. The Sexual Addiction Screening Test (SAST) is available in Appendix A (Carnes, 2012, ITAP).

The objective of Exercise Four is to encourage a deeper recognition of the features of the addict's sexual addiction.

Exercise 4: Attributes of Sexual Addiction

Read the following questions and relate in the space provided how each attribute of sexual addiction plays a role in your life as an addict. If you connect with any question, you have begun to peel another layer of the addiction onion and to gain a deeper recognition of your behavior.

Were You Sexually Abused As a Child or Adolescent?

Carnes (1992) found that 81 % of addicts remember sexual abuse in some way as a child. The abuse may have been blatant or subtle. If you were exposed to sex as a child, it may have created a lasting and troubling memory. The fact that you can recall the sexual event affirms that it did affect you (p. 109).

A child may react to sexual abuse by experiencing Post-Traumatic Stress Disorder (PTSD). When abuse is extreme and the child is sensitive, the shock to the child's psyche can be debilitating. Symptoms of PTSD can either begin congruently with abuse or show up later in life. Stress in adulthood can trigger PTSD symptoms related to childhood abuse.

A consequence of childhood sexual abuse is, as adults, they incorporate high-risk behavior and integrate fear into their arousal patterns. High-risk behavior may result in severe outcomes, such as loss of career or arrest.

Not all sexually abused children become addicted, but a large percentage do. What has been your experience?

_____
_____
_____
_____

Do you include a fear component into your acting out ritual and thus take risks?

_____
_____
_____
_____

Do You Regularly Purchase Sexually Explicit Magazines?

Exposing a child to pornography is a form of sexual abuse. Even a child knows such material is secretive and inappropriate. Sexually explicit material causes mental and possibly physical arousal in a child. The feeling of arousal is a new and a pleasurable experience—so much so that, as the child grows, she or he knows that a source of pleasure can be renewed by viewing pornography

Pornographic magazines are readily available. Do you purchase them? For many, it becomes habitual. What has been your experience?

_____

_____

_____

_____

Do You Regularly Pursue Online Pornography?

Although the Internet is a blessing for many, to those addicted to online pornography it is a curse. The addicted man or woman will spend many hours trying to find the ideal image only to fail. Searching the Internet becomes a never-ending pursuit of more tantalizing material. Visual stimulation from online pornography usually leads to masturbation.

You may tell yourself that what you do on your own computer is private and will not be discovered. Not so! For several technical reasons, private computers record and store downloaded images and Web sites visited. In an office environment with a centralized server, all online transactions are recorded and stored. Internet service providers record sites visited and, if requested, supply information to law enforcement officials. Family members frequently and inadvertently discover downloaded pornography.

The possibility of being caught is just one undesirable consequence. Do you waste many hours seeking online stimulation? Do you find your desire to checkout old or new web sites has become compulsive and repetitive. Do feelings of guilt follow your online pursuit of pornography?

_____

_____

_____

_____

_____

_____

Are You Often Preoccupied with Sexual Thoughts?

According to Hastings (1998), "Sexual fantasy is addictive when it is used to create a pleasant hum to make otherwise boring or distressing activities seem more appealing" (p. 71).

Preoccupation with sexual thoughts may begin in childhood. A young person learns that a sexual fantasy leads to pleasurable feelings—an escape from reality.

As an adult, you may engage in various forms of sexual fantasy and thinking. By analogy, when you are sexually hungry, is a sexual fantasy the first cookie you find to soothe your hunger? Do you have a favorite fantasy to which you return in the same way you look for a favorite type of cookie to eat?

Whenever feelings of distress or anxiety become troublesome, is sexual fantasy or thinking your solution?

_____
_____
_____
_____

An addict sees an image and stores it away for future processing. Over time, the addict will reserve a part of his or her memory for stimulating images. The memory is like an on-call secret sexual filing cabinet in the brain. When in need, the addict pulls out a *sexual file,* reviews and examines the contents and once enjoyed, stores it for future use.

Memories of past sexual encounters are also stored for future stimulation. What has been your experience?

_____
_____
_____
_____

What Is the Problem? Don't All of Us Have Sexual Memories?

All humans who have engaged in sexual behavior have memories. It would be abnormal for a married person not to have sexual thoughts about his or her partner. The sex addict processes fantasies well beyond any healthy fantasies related to his or her partner.

Do you use a sexual fantasy or a recalled memory as your first step to sexual activity?

_____
_____
_____
_____

Do Your Partner/Significant Other Ever Complain About Your Sexual Behavior?

Although your judgment of acceptable sexual behavior may be cross-wired, those around you may have a clearer view. If others express concern, take it as a wake-up call.

Is it time for you to ask a counselor to assist you to sort out the truth? Do you fear talking to a counselor about your sexual behavior? Describe your thinking.

_____
_____
_____
_____

Can You Stop Your Sexual Behavior When You Know It Is Inappropriate?

A fundamental feature of any addiction is difficulty in stopping. Can you stop your sexual behavior?

Share what it means to say that your sexual behavior has become obsessive and compulsive for you.

_____
_____
_____
_____

Do You Ever Feel Bad About Your Sexual Behavior?

When exposed to sex, the mind and body respond. When you engage in sexual behavior outside the marriage, do you feel guilty about your behavior?

Do you have guilt feelings after marital sex? If not, why do you think that is so?

_____
_____
_____
_____
_____
_____

Has Sexual Behavior Ever Created Problems for You or Your Family?

If your partner discovered your behavior, you may be either angry or remorseful that your sexual behavior was discovered. Perhaps discovery is the only way you will take steps to recover. Although you and your family may be in great pain, understand that pain is a significant motivator.

Has your sexual behavior been discovered? If not, why not?

_____
_____
_____
_____

Do You Worry About People Finding Out About Your Sexual Behavior?

Likely you are not proud of your behavior. Do you fear you will be castigated if your aberrant sexual behavior is discovered? You may even fear your sexual behavior will end. Do you fear social, employment, marriage, or legal consequences? Are your fears legitimate?

Are you concerned that others will find out about your sexual behavior? Describe your anticipated consequences.

_____

_____

_____

_____

Do You Lead a Double Life?

Do you want your family and friends to know you as an upstanding citizen, a person who is successfully tackling the challenges of life? Conversely, do you hide a second self who feels shame when you compulsively return to sexual stimulation? Living a double life leads to feelings of loneliness and isolation

Do you lead a good self and a bad self-double life? What does it mean to say your secret life is a constant reminder that you live a lie—a lie you fear will be discovered?

_____

_____

_____

_____

Do You Keep Secrets About Your Sexual Activities from Those Who Are Important To You?

An early step in recovery is disclosure. Disclosure to a counselor is a beginning step. If you have not disclosed your behavior to family and friends, first consult a counselor. Your life will begin to change upon disclosure.

Share the status of disclosure of your secrets.

_____

_____

_____

_____

Has Your Behavior Ever Emotionally Hurt Someone?

If a partner or family member discover your sexual behavior, it is likely they have experienced sex addiction induced-trauma.

- Your partner and family may feel betrayed, fear the loss of the family structure, or fear social and economic consequences.

- Their feelings may be very raw and it may take considerable time to heal.

- Requesting and receiving forgiveness does not make emotional pain vanish. For some it is an ongoing process.

- Trust is broken.

- Rebuilding trust takes commitment to end offending behavior and ultimately demonstrating a lasting period of sexual sobriety.

- Unless you change your addictive life, you cannot expect to be forgiven by others in your life.

It is common for an addict to believe s/he needs to say or do something to reassure his or her partner s/he is worthy of trust. The only loving action an addict can do to grow trust is to be fully honest. All other actions are self-serving and futile.

Who in your family is emotionally hurt by your sexual behavior? How can you help them?

_____
_____
_____
_____

Are Any of Your Sexual Activities Against the Law? (For example, sex with minors, exposure of genitals in public, peeping)

If your behavior is illegal, consult an attorney and a counselor. If you have abused a child or aged person, the counselor will report your behavior to the authorities. They are required to do so by professional ethics and by law. Consider the damage done to your victim and take the steps necessary to end the abuse.

What is your plan?

_____
_____
_____
_____

Have You Ever Felt Degraded by Your Sexual Activity?

Some have a psychological desire to be humiliated or experience pain to achieve arousal. If your behaviors fall within the definition of sexual sadism or masochism, and you want to change your thinking and behavior, seek the aid of a professional counselor who specializes in these behaviors.

Have you ever felt degraded by your sexual activity? How did you feel?

_____

_____

_____

_____

Do You Feel Depressed After Having Sex?

If you believe your sexual behavior is improper and you feel ashamed, a natural consequence is to experience depressed mood.

What has been your experience?

_____

_____

_____

_____

Do You Fear Sexual Intimacy? Do You Avoid Sex At All Costs?

If you avoid sex in order to cope with stress, it is likely that stress is adversely affecting many aspects of your life. Seek counseling to establish a perspective as to the effectiveness of your behavior.

Do you fear of sexual intimacy? Describe why.

_____

_____

_____

_____

Do You Frequently Feel Remorse, Shame, or Guilt After a Sexual Encounter?

When sexual behavior causes negative feelings, it is a sign that something is amiss. Sex is a precious gift. It is not intended to be a source of remorse, shame, or guilt. Your conscience is also a precious gift. If it tells you that one gift is at odds with another, it is time to seek counseling.

Carnes (1992) describes the link between shame and sexually acting out:

Addictive sex feels shameful. Often it is illicit, stolen, or exploitive. It compromises values and draws on fear to generate excitement. Addictive sex often reenacts childhood abuses, disconnecting one from self. A world of unreality is created, allowing self-destructive and dangerous behaviors. Based on conquest or power, it is seductive and dishonest. Serving to medicate and kill pain, addictive sex becomes routine, grim, and joyless. A tough taskmaster, the addiction requires a double life and demands perfection. (p. 254)

How do your feelings of remorse, shame, or guilt affect your life? Are these feelings particularly strong after illicit sex?

_____
_____
_____
_____

Have You Ever Tried To Limit Or Stop Masturbating?

Is masturbation normal and a healthy activity? Some health practitioners say masturbation is just part of life. However, when masturbation becomes:

- obsessive and compulsive,

- repeated multiple times a day or week,

- excessive time is spent thinking about the next time,

- rituals are used to enhance the effect,

- and, you wonder if you want to live your life this way, it is time to seek counseling.

Masturbation is not healthy for everyone. Masturbation in conjunction with Internet pornography is a leading reason for men and many women to enter therapy.

Has masturbation caused you stress? What has been your experience?

_____
_____
_____
_____
_____
_____

Do You Lose Your Sense of Identity Or Meaning in Life Without a Love Relationship?

Does your life lack satisfaction without a love relationship?

What does a *love relationship* mean to you?

_____

_____

_____

_____

Does Your Pursuit of Sex Interfere with Your Spiritual Development?

Humans have a conscience—an internal alarm. When out-of-bounds behavior is elevated, your alarm should sound. Conscience arouses humans to experience guilt. Appropriate guilt can lead to changed behavior. Adults usually know that the practice of certain sexual behaviors does not make for a good life. A right conscience is a blessing. Conversely, despair over weaknesses, empowers the devil. To which voice are you listening?

If you are not proud of your sexual behavior, it is the right time to seek guidance. Has feeling guilt affected your spiritual relationship?

Describe the consequences.

_____

_____

_____

_____

Are Your Sexual Practices Compulsive and Unmanageable?

What began as an occasional practice may increase to the point where you become powerless to stop.

Do you compulsively repeat your sexual behaviors after you promised you would stop? Has your addictive life become unmanageable? What is your solution?

_____

_____

_____

_____

Have You Experienced Life-damaging Consequences Because Of Your Sexual Behavior?

Isolation is a primary consequence of sexual addiction. Other consequences include self-loathing, depression, anxiety, anger, despair, and pervasive feelings of hopelessness. You may find relationships are damaged, particularly those with your family and your Higher Power (See Exercise 30). Shame and guilt become constant companions.

What life damaging consequences have you experienced? Explain

_____
_____
_____
_____

Has Your Sexual Behavior Caused a Change in Your Life Focus?

For some, sexual behavior becomes so consuming that it takes precedence over sleep, work, and healthy recreational activities. Paying for sex may take precedence over family expenses. Obtaining sexual gratification becomes consuming when it displaces day-to-day functions and pleasures.

Has your sex addiction interfered with your normal activities?

_____
_____
_____
_____

Has sexual activity become a primary motivator in your life? Explain.

_____
_____
_____
_____

Is Keeping Your Sexual Behavior a Secret Important To You?

Secrecy is a hallmark of sexual addiction. Do you fear being judged a bad person—someone with an out-of-control problem? Do you believe you are alone in your degeneration?

Does secrecy keep you bound to your sexual behavior?

_____
_____
_____
_____

154

Do You Fear Giving Up Your Sexual Behavior?

You may have lived with sexual behavior for many years. Is the thought of forfeiting your sexual behavior paralyzing? Intellectually, you may hear the call to change your life, but are you emotionally bound to your long-term habit, to your best friend?

Does attachment to your sexual addiction keep you locked into repeating your behavior?

_____
_____
_____
_____

Have You Denied That You Have a Problem Related to Sexual Behavior?

Invariably, when you engage in a pattern of repetitive addictive sex you will develop illogical thinking to justify your behavior. Frequently heard excuses include:

- I deserve a little happiness in my life,

- I plan to quit but I am under stress now,

- I have a much higher libido than my wife,

- I must have this outlet,

- I can control this when I want to and I don't want help,

- It only happens once in a while,

- and how else am I going to relieve my tremendous sexual tension?

Do you tell yourself lies? What lies do you tell to justify continuing your sexual behavior? Do you avoid counseling because you believe your lies?

Lies I believe. . .

_____
_____
_____
_____

Lies I believe. . .

_____
_____
_____
_____

Lies I believe. . .

_____
_____
_____
_____

What excuses do use to continue your sexual behavior?

My excuses

_____
_____
_____
_____

My excuses

_____
_____
_____
_____

My excuses

_____
_____
_____
_____

CHAPTER NINE: STAGE II - ADDRESSING BEHAVIORS THAT BOND A MAN OR WOMAN TO SEX ADDICTION

In addition to shame and denial, many factors keep a man or woman steeped in sexual addiction. Each needs to be addressed in recovery. Despite the addict's desire to change his or her way of life, these conditions are not easily dispelled. The factors addressed by therapeutic exercises in this chapter are:

- Sexual thinking and fantasy

- Acting-out cycle

- Acting-out rituals

- Chronic depressed mood

- Clinical anxiety

- Anger

- Habit

- Isolation and loneliness

- Dysfunctional marriage relationship

- Pornography

- Acting-out triggers

Therapist Introduction to Exercise Five:
Sexual Thinking and Fantasy

Sexual thinking and fantasy are the most difficult addictive behaviors to change. A goal is to greatly reduce and eventually eliminate addictive sexual thinking and fantasy.

TJ's story. When I engage in sexual fantasy and thinking, I find myself planning my next acting-out scenario. At the same time, I realize that if I do not engage in sexual fantasy and thinking I am not tempted to act out. After much thought, I reasoned I needed to end my current sexual behavior. I decided to declare *zero tolerance* for sexual fantasy and thinking. In time, I found it worked and my acting-out behaviors significantly decreased.

Clinical notes. Exercise Five explores the role of sexual thinking and fantasy in bonding the addict to sexual addiction. In addition to completing the exercise, encourage the addict to keep a log of the time and content of sexual fantasies and thinking. The period to keep the log does not need to be long. Usually within a couple weeks, the addict realizes how pervasive mental sexual processing dominates his or her life. An important session activity is to discuss what it would mean to end addictive sexual thinking and fantasy. The concept of zero tolerance for sexual fantasies and thinking is the ideal.

The objective is to confirm the relationship between sexual thinking, fantasy, and acting out. The long-term goal is for the addict to end sexual fantasy and thinking.

Exercise 5: Sexual Fantasy and Thinking

By analogy, sexual thinking and fantasy are the primary lubricants for sexual behavior. While a combustion engine needs oil to run, an addict needs sexual fantasies as a lubricant for acting out. If the brain is not stimulated, you will not achieve a euphoric feeling. Your most powerful and active sex organ is your brain. The dopamine flow begins as an addict engages in sexual fantasy or thinking.

The material to generate a sexual fantasy is found everywhere—the Internet, a person walking down the street or sitting in the restaurant, image in a magazine, and even in church. The addict's mind has the capacity to store and process an unending supply of thoughts and images.

The brain plays a vital role in human sexuality. Human beings require the brain to produce a flow of multiple chemicals for arousal to occur. You may not realize how much work your brain does in the buildup and sexual exchange. For example, the brain is solely responsible for imagining someone naked, processing sexual stimuli, manipulating a prospective sexual partner, and conceiving ways to increase your pleasure. Most sexual issues begin and end with brain-centered thinking and fantasy (Sbraga & O'Donohue, 2003, p. 80).

How do you avoid sexual thinking when random sexual thoughts are at work without being invited? An effective strategy is to use a mantra. A mantra is an active reiteration of commitment. For example, a mantra, "I don't want to go there," is invoked when you realize that a sexual thought has begun. A mantra is voiced aloud if possible. Doing so activates multiple cognitive sensors—mental, voice, hearing, and even face muscles. When actively repudiating sexual thinking, brain chemicals associated with stimulation tend to stabilize.

Some addicts, although committed to recovery, require more assistance. Some turn to prayer and others engage in an alternative non-sexual fantasy. One man's favorite time for sexual fantasy was before sleep. He said that a sexual fantasy calmed him, but he complained, "At times, they excite me to the point of masturbation." In his case, he needed an alternative to sexual thoughts to achieve calm and sleep. He chose a fantasy of playing a round of golf in his head. By the time he completed his alternative fantasy, eighteen holes of golf in his head, he was asleep or onto other acceptable thinking. Some use other sports fantasies, such as playing quarterback in the Super Bowl, pitching a no-hit game, catching the big fish, or winning a tennis championship. For a woman, decorating a house, taking a delightful walk on the beach, enjoying a game of tennis, making a grand slam in bridge, or visualizing a round of golf are examples of alternative fantasies.

Women engage in sexual fantasies that are personal and romantic. Their fantasies are interlaced with emotion and connection. Female sexual fantasies are often centered on a partner, loved ones, or fantasy mate (Ferree, 2010, pp. 61-62).

Men fantasize more than do women. Men, in particular, have a fine-tuned filter in their heads through which all visual images are processed for sexual content. For example, men may ogle body parts, sexy movement, attractive or revealing clothing, facial expressions, or a perceived come-on. The sexually addicted man either processes his sexual thinking in the present moment or stores the content as the source of fantasy at a later point.

Traumatic events and sexual fantasies are often related. One way of understanding why trauma is so powerful is to connect the dots between fantasy and trauma. Fantasies are a window into the meaning of trauma. For example, if an addict's fantasy depicts fondling, it is possible that the addict's early trauma relates to molestation. Fantasies may reflect the sexual content that occurred during childhood abuse. Trauma needs to be brought into the present time in order to normalize it. The addict needs to internalize that s/he was not responsible for the traumatic event.

When did your attraction to sexual fantasy and thinking begin?

_____
_____
_____
_____

When did your attraction to sexual fantasy or thinking become a concern to you?

_____
_____
_____
_____

Is sexual fantasy or thinking an important part of your life? Why?

_____
_____
_____
_____

How frequently do you engage in sexual fantasy or thinking? Why?

_____
_____
_____
_____

Does sexual fantasy and thinking consume a part of your day? What percent of the day does sexual fantasy or thinking occupy?

_____
_____

What is the typical time lapse between episodes of sexual fantasy or thinking?

_____
_____
_____
_____

What body parts, relationships, or feelings are particularly stimulating to you?

_____
_____
_____
_____
_____
_____
_____
_____

Is the primary subject of your fantasy a real person, a fantasy person, or body parts?

_____
_____
_____
_____

How do you stimulate the beginning of your sexual fantasy or thinking?

_____
_____
_____
_____

Do you have a preferred time of the day to engage in sexual fantasy or thinking? Why?

_____
_____
_____
_____

Do you find you are never satisfied with your latest sexual fantasy? Do you want more or better?

_____
_____
_____
_____

What consequences have you experienced by engaging in sexual fantasy or thinking? For example, do you find yourself isolated, wasting too much time, disconnected from important relationships, or a source of harmful procrastination?

_____
_____
_____
_____

Do you experience shame after having engaged in sexual fantasy or thinking? Describe.

_____
_____
_____
_____

Have you tried to end your sexual fantasy life? Why?

_____
_____
_____
_____

Have you been successful? If yes, why? If not, why not?

_____
_____
_____
_____

Do you stop for short periods but find yourself going back? Why do you think you find yourself going back? What are your triggers?

_____
_____
_____
_____

What sexual fantasy do you often repeat? Describe the fantasy in general terms.

_____
_____
_____
_____

Why is do you repeat this sexual fantasy?

_____
_____
_____
_____

What is the connection between your favorite sexual fantasy and your catalytic event? How do they relate?

_____
_____
_____
_____
_____
_____
_____
_____

What is the connection between your favorite sexual fantasy and your *desire* to act out? Explain?

_____
_____
_____
_____

What is the connection between your favorite sexual fantasy and your specific acting-out behavior?

_____
_____
_____
_____

If you ended your sexual fantasies and thinking, how would that change the frequency of your acting out? Explain.

_____
_____
_____
_____

Do you want to end this behavior? Why?

_____

_____

_____

_____

Has sexual fantasy or thinking affected your spiritual life? Describe how.

_____

_____

_____

_____

Sexual thinking and fantasy are the most challenging addictive behaviors to end. A goal is to greatly reduce and eventually eliminate addictive sexual thinking and fantasy.

TJ's story. When I engage in sexual fantasy and thinking, I find myself planning my next acting-out scenario. At the same time, I realize that if I do not engage in sexual fantasy and thinking I am not tempted to act out. After much thought, I reasoned I needed to end my current sexual behavior. I decided to declare *zero tolerance* for sexual fantasy and thinking. In time, I found it worked and my acting-out behaviors significantly decreased.

What would it mean to you to declare zero tolerance to sexual thinking and fantasy?

_____

_____

_____

_____

What is the content of your other sexual thinking or fantasies? (For example, I fantasize being seduced by. . .)

The content of my sexual thinking or fantasy is:

_____

_____

_____

_____

The content of my sexual thinking or fantasy is:

_____

_____

_____

The content of my sexual thinking or fantasy is:

_____
_____
_____
_____

The content of my sexual thinking or fantasy is:

_____
_____
_____
_____

What alternative non-sexual fantasy could you substitute for your sexual fantasy?

_____
_____
_____
_____

What mantra could you use as a substitute for your sexual thinking?

_____
_____
_____
_____
_____
_____
_____

Therapist Introduction to Exercise Six:
Acting-out Cycle

In *Out of the Shadows* (2001a) and *Contrary to Love*, (1994) Carnes presents the concepts of sex addiction cycle and sexual rituals. The presentation in this exercise of the *acting-out cycle* and *sexual ritual* are adaptations of his concepts (Carnes 2001, pp. 28-33).

Clinical notes. Exercise Six assists the addict to gain an understanding of his or her acting-out cycle. The acting-out cycle consists of sequential steps an addict follows in each sexual experience. It is essential for the addict to understand the components of the cycle and to begin to recognize these while in the process of acting out. After each incident, the addict needs to record the cycle, or stages of the event, in detail in order to gain insight into the mental process contributing to acting out.

Once the addiction cycle's components are understood, the addict will recognize a change of mood in phase one and the beginning of a fantasy in phase two. At this point, he/she will be able to reject acting-out in phase three. It is necessary for the addict to understand these components in order to interrupt the cycle and stop the process of acting out.

Exercise Seven addresses the acting-out ritual. The acting-out ritual is a component of the third phase of the cycle. Some therapists address the acting-out ritual before introducing the cycle.

Exercise 6: Sex Addiction Cycle

A sex addict repeats a *Sex Addiction Cycle*. The cycle consists of four sequential phases. (Carnes 2001b, pp. 28-33). It is akin to the proverbial donkey locked to a wine press. He goes round and round, even when he would rather not. The cycle makes it difficult or impossible for an addict to stop his or her acting-out behavior, as it is impossible for the proverbial donkey to stop going round and round.

- The first phase of the sex addiction cycle is triggers (shame and guilt, family wounds, depressed mood, loneliness, guilt, remorse, fear, anxiety, anger, negative thinking, boredom, and the poor me syndrome, etc.) which begin the cycle.

- The second phase is distorted thinking (sexual thinking, fantasy, pornography, and environmental elements) that promote arousal and a build-up to acting out.

- The third phase is an acting-out ritual (s). The ritual is a series of events (real or imagined) or illogical thinking that accompany an addict down the path to acting out.

- The fourth phase is the feeling of regret one experiences after acting out.

The addict returns to the first phase and it is only a matter of time before the cycle begins again.

In summary, the sex addiction cycle begins with a mood change, followed by a buildup of sexual desire, the actual sexual act, remorse, and a return to the beginning. Each time the addict completes the four phases, the acting-out cycle ends.

Note: If the addict alters phase one of the cycle, he or she can choose not to go to phase two. Awareness leads to choices. For example, the life condition that begins John's sex addiction cycle is low-grade depressed mood. Now when John recognizes he is experiencing depressed mood, he chooses to go to the gym. John has found that exercise brings him out of his depressed mood. John has taken an important recovery step.

The sex addiction cycle is presented in four tables. Each table represents a phase of the sex addiction cycle. Each table presents descriptive information and an understanding of the sex addiction cycle.

Sexual Addiction: Understanding and Treatment

Initial phase—life condition

Triggers begin the acting-out cycle. At the left side of the table are examples of life conditions, such as, shame and guilt, family wounds, depressed mood, loneliness, anxiety, remorse, fear, negative thinking and a pity party, in which you find yourself at the beginning of your sex addition cycle. Each condition or trigger is some form of negativity that exists in your life. You may not identify with all of the examples, but chances are that some of them will have meaning for you. At the right side of the table, note your understanding of the condition(s)

Sample Life Conditions:	Your reasoning:
Victim posture. In my belief system, I am a victim in this world and not responsible for my behavior.	My life condition(s) when I begin my acting-out cycles is: _____ _____ _____
Preoccupation. I am preoccupied with my sexual behavior or being romantic.	_____ _____
Shame and family wounds. I let shame and childhood abuse control me.	_____ _____
Low-grade depression. Life for me is an existence; I often think life is passing me by. Except when acting out, I am rarely happy.	_____ _____
Anticipated rejection. I create situations in which someone can reject me. I hold people at a distance. I cannot let people know my real self—I know they will not love me.	If I alter my negative life condition at the beginning of the cycle, I am ideally suited to choose not to go to phase two of the cycle. I can alter the condition by: _____ _____
Social isolation. I live behind a mask of respectability but underneath my mask is my real self. I simply cannot let anyone in. If I did, they would see that I am really a bad person. I have few or no real friends. No one really knows who I am.	_____ _____ _____ _____
Emotional isolation. I am not in touch with my own or other people's feelings. I do not understand that I hurt others. I do not understand my own feelings. For me, intimacy means sex.	_____ _____ _____ _____

Phase Two—reaction to life condition

Certain conditions promote arousal (sexual thinking, fantasy, pornography, and environmental elements) and a build-up to acting out. At the left side of the table are listed some common means that sex addicts use to cover the pain of negative life conditions. Each allows the addict to escape reality. You may not identify with all of the examples. Go back and review your entries related to sexual thinking and fantasies. At the right side of the table, note your understanding of the reaction(s) you use during phase two of your sex addiction cycle.

Sample Reactions to Life Conditions:	Your reasoning:
Escapism. Living life is boring or I feel like life is just one painful experience after another. I want to relieve my bad feelings. **Need fulfilling fantasy.** I don't know how to cope thus I daydream of a better life. I use sexual fantasy to get temporary relief. **Grooming.** I exchange provocative sexual messages, flirt, and participate in chat room sessions where I exploit emotional intimacies. **Stalking.** I feel a sense of intimacy when I stalk my conquest. **Sexual thinking and fantasy.** I use sexual thinking, fantasies, or visual sexual stimulation to escape my pain. My next act is often the subject of my fantasies and sexual thinking. My fantasy is my best friend; we see each other a lot. **Sexual materials.** I maintain a well-used stash of pornographic magazines and movies, web sites, and sex toys. Whenever I feel lonely, tired, or angry, my stash is nearby to lead me to act out. **Altered brain - habit.** I have acted out so many times I really don't require an external stimulus. I just act out every morning/ evening. I just have an overwhelming sexual feeling to which I respond.	My reaction(s) to my life condition(s) that propel me toward acting out are: _____ _____ _____ _____ _____ _____ _____ _____ _____ I can forgo acting out by changing my reaction(s) to my life conditions. I choose to do so by: _____ _____ _____ _____ _____ _____ _____ _____ _____ _____ _____ _____

Phase Three—acting out

The addict's acting-out ritual (s) begins in phase three. The ritual consists of a series of events (real or imagined) or illogical thinking that accompany an addict down the path to acting out. This is called a *slippery slope*, since once the ritual has begun; it is difficult for the addict to stop, just as it is difficult to stop skiing down a slippery slope. The actual acting out, or performing sexual behavior, ends the ritual.

At the left side of the table are examples of acting-out behavior. At the right side of the table, is your acting-out ritual and the action you take to act out.

Sample Ritual Thinking:	Your acting-out ritual (s) is:
Acting-out. I am mentally aroused but I play games with myself. I tell myself I will just go a little way but not all the way but then I go all the way. I tell myself I will check email but not go to porn but then I end up at a porn site. I often masturbate to relive my anxiety or my profound loneliness.	(See Exercise Seven for information on how to record a ritual and a worksheet to do so.) _____ _____ _____ _____ _____ _____
Romantic partners. I am involved with multiple partners. I enjoy the hunt but I bailout when serious talk begins.	_____ _____ _____
Online sex. I spend countless hours searching for the perfect image then I masturbate.	_____ _____ _____
Fantasy Partner. Just him and me… the love of my life. Some day we will get together.	If I interdict my acting-out ritual, I can forgo acting out. I choose to interdict my ritual by:
Sex. Sex is my most important requirement. I act out even when I do not want to. I visit massage parlors, strip clubs, or engage a prostitute.	_____ _____ _____ _____
Note: The next chapter presents the *Acting-Out Ritual*. The Ritual addresses the content of Phase Three in more detail.	_____ _____ _____ _____

Phase Four—reconciliation

The addict often experiences regret after acting out. To reconcile guilt feelings the addict may promise to change behavior or justify that acting out was not so bad.

At the left side of the table are possible reaction(s) you may have. Each keeps you glued to shame and guilt—even excuses which would seem to relieve you of responsibility. Intuitively you know such excuses are lies. You tell yourself lies to deal with shame and guilt. At the right side of the table, note which reaction(s) do you use after acting out.

Sample Reactions to Acting Out:	Your Reaction to Acting Out:
Transitory guilt. I feel ashamed of myself. I fear being caught. My focus is on what is going to happen to me. My feeling of guilt is short lived.	What is your reaction to acting out? _____ _____ _____
Reconstruction. I present myself outwardly as a good person. I will seek forgiveness. I am never going to do it again. I am going to make it right. I conceal my act.	_____ _____ _____
Mistaken beliefs. I didn't hurt anybody. I deserve some pleasure in life.	_____
Thinking errors. I can control my behavior if I want to. I don't need any help. What do they know about my problem?	My reaction to acting out is grounded in shame. I choose to change my acting-out cycle by: _____
Feelings of shame and guilt. I have profound feeling of shame and guilt that I need to get over.	_____ _____ _____
Despair. I am a terrible, horrible person. I deserve to be stoned.	_____ _____ _____
Shame. I feel overwhelmed by my behavior.	_____ _____ _____

Once the cycle is completed, the addict returns to the initial phase and begins the cycle anew.

Therapist Introduction to Exercise Seven:
Acting-out Ritual

An acting-out ritual is a series of events or thoughts that the addict processes before acting out.

Clinical notes. Exercise Seven helps the addict to recognize how his or her acting-out ritual is the precursor to acting out. The acting-out ritual is the principal component of phase three of the acting-out cycle (Becker, 2012c, pp. 57-61).

At the beginning of each therapy session, ask the addict to *check in*, that is, report any episodes of acting-out since the last session. The acting-out cycle and ritual are used to report.

The objective is to recognize the dynamics of the acting-out ritual (s) and identify a point at which the addict can interdicted his or her ritual to forgo acting out.

Exercise 7: Acting-Out Rituals

A ritual predisposes a person to act out. The ritual is a series of events or rationalizations in which an addict engages before sexual activity. They often connect to places, things, or activities. For example, Mason knew the location of massage parlors throughout the city. He would cruise the city, tell himself he was not going near a massage parlor, but found himself repeatedly parking nearby. His ritual is composed of all the thinking and actions that lead him to a massage parlor and to act out.

As a sexually addicted person, you have one or more acting out rituals. By analogy, once you pass through the initial steps of your ritual, it is common for you to hit a *slippery slope* that leads you to act out. Picture a ski slope. While you are at the bottom of the slope, you still have choices. Your mind does not correlate riding the chair lift with acting out, so you stand in line and ride to the top of the slope. While standing at the top, you convince yourself that a leisurely ride will not trigger you to act out. You tell yourself, "I must be careful not to gain too much speed or to hit a patch of ice or I will be out-of-control." While cruising through long sweeping turns, feeling comfortable, you want to go a little faster and even faster. Suddenly you are barreling down the slippery slope toward certain sexual acting out and you do not understand why.

Each step in the ritual brings you closer to acting out. The progressive nature of each step explains why your thinking and decisions cause you to barrel down the slippery slope. Instead, of blaming a patch of ice or the slope itself, your ritual began when you decided to ride the chair lift, not when your speed and direction no longer allowed you to stop.

Your ritual may be linked to pornography, TV or videos, or locations such as parks, swimming pools, beach, shopping malls, restrooms, movie theaters, porn shops, peep shows, or other places that are part of the pattern you use to set the stage for acting out. For example, the TV remote may be a curse for you. Your ritual may begin with feeling *bored* and wanting to be entertained. The second ritual step is to turn on the TV and the third is channel flipping—and so on. Channel flipping is compared to having a gun with one round in the chamber. Eventually a channel will provide the visual stimulation you want.

You may not realize how consistent are your ritual patterns until you record your thinking and events that lead you to act out. Often your ritual begins long before you act out. Initial ritual steps may begin with feelings of loneliness, boredom, discontent, anxiety, and any number of life conditions from which you seek relief. You, like most sexually addicted people, live in a state of low-grade depressed mood. The feeling of being down may trigger a choice to alter your mood. Negative feelings frequently begin an acting-out ritual.

For a woman a ritual may include grooming to be provocative, flirting; and connecting with a partner by phone or email; stalking, phone-sex, chat rooms, or exchanging sexually enticing intimacies. A woman may begin her ritual by daydreaming or fantasizing about a man or choosing certain clothing or makeup, making eye contact, drinking alcohol, dancing, or initiating casual touch. Any sexual thinking or progressive acts are part of a sex and love addict's acting-out ritual.

Carnes (1994) clarified the role of a sex addiction ritual,

The ritual seems magically to bring order out of chaos. Think of it as a dance—certain steps, certain sounds, ceremony, rhythm, special artifacts—which can be very elaborate but have one purpose, that is, to put addicts into another world so they can escape the conditions of real life over which they think they have no control. Fantasy is compounded by delusion at this point, for the mood-altered state is a 'world' in which the addicts no longer care about control in the same way. A sexual obsession is pursued to its peak regardless of risk, harm, or other consequences. There is only one kind of control that matters now—control of sexual pleasure. Once they start dancing, they rarely, if ever, can stop on their own. (p. 64)

Greg's story. As a manager of a high performance IT shop, I constantly live with stress and fear that my performance will be found wanting.

To reduce my stress I long for the touch of a female. Massage parlors that specialized in oral sex or masturbation are my sexual lifeline. Stress from my high paying job justifies my seeking relief. My answer is to go to a massage parlor each Friday afternoon.

I began to realize massage parlors did not make me happy. I constantly looked for a better experience. I told my counselor that I was tired of my behavior and I wanted it to end. Together we began to examine my acting out ritual. We looked for an event or change in emotions that began my descent to acting out. We called my descent my slippery slope. I learned I could stop the mental processing at an initial stage. Once I pasted the initial stage of my descent, I could no longer stop; I entered a trance like state, which did not end until I acted out.

Greg outlined his acting out ritual:

- During the week, I remembered past trips to one or more massage parlors. I fantasized about a woman with the best technique—a woman who satisfied me the most. Fantasies kept my sexual tension high during the week.

- I constantly looked for someone who could excite me more. I liked to try new parlors in search of a more tantalizing experience. I dream of the perfect touch.

- Wednesday's newspaper contains ads for massage parlors. I waited for my newspaper in anticipation of the ads. I often found new ads.

- When a new ad appeared, I called for an appointment.

- Friday morning was a time of high sexual energy. At times, I masturbated in my office to make the afternoon's experience last longer.

- I drove our older car to work on Fridays. I thought it was less likely I would be recognized in my wife's Honda Accord than in my BMW.

- I cleared my calendar for Friday afternoon so I could leave my office by 3:00 P.M.

- At times, I had second thoughts; maybe I can skip it today. I told myself I would just go to Starbucks for a coffee. Invariably I found myself driving near the massage parlor even when I told myself I was going to Starbucks.

- I went to a massage parlor just about every Friday afternoon. I found I could no longer stop myself.

- I believed my ritual began when I thought about past encounters. Although this step was part of my ritual, I learned that my mental processing began in riding the chair lift phase, that is, why I felt a compulsion to relieve stress.

- The issue I needed to address was my stress. Unless I managed my stress in a constructive way, I would likely return to my entitlement logic, I must have this to calm down from my charged-up daily life.

In summary, an acting-out ritual is a series of events or rationalizations that lead the addict to engage in sexual activity. The addict needs to connect with his or her ritual to identify at what point s/he can interdict the ritual to change the sexual response.

You can use the following chart to record your acting-out ritual(s). Begin with illogical thinking, feelings of entitlement, changes in mood or anxiety, and any other steps that precedes acting out. Early in the ritual is when you have the greatest potential to interdict your ritual and forgo going down the slippery slope. It is probable you have more than one ritual. Record as many as you can.

Your Acting-out ritual	Record your reasoning as to why you chose each step in your ritual.
Step # One	Reasoning # One
Step # Two	Reasoning # Two
Step # Three	Reasoning # Three
Step # Four	Reasoning # Four
Step # Five	Reasoning # Five
Step # Six	Reasoning # Six
Step # Seven	Reasoning # Seven
Step # Eight	Reasoning # Eight
Step # Nine	Reasoning # Nine
Step # 10	Reasoning # 10

Therapist Introduction to Exercise Eight:
Depressed Mood

Living in a depressed mood is nearly a universal characteristic of sexually addicted people. (A person who masturbates to *relieve chronic anxiety* is treated differently than a person who experiences the symptoms of depressed mood.)

Depressed mood is a significant part of an addicts' life and dominates his or her existence. It is hard for an addict to see beauty, or appreciate wholesome love, joy, or many other uplifting attributes that are normal to mentally healthy people. Instead, the addict focuses on what is going wrong in their life rather than what is going right. It is a condition which fosters acting out.

The mental health community calls chronic depressed mood, *Persistent Depressive Disorder* or *Dysthymia* (The full DSM-5 criteria for Dysthymia is in APPENDIX C) (APA, 2013). While not much in life is upbeat, the addict is not so deeply depressed that s/he cannot function. Another term for this condition is *low-grade depression* (pp. 68-169).

Depressed mood and isolation tend to coexist. Once exposed to sex and found arousal a pleasurable feeling, some children return to those behaviors as a source of relief from parental abandonment. Once s/he begins to engage in frequent sexual behavior, feelings of guilt convince the child that s/he is *defective*. Isolation is a consequence of living in a *chronic depressed mood*.

Clinical notes. Exercise Eight assists the addict to gain an appreciation of how low-grade depressed mood supports acting-out behavior. The exercise also introduces The *Addict's Life Scale*. It is a visual tool which explains the relationship between low-grade depressed mood and acting out.

Once the addict completes the exercise, ask him or her to share verbally what s/he wrote. During check in time, ask where people find themselves on the *Addict's Life Scale*.

The objective is to interdict the addict's persistent depressed mood.

Exercise 8: Depressed Mood

Living in a low-grade depressed mood keeps an addict bonded to sexual addiction. An addict awakens each morning to the symptoms of low-grade depressed. For example, an addict has few, if any, close friends, feel lonely much of the time, procrastinates because of fear of failure, and looks for more from life but does not seem to ever find it. Persistent feelings of shame and guilt accompany depressed mood.

Everyone experiences disappointment and depressed mood. A healthy person who has a bad day does not raise his or her mood through sexual behavior. On the other hand, to the addict a bad day confirms that life is just one bleak day after another. The addict uses sexual behavior to elevate his or her mood.

Living in low-grade depressed mood is nearly a universal characteristic of sexually addicted people. The mental health community calls it *Dysthymia*. (The full DSM-V criteria for Dysthymia is in APPENDIX C) (APA, 2013). Those who experience low-grade depressed mood have low energy, low self-esteem, and a general feeling of hopelessness. Although not much in the addict's life is upbeat, he or she still functions, just not very well. Chronically depressed people raise their mood by sexual stimulation, often because of viewing pornography (pp. 168-169).

The *Addict's Life Scale* is a visual tool which explains the relationship between low-grade depressed mood and acting out. This scale ranges from zero to 50, in 10-point increments. Each benchmark correlates with a relative mood level. At the top of the scale is the 50-point benchmark. This mood level coincides with acting out. It is called the *euphoric level*.

The addict may try to maintain life at the 50-point benchmark by acting out frequently. However, sustaining life at the 50-point benchmark is unrealistic because once the euphoria ends the brain replaces it with feelings of shame and guilt. It becomes a futile chase for the impossible.

One-step down from the *euphoric level* is the 40-point benchmark. It is the functioning *level of a normal mentally healthy adult*. It is the mood level of solid strength and energy. This is the, *great to be alive*, level. The margin of difference between the 40-point benchmark and the 50-point benchmark is 10-points. A person, who lives at the, great to be alive (40-point) benchmark, understands that acting out only yields a 10-point gain. For a normal person, a 10-point gain is not worth the feelings of shame and guilt that follow.

The next step down is the 30-point benchmark. It is one level below the great to be alive mood level. This is the *bad day* level. A normal person who regularly functions at the 40-point benchmark realizes life has its difficulties and it is okay to be down for a short period. The 30-point benchmark is a level a normal person visits but does not live there.

The 20-point benchmark is the level where most sex addicts live. It the level of a low-grade depressed mood or Dysthymia. Life does not meet the addict's expectations. One addict said,

"I got in a rut and I furnished it!" When asked, the addict talks about unfulfilled relationships with parents, siblings, and partner. The addict would like to find joy in life, but his or her search is futile. A woman who suffered from low-grade depressed mood used the cliché, "Life is a bitch, and then you die."

An addict who dwells at the 20-point benchmark lives with failed expectations and dreams. However, by acting out, the addict can raise his or her mood from 20 to 50—a 30-point jump—but only for a short period. The 30-point jump makes acting out worthwhile for the addict. Society teaches, when we are in pain, we are entitled to take medicine to relieve the pain. For the addict, pain relief medication is masturbation.

A recovering addict who maintains life at the 20-point benchmark is highly susceptible to slipping back into acting-out behavior.

The 10-point benchmark represents *full-scale depressed mood*. This person finds it difficult to eat, sleep, and to go about daily life. Sexually addicted people rarely experience full-scale depressed mood. Although the addict does not feel good about self, s/he tends to weather life's daily blows. However, public discovery, particularly when accompanied by legal or divorce implications, is an exception to the survivor mode and full-scale depression may follow.

The 0-*point* benchmark represents institutionalization. A person who finds self at the 0-point benchmark is out-of-control. The person is not capable of making rational decisions. Other than, to identify the 10 point and 0-point levels, they are not addressed further.

Can you identify with the addict's life scale?

Addict's Life Scale

50 - Acting-out mood. The euphoria one feels during the build-up and orgasm

40 - Normal Functioning Mood. The mood level of a normally functioning adult. It is the, great to be alive, mood level.

30 - Bad Day Mood. A level to visit but not to stay or live.

20 - Low-grade Depressed Mood or Dysthymia. Where most addicts live.

10 - Full Scale Depressed Mood. The person barely functions.

0 - Unable to Function Mood. The person is often institutionalized.

The critical concept illustrated by the Addict's Life Scale is the 30-point differential between the addict's low-grade depressed mood level (20) and the feeling of euphoria the addict experiences when he or she acts out (50). A 30-point gap justifies acting out for the addict.

However, is it possible for the addict to live more like a normal person (40) who, because of only a 10-point gap, does not act out? If the addict changed behavior to mimic a normal person, would the addict be less tempted to act out? (See Exercise 23).

Tina was in therapy to resolve her addictive sexual behavior. When asked if she lived in low-grade depressed mood, she declared, "No way, I am a happy go lucky gal!" As therapy progressed, she returned to her earlier assessment. She said, "I have been deceiving myself—I do live in depressed mood. I have no idea what normal feels like because I have never lived at normal." Most addicts never feel joy—they live in low-grade depressed mood and have nothing with which to compare it.

The key to change

The challenge for the addict is to change so the *great to be alive* mood level becomes more of the norm. When the addict choose to live like a normal healthy person, a 10-point differential is not a sufficient reward to offset the adverse consequences of acting out.

Because thinking, feelings, behavior, and moods have been ingrained over many years, it is unlikely that the addict can live like a normal healthy person every day. However, it is possible to include mood-lifting behaviors into one's life to change the power of addiction. It is possible to choose non-sexual activities to move out of life's rut. (See Living at 40, Exercise 23).

The change process takes time as the following vignette illustrates.

Pete's story. My wife, Jean, found my porn collection on my computer. She told me I either seek therapy or.... Not only do I have problem with pornography and masturbation, I work at least seventy hours a week including weekends. I am married more to my job than to Jean. As a workaholic mortgage broker, I spend very little time with my teenaged twin boys, Rob and Tom. I thought I needed to make hay while the sun shined. My stock portfolio is very fat but a lot of good it will do me if I die from working too hard!

My marriage is ok but I don't think Jean is my best friend. In fact, I don't have a best friend.

Pete admitted his life was not what he hoped it would be. He came to therapy scared. Jean went back to work when their boys were out of grade school and Pete knew Jean made enough money to support herself. He was afraid Jean was so unhappy that she might leave him. "Who could blame her? If she leaves me, how will I live? Yes, I have treated Jean very badly, but I need her."

After several months of therapy, I was open to make changes in my life. I now understood how healthy and uplifting activities would inspire me to reduce my self-medication. I will be a much happier if I change my priorities. I must address my relationships with my family. I need to put them first.

Pete agreed to participate in marriage therapy with Jean. They formulated a marriage plan. They agreed to incorporate non-sexual behavior into their marriage. He agreed to come home for dinner no later than 6:30 each evening. He and Jean agreed to spend one evening during the week getting to know each other again. They chose to read several books together and to discuss each other's views. They agreed to do something together each weekend, either a day or evening event. Other *changes* followed, as they became friends.

I also addressed my relationship with Rob and Tom. I am concerned that my boys will soon be grown and I missed it all. I want to let them know that I take responsibility for my failure to be present for them up to now. I want to 'walk the talk.'

I told my sons about my addiction to porn and masturbation and the reasons why, as I understood them. The boys already knew, all too well, about my addiction to work. I asked them to have patience as I try to repair the damage I did to our relationship. My sons love baseball. We agreed to attend minor league games together. I made a point to make time to talk with them. My boys are more than happy to get me, their dad back.

I attended a 12-step program and made a friend. He is now my sponsor.

Because I work so many hours, Sunday morning is my time to sleep and relax. I have not been to church for years. The next change then is to repair my relationship with God. I asked my family to join me on Sunday mornings at church. At first, they did not buy in. They too liked the family habit of sleeping in Sunday mornings. That is another bad habit I taught them!

As I showed by my actions, I am serious about changing my life; Jean joined me at church. One New Year's morning, Rob and Pete said, 'We talked about what kind of New Year's resolution we could make—something meaningful. Dad, we would like to join you and mom at church each Sunday.'

Pete made a conscious decision to include activities and make other changes to raise his mood to the 40-point level. The new activities reduced his desire to act out. His life became closer to the life he and his family wanted.

How does the *Addict's Life Scale* apply to your life? At what mood level do you awaken each day? Do you know why you live at low-grade depressed mood? What activities or changes can you make to experience life at the 40-point level more often? Exercise 23 addresses relationship changes you may wish to consider to live at the 40-point benchmark.

Take a few minutes to record your experience on the *Addict's Life Scale* below.

50 - Acting-out mood. The euphoria one feels during the build-up and orgasm.

_____
_____
_____
_____

40 - Normal Functioning Mood. The mood level of a normally functioning adult. It is the, great to be alive, mood level.

_____
_____
_____
_____

30 - Bad Day Mood. A level to visit but not stay.

_____
_____
_____
_____

20 - Low-grade Depressed Mood or Dysthymia. Where most addict live.

_____
_____
_____
_____

10 - Full Scale Depressed Mood. The person barely functions.

_____
_____
_____
_____

0 - Unable to Function Mood. The person is often institutionalized.

_____
_____
_____
_____

If the gap between depressed mood and living at 40 were narrower, would you still act out? (See Exercise 22) Share you assessment.

_____
_____
_____
_____

How would you characterize your low-grade depressed mood?

_____
_____
_____
_____

List the symptoms you experience related to your low-grade depressed mood. For example, do you focus on what is going wrong rather than on what is going right? Are you unable to sleep and eat healthily and regularly? Do you tolerate your day rather than experience the joy of being alive? Are you often sad? Do you frequently waste time or procrastinate? Do you seek sex to medicate depressed mood?

_____
_____
_____
_____

Do you *like to live* in a depressed mood? Most are quick to say, of course not. Nevertheless, the reality is many actually choose to live in depressed mood rather than take steps to change. Ida said, "I moved into a cave and I live in it alone." She knew what her cave looked like for it was her home for years. She hates the ugly color of her cave but she is fearful of the unknown outside of her cave. It takes courage to move out of one's cave. It takes giving up a comfortable place for one that is less comfortable, at least initially.

Do you have the courage to move out of your sex addiction cave? What would you have to give up?

_____
_____
_____
_____

What would move you out of your cave?

Condition one

_____
_____
_____

Condition two

_____
_____
_____

For a woman, the 50-point acting-out level may not include orgasm. It depends on the activity a woman chooses to medicate her depressed mood. A female sex addict may fight low-grade depressed mood by engaging in an interactive web conversation—seeking a new relationship or any other relational behavior favored by sex and love addicts. What is your experience?

_____
_____
_____

Therapist Introduction to Exercise Nine
Anxiety

For many, unless the roots of anxiety are laid bare and pruned, little progress will be made to change unwanted sexual behavior. A person who acts out because of anxiety induced stressors often *needs medication* to reduce his or her anxiety.

Anxiety is an emotion characterized by feelings of tension, worried thoughts, and physical changes like increased blood pressure. People with anxiety disorders usually have recurring intrusive thoughts or concerns and may avoid certain situations out of worry. They may also have physical symptoms such as sweating, trembling, dizziness or a rapid heartbeat. (APA, 2013, pp. 222-225)

Clinical notes. Exercise Nine discusses the link between anxiety and acting-out behavior. If anxiety is a problem, ask the addict to share what s/he wrote.

When anxiety is the primary condition and acting out is pervasive or chronic, anxiety is addressed first.

The objective is to identify the source of the trauma that is causing the anxiety. The addict can incorporate anxiety-reducing strategies into his or her daily routine such as conditioning or relaxation exercises.

Exercise 9: Anxiety

Anxiety is an emotion characterized by feelings of tension, worried thoughts, and physical changes like increased blood pressure. People with anxiety disorders usually have recurring intrusive thoughts or concerns and may avoid certain situations out of worry. They may also have physical symptoms such as sweating, trembling, dizziness or a rapid heartbeat (APA, 2013, pp. 222-225).

The link between anxiety and sexual behavior is strong Anxiety has multiple facets. They include sexual, situational, and chronic anxiety.

Sexual Anxiety. A man may experience sexual tension in his genital area that is triggered by a sexual stimulus, habit, or generalized anxiety. The man feels a strong urge to do something to quiet his sexual tension. Most often, sexual tension is relieved by masturbation.

Alex's story. I am a newly hired graphic designer and I receive new assignments regularly. I am concerned I might not meet my new supervisor's expectations. He is a very talented designer. Each time I receive a new assignment I feel overwhelmed and I can't concentrate. I feel muscular tension in my lower abdomen as if my genitals were going to explode. Changing my thinking does not change my condition nor does anything else I try, short of masturbating. After I masturbate, I feel relief and I am able to begin a new assignment. From time to time, I am stuck in the middle of a project and the sexual tension returns.

Alex's reaction to feeling overwhelmed is different from sexual arousal. His overwhelmed state is not accompanied by an erection. However, relief comes by the way of masturbation. It is unlikely that Alex is a sexually addicted man. He suffers from sexual anxiety. Medication, a Selective Serotonin Re-uptake Inhibitor (SSRI), and counseling may revitalize him.

Situational anxiety. Anxiety can be situational, for example, feeling very uncomfortable in social gatherings. A man or woman may react to an environmental stimulus, that is, a particular situation will trigger an anxious feeling and a desire to act out. The anxious person is unable to function normally, becomes tense, irritable, unable to think clearly, and obsessed with relieving the situational anxiety.

Clyde's story. I am a college student who has an eye for young women. In the classroom, I positioned myself so I can ogle exposed body parts—particularly legs. Some wear such short skirts that I am rewarded with a view of even more flesh. At the end of the day, my body reacts to the day's stimuli. I feel sexually aroused, my body is no longer under my control, and it is demanding release of body fluids. I experience an intense reaction to situational anxiety.

Chronic anxiety. Anxiety can be chronic, for example, feeling on the edge most days and for most of each day. For some, anxiety becomes a way of life. Martin lived in a constant state of unrest and a pervasive feeling of uneasiness or apprehension. Surviving each day was a formidable task.

Martin's story. From as early as I can remember I felt anxious. I believed I could not please my parents. I was continually reprimanded for my behavior. In school, I knew I did not measure up as each report card told the tale. I was drawn to work with computers. I found a job in computer programming. As long as I worked alone, my anxiety was low. However, most of the time, I was part of a team effort and my anxiety was high. I viewed pornography to quiet my nerves. I had difficulty sleeping and suffered reoccurring stomach distress. I experienced a mild breakdown and began therapy. My therapist addressed my generalized anxiety before we addressed my addiction.

Alex, Clyde, and Martin all suffer from anxiety. The source of the trauma that is causing their anxiety needs to be identified and therapeutically addressed.

As a young person, did sexual anxiety play a role in your life? Explain

_____
_____
_____
_____

What was your parents' response to your anxiety?

_____
_____
_____
_____

Do you masturbate to relieve anxiety? At what age did you begin to masturbate to relieve anxiety?

_____
_____
_____
_____

As an adult, do you experience *sexual* anxiety? For example, do you feel a tense feeling in your genital region that goes away by masturbating? Does procrastination cause you to feel sexually anxious? Describe a typical situation. How frequently do you experience sexual anxiety?

_____
_____

_____
_____
_____
_____
_____
_____

Did any member of your family have an anxiety problem/disorder? Which members?

_____
_____
_____
_____

Are you anxious when attending social gatherings? In other situations?

_____
_____
_____
_____

Did anxiety cause you problems in school, sports, or relationships? If so, share some examples.

_____
_____
_____
_____

Do you experience anxiety most days of your life?

_____
_____
_____
_____

Do you consider yourself an anxious person? Explain your condition.

_____
_____
_____
_____
_____
_____

As an adult, do you take medication for anxiety? If so, describe events that lead to taking anti-anxiety medication.

_____

_____

_____

_____

_____

Therapist Introduction to Exercise 10
Anger

Men in sexual addiction group therapy talk about their anger response. Most talk about situations while driving or in the family. The extent to which recovery is hampered by anger, particularly in the family, determines the need to address anger in therapy.

Achieving sobriety reduces the anger response.

Clinical notes. Exercise 10 links anger and acting-out behavior. If anger is a problem, ask the addict to share what s/he wrote.

The objective is to end the connection between aberrant sexual behavior and the anger response. Incorporating anger reducing strategies such as the use of relaxation exercises has proven effective. Positive response conditioning, such as replacing negative thinking with positive self-talk is also effective. Medication, that is, a Selective Serotonin Re-uptake Inhibitor (SSRI) has helped a number of group participants.

Exercise 10: Anger

Some men and women feel compelled to control the behavior of family members, peers, friends, employees, and others in their environment. The anger response stems from the lack of control they had over their lives while living in a dysfunctional family. Addicts are sensitive to a belief that they have been cheated, disrespected, or devalued. Their anger is also a response to shame and guilt associated with aberrant sexual behavior.

Sobriety and restored relationships promote positive feelings of self-worth and thus lower the trigger threshold for an anger response. A decrease in the anger response may improve the marriage relationship, particularly when non-sexual intimacy becomes more of the focus rather than sex.

Anger is manifested in different ways. For example, *active* anger is evident though fits of rage, yelling or screaming, destroying property, or attacking another person. *Passive* anger is evident by withdrawing from a conversation when the addict feels overwhelmed or unable to control the outcome of a disagreement. Frequently, anger is exhibited by expressing criticism, becoming cynical in the evaluation of others, or making sarcastic remarks to appear superior in comparison to others.

What role does anger play in your life? Give examples.

_____
_____
_____
_____
_____
_____
_____
_____

How is your anger and acting out connected?

_____
_____
_____
_____

Anger can be expressed though fits of rage, yelling or screaming, destroying property, or attacking another person. How do you outwardly express anger?

_____
_____
_____
_____

Anger is expressed passively when the addict withdraws from a conversation because s/he feels overwhelmed. Anger is exhibited by expressing criticism, becoming cynical in the evaluation of others, or making sarcastic remarks to appear superior in comparison to others. How do you express passive anger?

_____
_____
_____
_____

Do you remember expressions of anger in your family of origin? Which members? Were you the recipient of their anger? What did you do to protect yourself? Give examples.

_____
_____
_____
_____
_____
_____
_____
_____

As a child, if you expressed anger, what was your parent's response?

_____
_____
_____
_____

Did anger cause problems in school, sports, or relationships? If so, share some examples.

_____
_____
_____
_____
_____

How does anger affect your relationships with friends and co-workers?

_____
_____
_____
_____

In the present time, do you express anger? Assertive or passive? How often? If so, how? Share examples.

_____
_____
_____
_____

How has anger affected your marriage?

_____
_____
_____
_____

Do you feel that anger plays a role in keeping you isolated from friends or family? Explain the circumstances.

_____
_____
_____
_____

What role does anger play in your relationship with your children? Do you punish your children while in the state of anger? Explain the circumstances.

_____
_____
_____
_____

Are you angry with your Higher Power? If so, why

_____
_____
_____
_____

Therapist Introduction to Exercise 11
Habits

Sexual habits form neuropathways which promote acting out. The recovery journey calls the addict to create new habits, which circumvent old well-worn addictive neuropathways in the brain. The goal is to build healthy habits that take the place of destructive ones.

The addict can incorporate habit-reducing strategies such as replacing negative with positive self-talk, use of relaxation exercises, and changing the environment where the habitual behavior takes place. An addict, who habitually masturbated every morning while showering, added spiritual music to change his habit.

Clinical notes. In therapy, identify undesirable sexual habits. Adverse behavioral conditioning may be useful in reversing habitual behavior.

The objective is to end aberrant sexual behavior by making habitual behavior transparent and less subject to mindless repetition.

Exercise 11: Addressing Habits

Habitual behavior is a recurrent, often unconscious pattern of behavior acquired through repetition. For example, an addict does not require much thinking before initiating sexual stimulation. The fantasy or self-sexual touch is repeated out of habit. Habituation is a basic form of learning which, after a period of exposure to stimuli, allows the person to stop conscious thinking about how to respond to the stimulus.

New behaviors become automatic through habit formation. Old habits are hard to change because the behavior an addict repeats is imprinted on his or her brain's neuropathways. However, it is possible to form new habits through repetition of healthy behavior. It requires re-wiring all the neuropathway circuits to change the brain's demand for a reward.

The addict can incorporate habit reducing strategies such as replacing negative with positive self-talk, use of relaxation exercises, and, in particular, changing the environment where the habitual behavior takes place. An addict, who habitually masturbated every morning while showering, added spiritual music to change his habit.

What habits do you have in your life that you consider good and purposeful?

_____

_____

_____

_____

What habits do you have in your life that you consider bad and destructive?

_____

_____

_____

_____

Do you have a habit related to your sexual addiction? Describe.

_____

_____

_____

_____

How can you change the environment where you habitually act out so you are no longer comfortable acting out in that location? For example, would you dedicate your home to your Higher Power and choose never to act out in your home or play spiritual music in the place where you normally act out.

_____

_____

_____

_____

What strategies will you use to preclude repetition of a destructive habit? For example, do you plan to cancel cable TV to change the habit of searching for stimulating programs or images?

_____

_____

_____

_____

Therapist Introduction to Exercise 12:
Isolation and Loneliness

Sexually addicted people tend to isolate themselves. A causal factor of isolation is often traced back to childhood. A child's response to abuse, lack of emotional nurturing, lack of positive socialization, and the shame of engaging in sex, may cause a child to separate or withdraw from family and peers. A child who lives in an abusive home may displace loneliness by academic achievement or, conversely, by use of alcohol, drugs, or sexual behavior. When adult addicts are unable to feel loved, their response is to isolate further.

Even in marriage, the addict is often isolated and lonely. Isolation, loneliness, and boredom are toxic and a breeding ground for depressed mood and acting out.

Clinical notes. Exercise 12 provides an understanding of how isolation supports acting-out behavior.

The lack of healthy connections with other people (caused by isolation) keep the addict addicted. Isolation is revisited in Chapter 11 as a condition that needs to change in order to living a healthy life style. Exercise 22 explores how coming out of isolation supports sexual sobriety.

Exploring childhood environment, behaviors, and feelings will likely reveal the underpinning of an addict's tendency to isolate as an adult. One of the first steps in recovery is for the person to incorporate new behaviors that encourage coming out of isolation (See Living at 40, Exercise 23).

Ask the addict to share what s/he wrote.

The objective is to end isolation and loneliness to foster sex addiction recovery.

Exercise 12: Isolation

The roots of isolation often form when a child's mother was unable to bond during the formative years. Bonding occurs when an infant is held, rocked, cooed, through eye contact, and nurturing touch, If this was the case for you, the lack of attachment to your mother left you unable to feel love or to love. Later as a prepubescent child, it is likely you also experienced abandonment when your parents did not provide the emotional nurturing you needed to feel whole. Conversely, your parents provided conditional love, criticism, unwarranted punishment, and sexual, physical, or emotional abuse.

The framework for isolation is heard in the child's expressions, "I keep to myself; I have few friends; I am not as popular as I would like; I am bullied by siblings; I spend my time playing video games and watching TV; Kids laugh at me; I find it difficult to share my concerns and feelings with my parents; I engage in sex play; I find acceptance from the wrong crowd."

Isolation takes many forms. The isolated adult has few friends and little or no social life, feels unloved in marriage, acts out in secret, lacks social skills, and feels bad and unworthy of friendship. The isolated person often seeks an occupation where s/he works alone.

To survive abuse you likely separated or withdrew from the family environment. A male child tends to stay away from the source of stress, that is, he comes home to eat and sleep, but that is all. He may find a substitute for the lack of human connection such as alcohol, drugs, or sex. The female child may run away from home or, alternatively, is rebellious at home. She may engage in destructive behaviors such as running away from home, promiscuous behavior, cutting self, bingeing, and bulimia.

The severity of isolation varies and the above is the worst-case scenario. All sex addicts have some tendency to isolate. For most, it is less severe. For example, lack of close friends is a common form of isolation.

What is the role of isolation in your life?

_____
_____
_____
_____

Do you know if a lack of attachment to your mother as an infant contributed to your adult isolation? Explain your understanding.

_____
_____
_____
_____

Do you know if a lack of healthy emotional nurturing contributed to your isolation? Explain your understanding.

_____
_____
_____
_____

What is the connection between your isolation and acting out?

_____
_____
_____
_____

Would you describe yourself as isolated as a prepubescent child (five-12), as a young teenager (13-15), or as an older teenager (16 on)?

_____
_____
_____
_____

As an adult, do you find yourself alone much of the time? Do you experience loneliness and boredom? Does your isolation contribute to your acting-out behavior?

_____
_____
_____
_____

What were your feelings related to isolation? For example, "I just felt I wasn't normal; I felt parents and teachers didn't understand me; I felt sad that I was not part of the 'in' group; and I was often bullied by my siblings or kids at school." What was your experience?

_____
_____
_____
_____
_____

Give several examples of how you were isolated from parents, peers, or siblings.

_____
_____

_____
_____

Are you isolated as an adult? Describe your isolation. Give several examples.

_____
_____
_____
_____

Therapist Introduction to Exercise 13:
Dysfunctional Marital Relationship

The quality of the marital relationship is a factor when one of the partners is sexually addicted.

Ideally, this exercise would involve both partners in sex addiction therapy. Alternatively, refer the couple to marriage counseling. Ideally, marriage counseling is scheduled after the addict has been in sex addiction counseling for at least six months.

Clinical Notes: Assist married couples to explore changes they wish to make in order to enjoy a loving and joyful marriage in the future.

Exercise 13, The Marriage Interview, will aid the man or woman to gain an appreciation of how addiction may have led to distancing within the marriage. Explain the concept of unbalanced power in the marriage.

The objective is to understand how the marriage relationship plays a role in maintaining sexual addiction. A key element in recovery is to restore equality in their relationship and a loving respect for each other's position.

Exercise 13: Marital Relationship

Because self-esteem is damaged, it is difficult for many addicted men and women to comprehend how anyone could love them. When they find a partner who professes love for them, they live in fear that their partner will someday repudiate their expressed love and abandon them. At least half of the men in sex addiction group therapy have experienced this scenario.

An addict tends to marry a partner who has unfinished business with his or her parents. For example, a man in group therapy talked about how his partner had similar traits to those of his mother. If the addict's mother was condescending and critical, odds are, the addict will marry a partner who will exhibit the same traits. If the addict's father found it difficult to show affection, the addict will likely marry a partner who will exhibit the same trait.

During a disagreement, the male addict may feel the call to *walk on eggs*. He fears that his partner will criticize, chastise, or reject him if he expresses his thoughts, just as he feared crossing his parents during childhood. As an adult, he prefers to walk away from a disagreement rather than to work through it. Walking away is safer than dealing with what he considers his partner's superior position. Alternatively, in disagreements he may try to gain control by raising his voice or engaging in other dysfunctional behaviors. These coping mechanisms play havoc with any marriage.

Exercise 13: Marriage Interview

- How long have you and _____ been married? How did you meet? How long did you date?

- Did you love _____ when you married? What did love mean to you then and today?

- At the time you married, did you consider_____ your best friend? What did it mean to be your best friend?

- Early in the marriage, did _____ suggest behavior s/he thought you needed to change? Did s/he ask, beg, demand, cajole, or nag you to make changes?

- At some point, did your spouse's requests annoy you? Give some examples of discord in your marriage.

- Does your partner seem to have traits similar to those of one or both of your parents? What are they?

- Are you able to ask _____ to consider changing? If not, why?

- Do you feel you are *walking on eggs* when you discuss an issue with_____? Why? Have you ever discussed this with_____?

- In general, do you have difficulty sharing your thoughts, thinking, or feelings with_____? What do you fear if you did?

- Whenever you and _____ have a fight, what do you do? What is the role of anger in your disagreement? Who usually wins? Why?

- Do you refuse to participate in a fight or withdraw from a discussion prematurely? Why? On the other hand, if you do not withdraw from the discussion, what do you do?

- Are you compelled to control a disagreement by expressing your anger? What do you do to exercise control?

- How would you change your marriage if you could? Why?

- Do you feel that _____listens to you?

- Do you believe either of you is codependent? In what way?

- How does your marriage differ from what you consider an ideal marriage? Do you think _____would agree?

- When did sexual activity first enter your relationship? How important was sex in your premarital time together?

- After you married, how soon did you dishonor the marriage contract by acting out? Why? How?

- Have you disclosed your acting-out behavior to_____? What was her reaction to learning of your acting-out behavior? What was your reaction?

- What reaction did you have when your acting-out behavior was discovered? Did you make promises to change your behavior? Did you succeed?

- In what condition would you call your marriage?

- How do you see the future of your marriage? Is your desire for the future a dream or does it have a strong sense of reality?

- For your desire to become a reality what needs to change?

Therapist Introduction to Exercise 14:
Pornography

Pornography is like stepping on a paper covered with glue.

Because pornography is a primary factor that keeps people addicted, it is addressed in multiple chapters including:

- Chapter Three - Road to Addiction.

- Chapter Four - Conditions Which Bond an Addict to Sexual Addiction.

- Chapter Five - *Pornography.*

- Chapter Eight - Exposing Addictive Behavior.

- Exercise One - Roots of Sexual Addiction.

- Exercise Three - Do I Need to do Something About my Sexual Behavior?

- Exercise Four – Attributes of Sexual Addiction.

- Exercise 17 - Commitment.

Clinical notes. Use these materials as you deem appropriate. For those addicted to pornography, multiple sessions are appropriate to address this subject. Exercise 14 reviews the addict's experience with saying *no* to viewing pornography. Addiction to sexually stimulating images is a challenge but one that can be successful addressed.

In Chapter Five, viewing pornography is discussed. Read Chapter Five, before you address Exercise 14.

The objective is to end addiction to pornography.

Exercise 14: Saying No to Pornography

Saying *no* to Internet pornography starts with awareness that you have a choice to say no. Ending any addiction is not easy. However, if you are serious about saying no to viewing porn, accessing chat rooms, web cams, or other cybersex behaviors, you must change your environment sufficiently to make it easier to say no. For example, reducing the number of devices that connect to the web will limit your access to the Internet. The playing field is reasonably well defined and a choice to use an Internet blocker is reasonable.

If you are not particularly computer savvy, a number of commercial software programs are available to block access to Internet pornography. Searching the term, *blocking software*, will display multiple blocking programs.

If you are computer savvy enough to circumvent an Internet blocking program, software entitled *Covenant Eyes* goes beyond blocking access to web sites. It provides a weekly Internet access report to a person designated by you, the user. The report details the sites accessed during the week of reference. Having someone else involved reduces the propensity to deceive yourself and others. *Covenant Eyes* (2014) is found at www.covenanteyes.com/Accountability. It may be more difficult to change your environment at work, but it is possible.

Other changes are easily made. For example, relocate the family computer and TV to a public area within the home. Relocation is only effective when someone else is in the room or likely to enter. In addition to relocation, password protect your devices so that Internet access is dependent on another person to logon. Make a commitment not to use a computer when home alone. Commit to go to bed at the same time, as your spouse.

Other solutions which forestall access to pornography include canceling access to cable TV; avoiding TV shows that provided stimulating images; canceling subscriptions to certain sports magazines that feature advertising or articles with tantalizing images; and fast forwarding past provocative scenes or commercials. Ending access to pornography is possible, but it starts with a choice.

What is your experience with pornography, chat rooms, web cams, and social media and other forms of cybersex? Describe.

_____

_____

_____

_____

When did your attraction to cybersex begin? How and why?

_____

_____

_____

_____

When did cybersex activities begin to interest you?

_____

_____

_____

_____

When did your attraction to cybersex become a concern to you?

_____

_____

_____

_____

Do you view Internet pornography? Rent or purchase pornographic movies? View pay-for-view or TV porn channels? Read pornographic magazines? Exchange videos or images over the Internet? Use a web cam to engage in or view sexual activity? Which one(s)?

_____

_____

_____

_____

_____

_____

_____

Do images of straight sex, oral or anal sex, same sex partners, sadomasochism, younger/older women, body parts, or children arouse you? Which one(s)?

_____

_____

_____

_____

What body parts appeal to you? This could be genitals, male/female, breasts, legs, hair, buttocks, necks, anorexic bodies, or full-bodied people. Which one(s)?

_____

_____

_____

_____

Do you fear being caught when you view pornography? How close have you come?

Do you view pornography in your home, workplace, Internet Cafe, other? Which one(s)? Why?

Do you get aroused (mentally or physically) by images not regarded as pornographic by society in general (newspaper, magazines, catalogues, TV, etc.)? If they cause sexual stimulation, do you consider the images as pornographic? What type of images, and what sources, stimulates you?

How frequently do you view pornography? Why?

What is the typical time lapse between viewing pornography? Why?

Do you have a favorite time of the day during which you view pornography? Why?

Do you find you are never satisfied with finding the latest pornographic image—you want more or better? Has your search for pornography/cybersex become obsessive and compulsive?

_____

_____

_____

_____

Have you hurt someone in your life by viewing pornography? Who? How has it affected your relationship with that person(s)?

_____

_____

_____

_____

Do you experience shame or guilt after you view pornography? Describe.

_____

_____

_____

_____

Do you want to say no to viewing pornography and/or cybersex? Why?

_____

_____

_____

_____

What strategies will be effective for you to say no to viewing pornography and/or cybersex? (See Exercise 20).

_____

_____

_____

_____

Outline your plan to say no to viewing pornography and/or cybersex?

_____

_____

_____

_____

_____
_____
_____
_____
_____
_____
_____

Has pornography affected your spiritual life?

_____
_____
_____
_____

Therapist Introduction to Exercise 15:
Acting-Out Triggers

Knowledge empowers an addict to understand how acting-out triggers lead to orgasm. Although an addict may identify a change in mood or daily stress as the beginning of the cycle, others point to specific triggers. For example, boredom is Jim's trigger. Jim, who lives alone, often feels bored, and allows his mind to wander and so begins his acting-out cycle. Other triggers include specific places, stimulating images or body parts, sexual toys, procrastination, anxiety, or an encounter with another person who sends an availability message.

Clinical notes. During check in time, an addict may disclose episodes of acting-out. When acting out is reported, ask the addict to identify his trigger(s). Ask the addict to suggest how s/he would deal with the same trigger in the future.

This exercise assists addicts to avoid or disable triggers. In addition, the person can incorporate new and positive behaviors into his or her life to reduce the attachment to triggers. (See Living at 40, Exercise 23).

Use the *three-circle* exercise to identify nurturing activities (outer circle), sure fire acting-out triggers (inner circle) and potentially toxic activities that could cause the addict to either act out or reject the temptation to act out (middle circle).

The objective is to identify triggers and establish strategies to curtail their effectiveness.

Exercise 15: Recognizing Triggers

Triggers are specific forms of temptation that lead to acting out. For example, boredom is Jim's trigger. Jim, who lives alone, often feels bored, and allows his mind to wander, and so begins his acting-out ritual. Other common triggers include specific places, viewing stimulating images or body parts, sexual toys, procrastination, anxiety, and an encounter with another person who sends an availability message.

Awareness of the dynamics of the acting-out cycle enables an addict to interdict his or her acting-out triggers at the beginning of the cycle. Rituals begin with thinking, actions, or behavior; so do triggers. A trigger is often the first step in a ritual. Ann's trigger was using her computer to check email. Although she had no intention of surfing for pornography, clicking her email icon was her trigger to begin her acting-out ritual. John's trigger was leaving work early on Fridays. He told himself that he had errands to run but he always ended up at a strip club. Joseph found trips to the beach or community pool were triggers for him. Arleen's trigger was men dressed in tight clothing.

A technique to address triggers calls for the addict to train his or her mind to activate an *awareness alarm*. The alarm sounds in the addict's head when s/he is tempted to act on a trigger. Sounding an *awareness alarm* empowers the addict to preclude or shortcut the trigger. Once an addict goes beyond this early stage of awareness, s/he enters a *trance* like state which, all intentions to the contrary, leads him down the slippery slope to acting out.

Note: Because of relevance of addressing triggers in conjunction with the concept of awareness, an application of an awareness alarm is introduced in this exercise but is addressed more fully in Exercise 18.

From Exercise Seven, identify your sexual triggers that you consider destructive.

_____

_____

_____

_____

Do you have any other sexual triggers that were not mentioned in Exercise Seven?

_____

_____

_____

_____

How can you train your mind to recognize a trigger when it begins, for example, the beginning of a fantasy? Give an example.

_____
_____
_____
_____

How can you engage your *awareness alarm* before you allow acting-out triggers to begin your acting-out ritual? (See exercise 18 for more information related to use of an awareness alarm)

_____
_____
_____
_____

What strategies preclude repeating destructive triggers? (See Exercise 20 for an inventory of strategies that may be used to counter a trigger)

_____
_____
_____
_____
_____
_____

CHAPTER TEN: STAGE III - RECOVERY - MODIFYING BEHAVIOR

In Stage II, factors that bind an addict to sexual addiction were evaluated.

In Stage III, you are now introduced to recovery–modifying addictive behaviors.

In Stage IV, you will learn how living a healthy life style is a gateway to changing the addiction torment.

In Stage V, you will be challenged to prepare a relapse plan—to think through what elements would support your sexual sobriety.

Therapist Introduction to Exercise 16:
Agreement to Celibacy

For the addict, one recovery tool is to participate in a period of celibacy. A contract for a period of celibacy is referred to as an Abstinence Contract or an Abstinence Plan.

The benefits of celibacy are to lower the addict's sexual temperature, that is, give the addict time to focus on recovery, as well as, to improve the practice of non-sexual intimacy in order to rebuild trust and friendship in the marriage.

Marital relations often cease for a period after disclosure or discovery of the addict's sexual behavior. To be ahead of the curve, the addict may elect to enter voluntarily into a period of sexual abstinence. Voluntary celibacy is a sign to demonstrate the addict's commitment to recovery. Carnes (2000) suggests a period of abstinence of two to three months (p. 13).

Clinical notes. Explain to the addict the benefits of choosing a period of celibacy. If the addict agrees, form an abstinence contract with her or him.

The objective is to clear the addict's mind of sexual stimuli to become more aware of self and underlying behavior traits.

Exercise 16: Period of Celibacy

For the addict, a recovery tool is to participate in a period of celibacy. Marital relations often cease for a while after disclosure or discovery of the addict's sexual behavior. To be ahead of the curve, the addict may elect to enter voluntarily into a period of sexual abstinence. Voluntary celibacy demonstrates the addict's commitment to recovery.

The benefit of celibacy is to lower the addict's sexual temperature, that is, give the addict time to focus on recovery, as well as, to improve the practice of non-sexual intimacy in order to rebuild trust and friendship in the marriage. Carnes (2000) suggests a period of abstinence of two to three months (p. 13). A contract for a period of celibacy is referred to as an Abstinence Contract or an Abstinence Plan.

A period of celibacy excludes all forms of sexual activity. Celibacy reduces sexual chaos and allows a period of time during which the addict, with the aid of his or her therapist, can explore what constitutes healthy sexual behavior. During abstinence the brain repaves the sexual neuropathways—a necessary recovery task.

Goodman (1998) further defined the concept of abstinence.

Early in recovery, when the sex addict's judgment is still significantly distorted by a combination of denial, rationalization, vague or fragmented identity, and superego pathology, distinguishing healthy from pathological sexual behavior can be exceedingly difficult. During this initial period, some patients might benefit from total abstinence from any kind of sexual behavior.

The rationale for initial abstinence is that, early in recovery, individuals who have been using sexual behavior addictively may be incapable of selectively eliminating the self-regulatory functions from their sexual behavior; and, to the extent that they continue to use sexual behavior to regulate their affects and/or self-states, they are less likely to benefit from treatment.

Meanwhile, refraining from behaviors that could be used addictively pushes the individual into greater self-awareness. Therapeutic use of enhanced self-awareness to undermine denial and rationalization, to stabilize identity and sense of self, and to integrate healthy superego functions then brings patients to a point where they are more capable of distinguishing healthy from pathological sexual behavior. Abstinence from sexual behavior, though not a goal of treatment for sexual addiction, can on occasion be a helpful therapeutic technique. (para 5)

The abstinence contract includes specific content. The first is a list of sexual practices that will be excluded during the duration of the contract. Second is a list of strategies (See Exercise 20) the addict will employ when tempted to engage in sexual activity. The third is a plan to employ the addict's accountability partner or sponsor to support the addict's abstinence pledge. Finally, the contract should incorporate a goal statement that reflects the addict's long-term expectation of what a high-level commitment will look like as part of recovery (Carnes, 2000, pp. 9-12).

How would abstinence from all sexual activity for one to three months help your marriage?

_____
_____
_____
_____

Have you discussed abstinence from all sexual activity with your spouse, therapist, and sponsor?

_____
_____
_____
_____

What is your motivation to abstain from all sexual activity for one to three months?

_____
_____
_____
_____

What benefits would you derive from engaging in a period of sexual abstinence?

_____
_____
_____
_____

What would inspire you to make a decision to enter a period of sexual abstinence?

_____
_____
_____
_____

How would a period of sexual abstinence signal a commitment to recovery for you?

_____
_____
_____
_____

How would a period of abstinence help you to distinguish between healthy and pathological sexual activity?

_____

_____

_____

_____

**Therapist Introduction to Exercise 17:
Commitment**

Recovery means more than giving up aberrant sexual behavior. The *give-up road* results in an incomplete solution and is characterized as the *white-knuckle* syndrome. An addict who uses the white-knuckle approach fights temptation repeatedly. Each time a sexual thought begins, s/he entertain the thought but tell self that s/he is trying to put it out of his/her head. It is nearly impossible not to think about the thought you are thinking about. The white-knuckler plays a game with self. "Let me get this sexual thought out of my head, but not so far out that I can't bring it back later, if I want."

The white-knuckler struggles but never fully commits to end the struggle. The white-knuckler throws away sexually stimulating pornography but keeps a stash. Stash is a favorite image(s), which s/he keeps available for a future time when white-knuckling fails and relief from the struggle is in order. For example, stash is a magazine tucked under the mattress or a web link hidden away. The struggle is ongoing, whereas, a high-level commitment is an immutable decision and ends the struggle.

Clinical notes. Exercise 17 compares the difference between white-knuckling and high-level commitment. Ask the addict to read text from Exercise 17 aloud during the session. Conduct an extensive conversation as to what a high-level commitment would look like. Each time an addict reports acting out, ask how the experience would have been different if s/he had achieved a high-level commitment. Ask the addict if any of the white-knuckling techniques are working. What does a high-level commitment mean to the addict?

The objective is to appreciate what constitutes a high-level commitment and establish the expectation that the addict will choose to make a high-level commitment.

Exercise 17: Commitment

An important recovery task is to learn the difference between white knuckling and a high-level commitment.

White knuckling

White knuckling is the torture you put yourself through before you act out. You use strategies that amount to applying bandage strips over a serious wound. Bandage strips do nothing but temporarily cover the wound.

Recovery means more than giving up aberrant sexual behavior. An addict who travels the give-up road fights temptation repeatedly. Each time a sexual thought begins, s/he entertains the thought but tells self that s/he is trying to put it out of his/her head. The white-knuckler plays a game with self. "Let me get this sexual thought out of my head, but not so far that I can't bring it back later, if I want."

The white-knuckler struggles but never fully commits to ending sexual behavior. For example, a white-knuckler throws away sexually stimulating pornography but keeps a stash. Stash is a favorite image(s), which s/he keeps available for a future time when white-knuckling fails and relief from the struggle is rationalized. Stash is a magazine tucked under the mattress or a web link hidden away.

Temporary strategies may work from time to time but long-term sexual sobriety is rarely achieved. The alternative to temporary strategies is making a high-level commitment to end acting out. *A high-level commitment consists of making an irrevocable decision to end illicit sexual thinking, fantasy, and behavior.*

High-level Commitment

Recovery entails permanently ending acting-out behavior. A high-level commitment is far different from promises to change behavior. It is an order of magnitude greater. It is so compelling that the addict mentally *forms a paradigm in which acting-out is no longer part of his or her reality.* It is significantly easier to reject temptation after a high-level commitment has been made because the possibility of acting out has been eliminated. An irrevocable choice to end addictive behavior is best understood after you experience the post commitment state.

A high-level commitment is usually not realistic early in recovery. If it were that simple, this book would not be necessary. For example, an addict needs to understand the roots of addiction, how shame binds an addict to addiction, how the characteristics of sexual addiction apply to the addict's life, and why white knuckling fails, before the addict is ready to move to a higher order of commitment. Making a high-level commitment is the core of recovery. However, it is not a stand-alone element.

An addict who makes a high-level commitment rejects all improper sexual thinking. When the battle of the mind is won, sexual sobriety follows. A major premise of the 12-step program is that "we are powerless to stop our behavior"—that applies to all addicts in the initial stages of recovery. Therapy, prayer, and attendance at a 12-step program and working the steps eventually prepare the addict to make a choice.

In group therapy programs, men discuss the difficulty they have in understanding what constitutes a high-level commitment. It is a challenge to conceptualize what one lacks in experience. Perhaps an example will enlighten. A high-level commitment happened when a man decided to end his addiction to masturbation. His home was the environmental setting for his addiction. He reasoned that a decision to end masturbation would be part of his high-level commitment. It just so happened he was moving into a new home. He made a covenant with his Higher Power that he would never act out in his new home. His covenant was the basis for his irrevocable commitment to end his masturbation. While he has been tempted, his high-level commitment has remained intact for the past 20 years.

Where are you? Are you white knuckling or have you made a high-level commitment?

_____
_____
_____
_____

Describe in your own words the difference between white knuckling and a high-level commitment.

_____
_____
_____
_____
_____
_____
_____
_____
_____
_____
_____

Described the white-knuckling strategies you use.

_____
_____

How would your strategies change if you made a high-level commitment?

Is it reasonable to expect you will make a high-level commitment in the near future? Share your thinking.

What *stash* do you keep hidden away?

What would a high-level commitment look like to you? For example, could you dedicate your home as a place where you will not act out?

Those who win the battle of the mind, find that a reduction in acting out follows. What does it mean to banish sexual thinking and fantasy?

My high-level commitment is:

_____
_____
_____
_____
_____
_____
_____
_____
_____
_____

Therapist Introduction to Exercise 18
Awareness

With the assistance of a therapist, an addict can develop an *awareness alarm* that sounds when s/he is tempted to engage in sexual behavior. *The awareness alarm is activated when one realizes s/he is becoming stimulated by a new sexual thought, fantasy, or by a trigger.* If the awareness alarm sounds before pleasure-seeking chemicals begin to act, the addict can choose to reject a trip down the slippery slope.

Clinical notes. Exercise 18 seeks the meaning of awareness as part of commitment. Ask the participant(s) to read the introduction and stories aloud during the session. Conduct a discussion as to what Maggie did to support herself. Ask the addict to describe what awareness means and the changes that happen as awareness grows.

The objective is to adopt an *awareness alarm* and exercise choice to forgo acting out.

Exercise 18: Awareness Alarm

Visual sexual stimulation is a curse. Even when you seek sexual sobriety, the media, television, newspaper, and billboard advertisements all sell sex. Merchants make their wares attractive by adding visual sexual stimulation. The Internet is the king of sexual stimulation. The book, *Every Man's Battle,* instructs you to bounce your eyes in the face of visual sexual stimulation (Arterburn, Stoeker and Yorkey, 2000). Bouncing your eyes means to shift your eyes away from viewing sexually stimulating images. It is solid advice. However, you may find it difficult to bounce your eyes in every situation (p. 125).

When a sexual stimulating image is forming, you can reject the image—that is, drop it. The three-second rule says you have three seconds in which to make a decision to reject temptation. At the end of three seconds, the processing switch is turned off.

Other techniques defuse the brain's pleasure-seeking chemicals. Pornographic or visual images are not real. To the addict they have become objects. The visual sexual images are means of gratification, not opportunities for friendship and relationship. By taking the object and adding human qualities, you may end the acting-out ritual. When you see a visual sexual image, instead of saying, "I want that," say, "That person is someone's mother; or that person is someone's daughter; or that person could be my sister (or my daughter)." Exploiting someone's mother, daughters, or your sister is not attractive to most.

Another technique is to employ an *awareness alarm*. The awareness alarm is the sudden realization that you are being tempted. As such, the addict trains his or her mind to sound a mental awareness alarm when s/he is tempted to engage in sexual behavior. *The awareness alarm is activated at the moment when one realizes s/he is becoming stimulated by a new sexual thought, fantasy, or trigger.* If the awareness alarm sounds before pleasure-seeking chemicals begin to act, the addict can choose to forgo a trip down the slippery slope.

Let us see how several men reacted to environmental temptation.

Mark's story. I was on my way to pick up my young son from a local campus day care center. Driving that warm day in May through campus set off fire alarms in my brain.

Flesh was everywhere I looked! My intent was not to look but how do you not look when two half-clad students jaywalk right in front you. I know it is my problem but, my heavens. I often think like a child in a candy store—so many sweets. I get sick just thinking of sampling it all.

I remembered to invoke my awareness alarm. It helped to change my mental processing…all those young things were somebody's daughter.

My reaction to temptation…my *awareness alarm*—allowed me to avoid sampling the sweets.

Jay's story. Jay checks his email each day.

I have been quite good lately. I know porn leads me to fantasies and fantasies lead me to masturbate. I used to tell myself that I was only checking out the latest pics of *Jannie Harbenure*, but I lied to myself. Once I was online, I couldn't stop from checking out a few other sites and I was off to the races.

As I said, I have done well over the past few months but last week, I really had a challenge. I received an email message that I knew was going to be provocative to say the least. I didn't even have to click to know it would get my juices running. I was a click away from opening the email or turning off my computer. I heard my *awareness alarm* sound—I turned off the machine.

Monty's story. I like to watch TV. It helps me to relax after a hard day at work. I find that visual stimulation, particularly images of women with healthy buttocks begins my ritual. I do not act out if I am not visually stimulated. I was surfing the channels. I like to watch sports—any kind of sports. Thursday evening, I was home alone and wanted to watch some hockey. Acting out was the farthest thing from my mind. I just wanted to relax and enjoy. I was not prepared for what happened next. I hit a channel (just passing through) and, oh my! My reaction was immediate—I could not take my eyes off her. I went down the slippery slope. Why?

Monty asked a good question, why? Monty, like many who deal with sexual stimulation, needs a better appreciation of what triggers pleasure. Monty needs an *awareness alarm* that sounds within the first few seconds of his encountering visual stimulation or the possibility of giving in to a tempting new sexual thought. If Monty allows an awareness alarm to sound before pleasure-seeking chemicals begin to run in his brain, he can choose not to act out. With about six months of repeated success, that is, sounding his awareness alarm at the beginning of erotic stimulation, he will have formed a new habit. An addict finds that once an awareness alarm becomes part of his or her being, it is very difficult to allow visual sexual stimulation to take over.

Maggie's story. Whenever I see a man dressed in tight short shorts, I am off into my fantasy—just he and me. I have been going to my fantasies for so long, how could I give them up? While I tell myself, I don't want to act out, I have grown to like how it makes me feel.

I also saw what it was doing to me. Acting out is the most dishonest thing I do. I want my partner, Bill, and my friends to see me as a good person, but I carry around a secret that, if they knew—well, so much for the good person. When am I going to beat this? When am I going to become the person I want to be? When am I going to put Bill, not my fantasies, first? I have to try.

I learned that the moment of choice is the instant I become aware of an impending fantasy or sexual thinking. Awareness precedes my choice. Once aware, I can ask myself; do I want to go there?

Maggie decided to try sounding her *awareness alarm* with changing how she viewed scantily clad men. She began to say to herself, "That person could be my brother." It helped but she found she did not fully drop the image. She stored the images in her brain and brought it out and enjoyed it before sleep.

Maggie talked about her commitment, "I am delaying gratification, but I don't seem to be committed to doing away with it. I want to do better. I need to do better. I am sick and tired of the pain. I am sick of being sick."

She went back to the drawing board and mapped out a different approach to her awareness alarm. She began individual therapy with a competent sex addiction therapist and she attended a 12-step program. She found an accountability partner at her church who had struggled with alcohol as a younger woman. She talked about Bill. She said she loved him and thought she did not have the right to put fantasies of other men ahead of her relationship with him. She first dealt with her secrets. With the assistance of a therapist, Maggie shared her secret life with Bill. He was shocked and hurt but with time he understood the courage it took Maggie to share her shame—her secrets. He understood her desire to make a commitment to put him first.

I have a new approach; I want to make a high-level commitment. I want to stop the pain. To put my fantasies first—myself first—is acting like a selfish child. It is not fair to Bill or our children. I am going to adopt a new mantra. When I am tempted by a visual sexual image, I will invoke my awareness alarm, and I will say to myself, 'God give me the power to not go there.'

I found that making an irrevocable commitment was not easy. I had been in the habit of entertaining sexual images since childhood. With time, and with the aid of my counselor, 12-step program, and accountability partner, I surrendered myself and began to experience repeated success. I worked to become aware of an impending fantasy and began to exercise choice. I used alternative healthy fantasies, prayer, and other techniques to clear my mind of sexual thoughts.

After about eight months, I told my therapist, I really wondered if I could defeat my addiction. It had been part of my life since I was a wet-behind-the-ears little girl. My fantasies and masturbation are where I went to deal with stress in my life. I know that now.

An interesting thing happened a few days ago. You know the gym on 8th Street. I was working out and a couple young men came in. They had much flesh exposed. In the past, this would have been more than I could have handled—you know what I mean. This time, my awareness alarm sounded and my mantra came into my head— 'God give me the power to not go there.' I actually found it easy to continue exercising and leave the young men (someone's sons) on the weight pile. In fact, I think it is becoming impossible for me to fantasize about such men. After having invested eight months to change my response to environmental temptation, I would be so disappointed in myself if I went back to my old ways. I have too much invested now in my sobriety. Going back is no longer an option.

Maggie found strong reasons for changing her behavior and she used techniques to clear her mind of offending thoughts. Techniques, by themselves, did not make the difference. However, a strong commitment along with techniques made the difference.

As time went by Maggie and Bill found that their marriage, while better, still had weaknesses. A therapist explained to them that they had a codependent relationship. Through family therapy, they understood the roles each played in their marriage and how codependency was an underlying illness that facilitated Maggie's sexual addiction.

Her individual therapist also taught Maggie to change her lifestyle. She programmed in more healthy activities, made new friends, and became closer to her God. She learned that the recovery journey is multifaceted but it begins with awareness.

Maggie did the following to support herself. The components of her actions, taken together, constitute a recovery plan.

- Found reasons to change her behavior—her relationship with herself, friends, and most important, Bill, her partner.

- Asked a sex addiction therapist to assist her.

- Exposed her secrets to Bill and the light of day.

- Joined a 12-step program.

- Asked a sponsor to assist her.

- Made a high-level commitment to herself and her loved ones to change her behavior.

- Sounded her awareness alarm and used a mantra each time she came across environmental temptation—"God give me the power not to go there."

- Began to see men, not as objects, but as people—someone's father, brother, or son.

- Worked her commitment day-by-day until it became a part of her.

What about you?

Describe a time when an unexpected sexual urge caused you to become stimulated.

_____
_____
_____
_____

What environmental conditions facilitate your addiction?

_____
_____
_____
_____

What does the following mean to you? *Awareness is part of my commitment.*

_____
_____
_____
_____

What does awareness in the present moment mean to you?

_____
_____
_____
_____

Are you aware of environmental urges before they trigger acting out?

_____
_____
_____
_____

What is an awareness alarm and how do you develop an alarm in your life?

_____
_____
_____
_____

The components of Maggie's actions taken together constitute a recovery plan. What component(s) would you include in your recovery plan?

_____
_____
_____
_____
_____
_____

Therapist Introduction to Exercise 19:
Addiction Causes More Pain than Pleasure

When an addict approaches a high-level commitment, she or he finally comprehends that the consequences of sexual addition are no longer palatable. A turning point for the addict is to realize that addiction causes more pain in contrast to the short-time pleasure of acting out. It is an important change in the addict's attitude toward addictive behavior.

Clinical notes. Exercise 19 addresses why addiction causes more pain than pleasure. Ask the addict to relate to the statement, for me, the pain-pleasure equation is out of balance. Ask the addict if a short period of pleasure (acting out) is worth the long period of self-loathing and guilt. Ask the addict to discuss, "It is dumb what I do to myself." Ask how the pain/pleasure equation could be changed. What would a changed equation look like? Empower the addict to change thinking and to choose sexual sobriety as a long-term answer to the pain of addiction.

The objective is to become aware that aberrant sexual behavior is paying negative dividends.

Exercise 19: Addiction Causes More Pain than Pleasure

When an addict approaches a high-level commitment, she or he finally comprehends that the consequences of sexual addition are no longer palatable. A turning point for the addict is to realize that addiction causes more pain in contrast to the pleasure of acting out. It is an important change in the addict's attitude toward addictive behavior.

Sex is pleasurable; nature intended it to be so. However, in the end, the euphoric feeling is more than offset by feelings of shame, guilt, and fear of discovery. This is the pain-pleasure equation. When men and women think about the pain-pleasure equation, they begin to recognize that it is far out of balance.

For men the period of euphoric pleasure is short. For women the fantasy, build-up, and the hunt may span more time. Humans trade pleasure for shame and guilt because they do not think through the consequences. One woman said, "I never thought of it that way; It is dumb what I do to myself."

If you have lived years in emotional pain, do you accept pain as part of your life? Does choosing pain of addiction actually become a comfortable place for you? Does the fear of change, keep you stuck in your rut? Perhaps it is time to address your irrational thinking. A change in prospective is essential to make a high-level commitment.

Do you feel bad about your inability to change your behavior? Do you realize that your life is in disarray? Explain.

_____
_____
_____
_____

Is it more comfortable to live in the known squalor of shame and guilt than to opt for a different but unknown environment? At least you know how pain feels. Some call such conclusions, irrational. What do you call it?

_____
_____
_____
_____
_____

If you have lived in emotional pain for years, do you accept pain as part of life? Are you at ease with your emotional pain?

_____
_____

What are your components of addiction pain? (Isolation, depressed mood, and shame)

Is it time for you to give up this pain? Explain.

What changes would you make to rid yourself of the pain of addiction?

Envision your life without the pain of addiction. What would your life look like?

Addiction causes more pain than pleasure is just one more condition, along with others presented in this chapter, which encourage you to make a high-level commitment to end aberrant sexual behavior.

Are you ready to make a high-level commitment?

Therapist Introduction to Exercise 20:
Strategies

Over the years, men in sex addiction therapy shared the strategies that they used to ward off temptation (Becker, 2012b). The ultimate strategy is to make a high-level commitment to end sexually addictive thinking and behavior. Time and a new way of thinking are needed to understand the real difference between white-knuckling and high-level commitment (See Exercise 17). The strategies employed before making a high-level commitment are analogous to bandages. Bandages are temporary coverings; they do not cure the wound. The use of strategies alone does not constitute a recovery program (pp. 105-108).

Paradoxically, once a high-level commitment is made, these same strategies support the addict's decision to eliminate permanently sexual thinking and behavior. As such, they become part of her/his recovery program.

Clinical notes. A list of strategies is included in Exercise 20. Ask the participant(s) to read the strategies aloud during the session. Discuss which of the strategies they wish to adopt. During check in at the next session, ask which strategies were actually used by the group members.

The objective is to select strategies to ward off sexual temptation in the quest for sexual sobriety.

Exercise 20: Strategies

Addicts in therapy have shared strategies they found effective in supporting their commitment. However, a high-level commitment is the ultimate strategy. Because every person is unique, you need to select strategies you expect will work for you in time of temptation. The strategies employed before making a high-level commitment are analogous to bandages. Bandages are temporary coverings; they do not cure the wound. Paradoxically, once you make a high-level commitment, these same strategies support your decision to eliminate permanently sexual thinking and behavior. As such, they are part of your recovery program.

Strategies in this exercise have been proven valuable to addicts in their quest for sexual sobriety. However, the use of strategies alone does not constitute a recovery program.

The recovery triad includes behavior modification, normalizing shame, and reconnecting addicts with normal feelings. For example, a strategy to reconnect with feelings is to name them, as they are experienced in the present moment. They can also be written down on a small pad as a means of tracking the number of feelings felt during the day. After a few weeks, awareness of feelings will become part of your recovery program.

You are encouraged to create and carry two index cards with two strategies. On one card, include strategies you plan to use to ward off temptation. When you are tempted to act out, read your card and select a strategy. The card will assist you to recall a strategy. It is difficult to think clearly, when you are in the throes of temptation. Make a similar index card with a list of strategies that address ways you can improve the quality of your life.

The strategies developed by group members are:

- Actively participate in 12-step and counseling programs.

- Be accountable to yourself—make a conscious choice to eliminate sexual thinking, and fantasy. Each success you have today is one more than you had yesterday.

- With the assistance of a therapist, disclose your addictive behavior to your partner.

- Be aware of your own needs, resentments, stresses, anxiety, and loneliness and how each feeling sets the stage for acting-out sexually. Deal with underlying issues through counseling.

- Medicate anxiety. If masturbation relieves your anxiety, anti-anxiety medication may be a better solution until the source of anxiety is removed. Dealing with chronic anxiety is toxic both to mental and physical health. (Medication is always taken under medical supervision. Consult your physician or a psychiatrist for a full evaluation and an appropriate prescription.)

- Become aware of your various acting-out rituals and learn to recognize when a ritual is beginning. If you experience an acting-out incidence, and while your memory is fresh, write down the steps which led you down the slippery slope to acting out. Focus on early steps and identify a step at which you became aware you were heading toward a slip. Pre-plan a strategy for that stage (See Exercise Seven).

- Develop a support network. Reach out—call a friend, sponsor, or your accountability partner in time of deteriorating mood or when sexual urges begin your acting out ritual.

- Use a journal to keep in touch with reality—to track moods, lies, triggers, or rituals.

- Think through, "Where am I heading," when you feel an urge to begin your acting-out ritual. Form a mantra that works for you, for example, "I don't have the right to go there;" or "Don't go there;" or "I don't have to be a pursuer of my past."

- Become fully aware of the persons, places, feelings, thinking, or things that leads you to begin your acting-out ritual. Pre-plan a strategy that will diffuse temptations related to persons, places, feelings, thinking, or things that lead you to act out.

- If you are more likely to begin your acting-out ritual when you are alone, plan ahead to avoid being alone.

- Make environmental adjustments to preclude an acting out ritual from beginning—get rid of cable TV or the Internet or choose safe routes.

- Become aware of your unique triggers. Reject them before they lead you to act out.

- Put a pornography filter on your computer(s).

- Forgo watching TV programs with sexual content. Alternatively, record TV programs you like to watch and fast-forward through sexual material, ads, or other difficult parts.

- Tape a note to the edge of your computer screen with a mantra, for example, "I will not use this computer to gain access to pornographic material."

- Make a high-level commitment to end addictive behavior. Draw a line in the sand...a line never to be crossed.

- Verbalize your thinking to defuse sexual feelings. In other words, talk aloud to yourself when you face temptation.

- Use an alternative healthy fantasy in place of a sexual fantasy. For example, play fantasy football or a round of golf in your head, or remember a time when you felt relaxed and enjoyed life.

- Plan for more healthy personal time to deal with stress. For example, regularly exercise to reduce stress. In case of a sexual urge, use an immediate exercise strategy such as 20 pushups.

- Learn to practice and enjoy non-sexual intimacy with your partner. For example, take a walk together, talk about what is important to your relationship, and plan other activities that build your relationship. Work to make your partner your best friend. Spend quality time with your family. (See Exercise 23).

- Understand the factors that encourage your choice to live at the mood level of a normal person (40-point benchmark) and program them into your life. (See Exercise 23).

- If you find yourself living below the mood level of a normal person (40-point benchmark) for weeks at a time, consider taking an anti-depression medication (SSRI) combined with individual therapy.

- Treat yourself to small rewards for not acting out. One man's self-reward is one hour of shooting pool for every four days of sobriety.

- Contrast the degree of pleasure derived from acting out versus the pain of guilt, shame, and time wasted. If the balance is negative, ask yourself why you want to do something that is causing you more pain than gain. (See Exercise 19).

- Dispute illogical thinking. If you are lying to yourself or engaging in illogical thinking, admit it and look for the truth.

- Implement the three-second rule. If tempted by an image of an attractive person, at three seconds look away and drop the image.

- Learn to bounce your eyes away from sexually titillating images or persons.

- Instead of seeing a person as a sex object, see the person as someone's mother or daughter, father or son. "Thank God for making a beautiful person and let it go."

- Personalize a sexual image. See the humanness of the person by focusing on the person's face, eyes, smile, and facial expressions.

- Sexual temptation will continue throughout your life. Learn to turn away.

- If you are married, transfer your thinking and your gaze to your partner.

- Work to gain greater awareness of who you are as a person and how your self-talk either promotes acting out or sexual sobriety. (See Exercise 18).

- Carry a picture of your family. Take it out when your feel the urge to act out.

- Trash stash. *Stash* is sexually stimulating material hidden away in anticipation of a future time of need. Examples include a hidden porn magazine or an Internet URL to connect to a sexually stimulating web page. Throw it away, so that it will not come back to tempt you!

- Address other addictions—alcohol, drugs, gambling, eating disorders, anger, etc.

- Imagine God's presence in the room when you feel the urge to act out.

- Take a walk. That is, remove yourself physically from the locus of your sexual urge.

- Carry a motivational verse or scriptural passage to bring you back to reality when you feel the urge to act out. Make prayer or other spiritual reading part of your life.

- Play spiritual music to ward off the urge to act out. For example, if you act out in the shower, play spiritual music.

- Surrender—in the 12-step traditions understand and acknowledge it will take both you and God to travel your recovery journey. Ask God's help—you are powerless.

- Dedicate your home to your God and refrain from acting out in your home.

- Plan and practice an active spiritual life.

- Learn to forgive yourself.

- If you engage in outbursts of anger, consider individual therapy.

- If you find your unwanted sexual behavior is continuing, consider individual therapy.

- Make a list of strategies you want to use, post the list where you normally act out, and use it to support yourself.

Note: The above strategies address quality of life or temptations. The road to recovery must address both. Make two lists of strategies, one to address quality of life and one to address specific temptations.

Therapist Introduction to Exercise 21:
Fear of Giving-up Their Best Friend

Sexual release is the addict's panacea for life, his or her best friend. The addict has enjoyed the company of his or her best friend for years. No other friend occupies so much time. The possibility of giving up a best friend can be frightening. It means that the addict has to choose a different way of living. The lost friend will not be available to soothe depressed mood, stress, and isolation.

Clinical notes. Discuss what life will be like without their best friend. Explain the five phases of grief. Ask the addict to discuss each phase and what it will mean.

The objective is to become aware of the loss involved in a high-level commitment. The grief stages may be revisited during several sessions.

Exercise 21: - Fear of Giving-up Their Best Friend

Your best friend, sexual addiction, has been your companion for years. The possibility of giving up your best friend can be frightening. It means you have to choose a different way of living. Can you live without your old friend to soothe you?

What does it mean to say that sexual behavior is your best friend?

_____
_____
_____
_____

How long have you known your best friend? Do you fear giving-up your best friend? Why

_____
_____
_____
_____

What effect will saying goodbye to your best friend have?

_____
_____
_____
_____

How will you grieve the loss of your best friend?

_____
_____
_____
_____

Is it time for your best friend to exit your life? Explain.

_____
_____
_____
_____

What steps can you take to say good-by to your friend?

_____

_____

_____

_____

_____

_____

CHAPTER ELEVEN: STAGE IV - LIVING A HEALTHY LIFE STYLE

To hasten recovery, the addict can choose to live a healthier lifestyle.

Improving one's lifestyle diminishes the propensity to act out. For example, when a man or woman chooses to come out of isolation, chooses to improve relationships with family and friends, chooses to promote a healthy mind and body, and chooses to put their Higher Power first, they have chosen to change their lives and thus their addiction dance. A healthier lifestyle reduces anger, anxiety, isolation and loneliness, and depressed mood. A reduction in negativity yields a corresponding reduction in acting out. Life becomes more satisfying. Addressing sexual addiction is not one-dimensional. Rejecting sexual addiction also means choosing to become a healthier person physically and mentally.

Making a major change in life is an intricate part of recovery. An addict may choose the following to live a healthier lifestyle:

- Employ strategies to help come out of isolation.

- Engage in new behaviors that will reduce depressed mood.

- Forgive self and others.

- Adopt new behaviors in place of old behaviors.

- Back-off addictive behaviors.

- Incorporate non-sexual intimacy (Living at 40 – Exercise 23) and affirmations of true intimacy.

- Reject compartmentalization.

- Change codependent behavior.

- Commit to total honesty.

- Commit to healthy spirituality.

- Develop a support system.

Therapist Introduction to Exercise 22:
Come Out of Isolation

To survive, an abused child lives behind a wall of isolation—out of harm's way. Because the child's parents were unable to provide emotional nurturing, the child learned to go it alone. As an adult, s/he continues to live in isolation and sexual processing dominates the addict's brain waves. Addiction is valued more than relationships. Although this is not a universal characterization of everyone, the scenario applies to 81 percent of addicts who were abused as children (Carnes, 1998, p. 1).

Because the addict thinks badly about self, he or she lack the self-respect necessary to be loving and gregarious. S/he does not form supportive relationships. It is likely that that the addict does not have a good friend with whom s/he can share the addiction struggle. It is also likely the addict's marriage is less than what his or her partner desires.

Coming out of isolation sets the stage for sexual sobriety.

Clinical notes. Exercise 22 provides the rationale for coming out of isolation and other social issues that may be addressed. Elements in fostering a healthy life style found in this exercise include:

- Come out of isolation by cultivating a strong same sex friendship.

- Come out of isolation by improving family of origin relationships.

- Come out of isolation by improving relationships with partner and children.

Conduct a conversation on each of the above topics. Ask how cultivating a strong same sex friendship, improving family of origin relationships, and improving relationships with partner and children contribute to sexual sobriety. Discuss why coming out of isolation is included as a recovery task. Ask why the practice of a healthy life style makes a difference to the addict and his or her partner. Ask what it means to the addict to find friendship in his or her marriage.

The objective is to end isolation, to live a healthy life style, and to enjoy sexual sobriety.

Exercise 22: Coming out of Isolation

"I tend to live in isolation. I live in my head. Sexual fantasy and thinking dominate my brain waves. Unfortunately, I value my addiction more than my relationships." Do these statements apply to you? If yes, how? If not, why?

_____
_____
_____
_____

"I have only a few friends. I don't let my friends know about my sexual thinking, fantasies, and behavior." Do these statements apply to you? If yes, how? If not, why?

_____
_____
_____
_____

If you were abused as a child, to survive you lived behind an emotional wall—out of harm's way. When your parents were unable to provide emotional nurturing, you learned to go it alone. As an adult, you continue to live in isolation.

Because of your sexual behavior, you think badly about yourself and you lack the self-respect necessary to be loving and gregarious. Your social skills are lacking and thus you have difficulty forming healthy relationships. It is likely that you do not have a good friend with whom you share your addiction struggle. It is also likely your marriage is less then satisfying to you and your partner.

Your past is not necessarily prolog. Better news can follow. The following are some changes to consider. Coming out of isolation supports sexual sobriety and a healthy lifestyle. Is it time to come out of your isolation and to live a joyful life?

Coming Out of Isolation by Cultivating a Strong Same Sex Friendship

A healthy life style includes cultivating a strong friendship—a friendship which, in time, allows you to share the real you—your problems and your journey.

Life is often a paradox. It is precisely the necessity to share your weakness and allow another person to pierce your veil of secrecy, which makes finding a new same sex friend therapeutic. Sharing and thus defusing shame reduces the underlying call to medicate pain.

Ideally, you will trust this friend to be your sponsor or accountability partner. A sponsor or accountability partner is someone who you can call to say, "I had a strong urge to act out today." Developing a strong same sex relationship takes time. Twelve-step meetings are often a good source of candidates. After all, others in 12-step groups understand your struggle and you appreciate theirs as well. Another source is Celebrate Recovery in which men and women with various addictions come together to seek friendship and mutual support.

Interestingly, men generally find it very difficult to cultivate a strong male friendship. During childhood, males are taught to be competitive. Life experiences enforce the stereotype. For the addicted man, forming a strong male relationship means he lets another male into his shame based world of addiction—a very frightening thought. An addicted man thinks he would rather suffer alone in his secret world than to share his weakness.

Women are relational. They may have the same fears as a male but most women have a clearer vision of the benefits of same-sex support. They realize that friends care, listen, and provide support.

A man or woman, who steps out of isolation by forming a strong friendship, finds the nurturing they never received from their family of origin—a healing experience.

What about You?

"I fear sharing my weakness with another person. I fear rejection more than isolation." Do these statements apply to you? If yes, describe your fear. If not, why?

_____
_____
_____
_____

If the above statement applies to you, test reality. Do you really think it is a sign of weakness to be vulnerable to a fellow traveler? Group members report that when they are vulnerable to another person they receive even more respect and the other person becomes vulnerable too. Perhaps you can also be a healing catalyst to the man or woman with whom you share your journey.

Are you willing to come out of isolation by cultivating a strong same sex relationship? If yes, how?

_____
_____
_____
_____

How would you cultivate a new friendship? What steps would you take?

_____
_____

_____
_____

Coming Out of Isolation by Improving Family Relationships

Improving relationships with your parents and siblings is another relationship restoration task. An addict often lacks a close family relationship because his or her family-of-origin played a role in fostering his or her isolation. It is difficult to love and cherish those who hurt you. Second, the secret world in which an addict lives is bounded by shame. Taking a risk that mom, dad, sis, or junior may discover your real identity is disconcerting. Again, it is by piercing the shame barrier that begins to defuse the underlying call to medicate pain.

The first step is to engage family members in a dialog. The dialog is deeper than talking about sports or the weather. A reasonably safe place to begin is to ask parents or siblings to share memories of their early family life. Siblings may have a different perspective than you. Hearing another family member's story establishes a more accurate perception of reality.

Becoming reconnected in a healthy way takes time. Your isolation is what those close to you have witnessed over time. It may take more than one try for them to respond.

What benefits do you anticipate from renewing healthy intimacy with your family?

_____
_____
_____
_____

Are you willing to come out of isolation by cultivating new friendships with members of your family? If yes, how?

_____
_____
_____
_____

How would you cultivate a new friendship with a family member? Which family member would you approach first? What steps would you take?

_____
_____
_____
_____
_____
_____
_____

Note: Sharing sexual addiction information with family members is a secondary objective to establishing friendship with them. The primary objective is to come out of isolation by fostering healthy family relationships. Although it may be beneficial for family members to know your weaknesses, sharing your sexual addiction is not mandatory. That knowledge can be shared when you feel it will contribute to a deeper understanding and intimacy.

Coming Out of Isolation by Improving Relationships with Your Partner and Children

Improving relationships with your partner and children is perhaps the most important task in coming out of isolation.

Intimacy always equates to sex for the addict. Because the relationship lacks self-sacrificing love, it is not difficult then to understand why most couples find their marriage less than satisfying. It does not have to be that way; you and your partner can live a more satisfying life. Partners must learn to be truly intimate—and intimacy does not mean sex. It means enjoying fun activities together. Examples include talking, cooking, and hiking, or enjoying an inexpensive dinner together. Sex is the dessert, not the nutrition in the meal. Sex is best enjoyed when it is relationship-based and when healthy non-sexual intimacy precedes sex. (See Exercise 23 for an understanding of non-sexual intimacy.)

"When I think about it, my relationship with my partner is based on sex. Only when we engage in frequent sexual activity am I satisfied with our relationship." Do these statements of apply to you? If yes, how? If not, why?

_____
_____
_____
_____

"I fear sharing my secrets with my partner because I know s/he will try to fix me. I know I am an addict, but I hate it when s/he points it out to me. I fear rejection." Do these statements apply to you? If yes, how? If not, why?

_____
_____
_____
_____

Again, test reality, do you think your partner will reject you? Even if s/he did, how much worse off would you be than you are today?

_____
_____
_____
_____

"I wish my partner were my best friend. Although we live under the same roof, I often feel we are distant relatives." Do these statements apply to you? If yes, how? If not, why?

_____

_____

_____

_____

What does non-sexual intimacy mean to you? What benefits do you perceive from gaining a deeper level of intimacy with your partner and children? (See Exercise 23 for an understanding of non-sexual intimacy.)

_____

_____

_____

_____

Are you ready to come out of isolation by cultivating a new friendship with your partner and children? What forms of non-sexual intimacy would you incorporate into your partnership? (See Exercise 23 for an understanding of non-sexual intimacy.)

_____

_____

_____

_____

How would you cultivate a new friendship with your partner and children? How you and your spouse benefit from marriage counseling? Why?

_____

_____

_____

_____

Improving family relationships is a major task in coming out of isolation. Sharing the knowledge of your sexual addiction with your partner for the first time is best done with the assistance of a sex addiction therapist. The therapist can set disclosure boundaries, normalize disclosure, and explain the nature of sexual addiction to your partner. In addition, the book, *Getting the Love You Want*, by Harville Hendrix (2007), has been beneficial to many men and women.

Therapist Introduction to Exercise 23:
Living at 40

To improve the quality of life is another important recovery task. When the addict begins to live at a normal person's mood level that is, at the *40* benchmark on the *Addict's Life Scale*, rather than at a low-grade depressed mood level, that is at 20, the desire to act out is reduced.

Living at 40 concepts and exercise were clinically tested and proved very effective (Becker, 2012c, pp. 4-130).

Clinical notes. Exercise 23 provides an alternative to living in low-grade depressed mood. A table is provided for the couple to record their non-sexual intimacy activities. These activities, when practiced by the couple, will help them live at a normal person's mood level that is the 40-benchmark level on the *Addict's Life Scale.*

Those who are sexually addicted live in low-grade depressed mood and to improve mood, they act out. Once the addict concurs in this premise, he or she is introduced to a new concept. It is called *living at 40* on the Addict's Life Scale. People who live at 40 enjoy activities that happily married couples practice all the time. Living at 40 is codified by preparing a weekly plan that includes daily, no or low-cost, non-sexual activities. Engaging in non-sexual activities, over time, fosters a healthy marital relationship. In turn, the mood level of the addict is raised so that the reward for acting out is diminished.

Ask the addict to read the text aloud during the session. Conduct a conversation on choosing to live at 40. Living at 40 reduces the time the addict lives in a depressed mood in favor of living at the mood level of a normal person. Discuss why a healthy life style is important to the recovery journey.

The objective is to adopt healthy activities as a means of reducing negativity and thus acting out.

Exercise 23: Living at 40.

The *Addict's Life Scale* is a visual tool which explains the relationship between low-grade depressed mood and acting out. This scale ranges from zero to 50, in 10-point increments. Each benchmark correlates with a relative mood level. At the top of the scale is the 50-point benchmark. This mood level coincides with acting out. It is called the *euphoric level.*

One-step down from the euphoric level is the 40-point benchmark. It is the functioning level of a normal mentally healthy adult. This is the *great to be alive* level. The difference between the 40-point benchmark and the 50-point benchmark is 10-points. A person who lives at the great to be alive (40-point) benchmark, does not act out because acting out only yields a 10-point gain. For a normal person, a 10-point gain is not worth the experience of shame and guilt that follow.

The next step down is the 30-point benchmark. It is a level below the, great to be alive, mood level. This is the *bad day* level. The 30-point benchmark is a level which a normal person visits but does not live there.

The 20-point benchmark is the level where most sex addicts live. An addict who dwells at the 20-point benchmark lives in a constant low-grade depressed mood. However, relief from depressed mood comes with sexually acting out. Acting out raises the addict's mood level by 30-points—from 20 to 50 but only for a short period.

The 10-point benchmark represents *full-scale depressed mood.* This person finds it difficult to eat, sleep, and to go about daily life. Sexually addicted people rarely experience full-scale depressed mood.

The 0-*point* benchmark represents institutionalization. A person who finds self at the 0-point benchmark is out-of-control.

With this introduction, let us look at the *Addict's Life Scale.* For the addict relief from depressed mood comes with sexually acting out.

50 - Acting-out mood. The euphoria one feels ← ——— during the build-up and experience of an orgasm. ← ———
   10 pt. jump ↑

40 - Normal Functioning Mood. Mood level of a normally functioning → ——— adult. It is the great to be alive mood level. ↑

30 - Bad Day Mood. A level to visit but not to live
   30 pt. jump

20 - Low-grade Depressed Mood. Where the addict lives → ———

10 - Full Scale Depressed Mood. The person barely functions.

0 - Unable to Function Mood. The person is often institutionalized.

What Has to Change?

In order to raise his or her mood without acting out, the addict has to live more like a normal healthy person. A normal person does not act out because a 10-point gain is not a sufficient reason. If an addict lived at the mood level of a normal person, his or her incentive to act out would match that of a normal person. This is called living at 40.

What Do I do to Live at 40?

A married couple, who live at 40, incorporates non-sexual intimacy activities into their lives; a major factor in fostering healthy marital living. It begins with preparing a weekly plan to engage in *no or low-cost activities* each day. The 40 type activities are those in which happily married couples engage as a matter of course. Non-sexual intimacy behaviors become the basis for a healthy marriage. When you raise your mood level by engaging in healthy activities, you begin to perceive what it is like to feel normal.

Courting Went Wrong

Although the following scenario is common, it may not resonate with your dating history. For the sex addict, the goal during courting was to engage in sexual activities. Once sex entered the relationship, efforts to build a friendship ended. You had what you wanted and you reasoned that if you were having sex, you and your partner loved one another. However, your definition of love equated to nothing more than having sex. In recovery, it is prudent to go back to square one and build the friendship that ideally should have been built during courting. Married couples who, from the beginning of their courting relationship, engage in continuing friendship building do not deal with sexual addiction—they live at 40.

Below is a representation of how relationship-building activities that can be practiced by you and your partner.

Sample 40 Activities Worksheet

Living at 40 begins when the couple develops a non-sexual activities plan. The activities chosen by the couple are reasonably simple, such as taking a walk together, going to the gym together, or talking for 20 minutes after dinner. Each plan covers a week, is in writing, and is posted on the family refrigerator. If the plan is just verbal, the addict, who lives in a low-grade depressed mood and has a tendency to procrastinate, will not fulfill his or her end of the commitment. The addict needs external motivation to overcome mood-induced ambivalence.

Ideally, healthy joint activities are planned for each day of the week.

Although the plan is composed primarily of non-sexual activities, the plan below includes an instance of sexual intimacy (Wednesday). Marital relations is included to affirm that sexual intimacy is still part of the marital bond—*when and if the couple so desire.*

The non-sexual intimacy activities vary according to the needs of the couple.

Sunday	Monday	Tuesday	Wednesday	Thursday	Friday	Saturday
Family Activity Written Plan for the coming week	Take a Walk together and hold hands	Go to the gym and work out together	Discuss a book that both are reading Marital Relation	Watch a movie together with close proximity to each other but no marital relations	Pizza & (Root) beer night Dinner at a low-cost restaurant	Family activity with or without children

When you live a normal life (40), the urge to act out is significantly lower than when you live in a state of a low-grade depressed mood (20).

Living at 40, that is, the 40-point level can mean taking different steps to different people but some additional steps include:

• Engaging in healthy recreation. Carving out a period of each week to enjoy life such as biking, walking, and playing with their children, taking one's partner out to dinner, etc.

• Becoming active together in a club, service organization, or church.

• Engaging your partner or friend in good conversation. Start with fifteen minutes a day and continue to add time.

• Calling one or more friends every day.

• Cultivating a strong same sex friendship.

• Focusing on what is going right in your life—not what is going wrong.

• Serving others. Part of coming out of isolation is choosing to serve others. Examples include serving periodically at a soup kitchen, coaching children's sports, or joining a prison ministry. The addict benefits from changing from being a *taker* and becoming a *giver.*

Living at 40, Activities Worksheet. Your 40 activities chart is below. Your daily activities will vary according to the needs of you and your partner. Add your examples of non-sexual intimacy to the chart below

Sunday	Monday	Tuesday	Wednesday	Thursday	Friday	Saturday

Your comments regarding living at 40 are:

_____
_____
_____
_____
_____
_____
_____
_____
_____
_____
_____
_____
_____
_____

Affirmations of True Non-sexual Intimacy

Men and women benefit by changing the focus of their marriage relationship. When the couple is able to say *yes* to many of the non-sexual intimacy statements below, isolation in the marriage has dissipated. Marriage counseling may assist you to achieve some of these lofty aspirations.

I know that I have intimacy in my marriage when:

• I consider my partner to be a very good listener.

• My partner understands how I feel.

• We have a good balance of leisure time spent together and separately.

• I look forward to spending time with my partner.

- We find it easy to think of activities to do together.

- I am very satisfied with how we talk to each other.

- We frequently do something nice for each other (without looking for thanks).

- We are creative in how we handle our differences.

- Making joint financial decisions is not difficult.

- We are equally willing to make adjustments in our relationship.

- I can share feelings and ideas with my partner, even during disagreements.

- My partner understands my opinions and ideas.

- My partner is my best friend.

- My partner does not try to fix me. We agree it is my job to fix me.

What do you want to change so that you and your partner focus on true intimacy?

_____

_____

_____

_____

_____

_____

_____

Therapist Introduction to Exercise 24:
Forgiveness of Self and Others

Forgiving is the next logical step in living a healthy life style.

The addict needs to forgive both self and others who contributed to the pain of sexual addiction. Forgiveness begins at home and includes family members. If a non-family member abused the addict, forgiveness may extend beyond the home.

In Step nine of the 12-step program the addict makes amends to those people that the addict has hurt, including his or her partner, children, family members, and any other affected person. Ideally, the addict asks forgiveness from his or her victims, but not if it is likely to cause victims more pain (Sexaholics Anonymous, 1989, p. 6).

Clinical notes. The addict needs to discuss what it means to forgive those who hurt him or her as well as those s/he hurt.

Ask the addict to write a letters to begin forgiveness. The first letter forgives parents who failed to provide emotional nurturing. The second letter, if applicable, is written to the person or persons who abused the addict. The next letter is to the child within in which s/he expresses sorrow for what happened and pledges to be present for the child within in the future. Ask the addict to write a forgiveness letter to those who s/he hurt. Forgiveness of the adult self can be included in this letter or in a separate letter. Ask the addict to read the letters aloud during a session. Discuss why forgiving self and others takes a burden from the addict. *Only with your agreement may any of the letters be mailed.*

Confrontation with members of the family of origin and abusers may or may not be appropriate. The addict, in conjunction with his or her therapist, determines if a confrontation is likely to support his/her recovery.

The objective is to guide the forgiving process as part of recovery.

Exercise 24: Forgiving Self and Others

Do you want to forgive yourself and others who contributed to the pain of sexual addiction? Forgiving begins at home and includes family members. If a non-family member abused you, forgiveness may extend beyond the home.

In Step nine of the 12-step program the addict makes amends to those people that the addict hurt, including his or her partner, children, family members and any other affected person. Ideally, the addict asks forgiveness from his or her victims, but not if it is likely to cause victims more pain (Sexaholics Anonymous, 1989, p. 6).

Your therapist will direct you to write letters in which you forgive those who hurt you and other letters in which you ask to be forgiven by those whom you have hurt through your addiction.

Letters of forgiveness may include:

- A letter in which you forgive your parents for not providing the emotional nurturing you needed to grow into a healthy adult.

- A letter, if appropriate, in which you forgive those who abused you.

- Letters in which you ask forgiveness from those whom you have hurt: your victims, including spouse, children, and other family members.

- A letter to yourself in which you normalize what happened in your past life and pledge to bring joy into your life by making a high-level commitment to end your acting-out behavior.

- A letter to the child within in which you expresses sorrow for what happened to your inner child. Pledge to be present for the child in the future and comfort the wounded child.

Only with the agreement of your therapist may any of the letters be mailed.

Therapist Introduction to Exercise 25:
New Behaviors in Place of Old Behaviors

It is more productive to add new and healthy behaviors to the addict's life than subtract old behaviors.

Clinical notes. Exercise 25 provides a narrative and several stories, which explain the principle of adding new and healthy behaviors as an alternative to subtracting old.

Ask the participant(s) to read the text aloud during the session. Discuss the benefits of adding new and healthy behaviors as a means of interdicting acting out. Ask the addict to suggest new behaviors that s/he could use to combat sexual temptation.

The objective is to curtail acting-out behaviors by adopting new, healthy behaviors in place of addictive ones.

Exercise 25: New Behaviors in Place of Old Behaviors

An addict faces a daunting task in giving up addictive behaviors. At some point, a line is drawn in the sand, which symbolizes an end to acting out. Once the addict stops acting out, a new life without old destructive acting-out behaviors can begin.

Men and woman in sexual addiction therapy find *subtracting* behaviors is more difficult than establishing new healthy behaviors. For example, when a sexual thought begins, it is difficult to curtail the thought, particularly when it is tantalizing. Often you just chase the thought out of your mind for a few moments but the thought continues to return.

Changing the subject of your thinking or engaging in a distracting activity is easier than trying to blot out an aberrant thought or behavior. An example is to engage in a healthy alternative fantasy. An alternative fantasy can be tantalizing but not sexual. For example, Gene enjoys soccer. When a sexual thought comes into his head, he plays a game in his head as an alternative fantasy. He scores the winning goal! Another substitute is employing a mantra to override an aberrant thought or behavior.

Substituting new behaviors tends to work well as a strategy to curtail acting out. Frank who frequented massage parlors each Friday afternoon found that making a date with his partner for an early dinner on Friday evenings worked well for him. Substituting new, healthy behaviors supports a high-level commitment when the new behaviors become habitual.

Jude's story. I find it difficult to stop channel surfing. As much as I try to white-knuckle through a temptation, I usually fail. I told Beth, my partner how much I enjoyed playing pool in my younger days. She encouraged me to purchase a pool table. Instead of watching TV each evening, Jude now engages in a healthy new behavior, playing pool with Beth. As a bonus, they are enjoying each other's company.

Adam's story. To resist the temptation to drive near my favorite strip club is difficult. It just seems to happen. I keep telling myself I am not going to act out this time, but I do. Why is it that when I am in my car I get this insatiable urge? What am I going to do?

Adam's counselor asked him to change his acting-out environment in order to forgo his acting-out ritual. Adam pondered how he could change his driving habits. As they talked, Adam revealed other parts of his acting-out ritual.

Adam always played oldie-but-goodie music that set his mood for cruising the strip club neighborhoods. Adam agreed to change the music. Adam's new behavior is to listen to praise and worship music. He reported that the music—his new behavior—changed his mood and his thinking. "It was hard to listen to sacred music and search for sex at the same time," he said.

Both Jude and Adam put new behaviors in place of old behaviors. New behaviors changed their addiction dance.

Your New Behaviors

Identify current situations where refraining from acting out is difficult for you? Identify two.

_____
_____
_____
_____
_____
_____
_____
_____

What new uplifting behaviors could you adopt to change your acting-out environment for these two situations?

_____
_____
_____
_____

Why is it better to add a new and uplifting behavior rather than to subtract a dysfunctional (acting out) behavior?

_____
_____
_____
_____

What new behaviors could you put in place in place of old behaviors? Name three.

One.

_____
_____
_____

Two.

_____
_____
_____

Three.

_____
_____
_____
_____

Therapist Introduction to Exercise 26:
Backing-off Behaviors

An addict often has more than one form of acting-out behavior. The behaviors vary in degree of perceived societal acceptance. It is usually easier to end the more egregious behaviors first.

Clinical notes. Exercise 26 provides a narrative and a story that explain the concept of sequentially ending sexual behaviors.

Ask the addict to read the text aloud during the session and disclose the layers of his or her addictive behaviors, and suggest a timetable for addressing each layer.

The objective is to curtail acting-out by choosing to address sexual behavior in stages.

Exercise 26: Backing-off Behaviors

An addict may parse his or her sexual behavior into three layers. The top is sexual behaviors, which are frowned upon by society. An addict may find this layer the easiest to forgo because of the fear of being caught. Such behaviors include extramarital affairs, one-night stands, frequenting strip clubs, massage parlors, and prostitution.

The second layer is viewing pornography and engaging in masturbation. An addict believes the potential for being caught is lower because of the privacy involved. Usually the addict finds it more difficult to abstain from this level of sexual behavior than the first level.

Of all the conditions that keep an addict sexually addicted, sexual thinking and fantasy head the list. This is the third layer. Each time the addict needs a dopamine reward s/he can engage a sexual thought or a sexual fantasy. The brain continues to supply lustful sexual material. Because acting out begins with mental processing, the addict needs to become aware of what is happening in the present moment. Early in the mental processing state, the addict has more control to forgo sexual fantasy or thinking.

Generally, those in therapy found they could end sexual behaviors sequentially. For example, Jesse found it easier to give up massage parlors than to give up pornography and masturbation. After a period of sexual sobriety related to massage parlors, Jesse wanted to address pornography and masturbation. After a period of sexual sobriety related to pornography and masturbation, Jesse addressed his sexual thinking and fantasy.

Dennis's story. I really enjoy the company of a woman. I first visited prostitutes when I was in the military. Overseas, you can find all kinds of services—which used to be cheap. When I was back home and could afford to treat myself, I had a list of 10 or so prostitutes and I made the rounds. At the peak, I guess I was spending $1,000 a month. I also liked phone sex. The sound of a sexy woman was all I needed. Of course, the Internet and masturbation were also available.

I found I was spending more and more money on sex. I bet I spent enough money to buy a 28-foot boat that sleeps six. While spending less money was a plus, the real motivator for me was fear of discovery. Can you imagine what it would have done for my career if I were busted in one of those places? I also feared VD. I sure did not want to become an HIV statistic. You just never know. After a month of therapy, I felt I could try to do without prostitutes and phone sex.

I found I could back away from behaviors that I thought could harm me. I had a more difficult time giving-up pornography and masturbation.

Yes, I want to be sexually sober—but even after a year of therapy I am still doing pornography and masturbation.

It seems like it is who I am. The urges keep bombarding me. I have a few clean days but I just can't seem to stick with it.

I resisted attending 12-step meetings. I thought I was different. I really hoped that in time I could control of my behavior. My efforts were not working. I am desperate to end my pain. I agreed with my therapist to attend 90, 12-step meetings in 90 days.

I have not viewed pornography nor masturbated in several months. My accountability partner is present for me. I still have another hurdle before I can say that I am on my recovery journey. I want to end my sexual thinking and fantasy. It is now time for that to go too.

For some, backing off behaviors, one layer at a time works. Ideally, foregoing all acting-out behaviors at once would be ideal. For some it takes steps—one after another.

Acting-out layers

Identify and describe your acting-out layers.

_____
_____
_____
_____
_____
_____
_____

Which layer are you planning to end?

_____
_____
_____
_____

Which layer(s) are yet to be addressed?

_____
_____
_____
_____

What is your plan?

_____
_____
_____
_____

Therapist Introduction to Exercise 27:
Compartmentalization

An addict has a unique mental ability. The addict is capable of separating thinking into multiple categories or boxes. Assume four boxes. Box number one represents employment. Box two represents his or her relationship with one's partner. Box three represents the rest of the addict's world: friends, hobbies, etc. Box four represents acting-out behavior.

An addict's mind keeps the boxes separate from each other. Thinking housed in one box does not cross over to any other box. Thus, the addict's relationship with his or her partner is in one box and acting-out behavior in a separate box. Box four, sexual addiction, was formed long before box two came along. Box four became self-contained and part of the addict's secret world at a time when s/he was unable to choose. An addict hopes that box four will go away in marriage, but it does not.

Clinical notes. Exercise 27 provides a theory of how a sex addict acts out and, at the same time, professes fidelity in marriage.

Ask the addict to read the text aloud during the session and share thoughts about compartmentalization in his or her life.

The objective is to curtail acting-out by choosing to reject compartmentalized thinking.

Exercise 27: Compartmentalization

"I have been found out by my partner," led Ben and others like him to begin therapy. In time, Ben understood that appeasing his partner's anger was not a sufficient reason to do his recovery work. Ben had to want it for his own sake. While self-realization is the best and most productive reason to seek therapy, doing so because of being caught is better than not seeking it at all.

Typically, the marriage is in crisis when an addict is found out. Many who find that their spouse is engaged in sexual activity outside the marriage assume that they are married to a sick person. Some even believe they may have played a role in causing their spouse to be sexually addicted. Some believe they can change the spouse's sexual behavior by enticing him or her back into the marriage bed. Such thinking is fallacious—a married spouse did not cause the addict's sexual addiction and more sex does not solve the addiction.

An innocent partner's common reaction is, "If my spouse loved me, s/he would not go outside the marriage for sex." The offender is seen as self-centered, unloving, sex-crazed, dishonest, and untrustworthy. Trust has been shattered. Conversely, the offending partner usually does not see that sexual activity outside the marriage as having anything to do with love for his or her spouse or children. An addict's mind works differently from that of his or her partner. The addict is able to separate his or her sexual world from the real world. This is called compartmentalization.

An addict has a unique mental ability. The addict is capable of separating thinking into multiple categories or boxes

Visualize compartmentalization in this way. Assume there are four boxes in the addict's brain. Box number one represents employment. Box two represents a relationship with one's partner. Box three represents the rest of the addict's world, friends, hobbies... Box four represents acting out behavior. An addict's mind keeps the boxes separate from each other.

Thinking housed in one box does not cross over to any other box. Thus, the marital relationship is in one box and acting-out behavior is in a separate box. Box four, sexual addiction, was formed long before box two came along. Box four was self-contained and part of the addict's secret world from early in life. An addict hopes that box four will go away in marriage, but it does not. It plagues the addict until a choice is made to change.

Although women may compartmentalize, for the most part, they are less prone to do so. For most women all of the boxes are integrated, none of the boxes is separate. Non-addicted women comprehend the consequences that box four has on the family. It is difficult for women to understand the ability of men to compartmentalize. To women it is illogical that men do not see how acting-out affects the other boxes.

The following provides a visual representation of a man's four boxes and the woman's integrated box. The addicted man faces a challenge to integrate his boxes.

A Sex Addicted Man's Compartmentalized Brain Boxes

Work interests Box One	Relationship with partner Box Two	Hobbies, sports, friends Box Three	Acting-out behavior Box Four

A Woman's Integrated Brain Box

Work <----> Relationship with partner <----> Hobbies, sports, friends <----> Marital relations

The brain box of a non-addicted woman is the ideal. A man's acting-out behavior adversely affects all boxes, and in particular, the relationship with his or her partner.

The wife's reaction, when she learns of her husband's addiction, is traumatic. She is angry and hurt. The husband's reaction to his partner's anger is guilt and shame. A man often expects his partner to forgive and forget—to compartmentalize. His expectations are unreasonable. For women, trust is rebuilt slowly.

What does compartmentalization mean to you? Do you identify with the concept?

_____

_____

_____

Explain your compartmentalized thinking. How has it affected your marriage?

_____

_____

_____

What would change if you rejected compartmentalized thinking?

_____

_____

_____

Therapist Introduction to Exercise 28:
Codependent Marriage

Bradshaw (1998) found that dysfunctional families often engage in codependent behavior. Although addressing the primary sexual addiction is the first order of business, it is necessary to address codependency in marital therapy (p. 173).

Clinical notes. Before beginning Exercise 28, read or distribute copies of codependency section from Chapter Six.

Chapter Six addresses codependency and the impact it may have on a marriage where one of the partners is sexually addicted. If symptoms of codependency are revealed during therapy, suggest couple's counseling.

Exercise 28 explores how codependency inhibits the formation of a deeper marital relationship. Ask the addict to discuss how codependency affects his or her recovery. Ask how it will affect the relationship with his or her spouse. Ask participant(s) to discuss their marriage in relation to the two stories contained in the text.

The objective is to educate the addict about marital codependency as an aid to sexual sobriety.

Exercise 28: Codependent Marriage

Codependency is fully addressed in Chapter Six. Read Chapter Six before proceeding with this exercise.

Marriage partners, where one of the partners is sexually addicted, have a greater possibility that codependent behavior will play an adverse role in their marriage. Bradshaw (1988) believes that "codependence is the most common family illness because it is what happens to anyone in any kind of dysfunctional family." Although addressing sexual addiction is the first order of business, codependency also needs to be addressed as part of therapy (p. 164).

Change the Codependent Response (To improve the readability, the following is in the male voice. The scenario applies to both sexes.)

In codependency, a man may depend on his spouse to behave in a manner that determines his happiness. For example, he raises the possibility of buying a new family TV. In codependency, if his spouse agrees, he is happy. If his spouse does not agree, he is unhappy. He gives his spouse the power to make him happy or unhappy. Codependency shifts the issue from the merits of buying a TV to how the relationship functions.

His spouse's response can be treated as neutral. When his reaction is neutral, he has introduced loving independence rather than starting an argument. In loving independence, each is responsible for their own happiness regardless of the response. He can be disappointed but not angry that she did not make him happy.

A change is needed to remove the power to make each other happy or unhappy from the marriage relationship. Without the power factor, the relationship remains focused on real issues rather than on spurious relationship issues that can fog the effectiveness of practicing non-sexual intimacy.

Partners do not cause each other's addiction or codependency. Addiction began long before the couple met and before codependency entered their lives. Banish the thought of blaming each other. Partners need to accept responsibility for their own behavior and happiness.

Some partners use accountability information to chastise their spouses. In a relationship where each partner is committed to do his or her own healing, information shared about his or her journey must be treated as neutral in contrast to damning. Each partner is responsible for fixing himself or herself.

What does codependency mean to you? Do you identify with the concept?

_____
_____
_____
_____

Explain your codependency behavior. How has it affected you marriage relationship?

_____

_____

_____

_____

What would change if you rejected codependency thinking?

_____

_____

_____

_____

Record your thoughts related to your codependency after reading the two scenarios in the codependency section of Chapter Six. Do you identify with the people in those stories?

_____

_____

_____

_____

_____

_____

_____

_____

What changes do you envision to minimize codependency? List three.

One.

_____

_____

Two.

_____

_____

Three.

_____

_____

_____

Therapist Introduction to Exercise 29:
Sexual Honesty

Disclosure is usually a process: rarely is it a single event. Although the addict will reveal certain practices, other information may be withheld. It is common for full disclosure to take time, even months.

Corley and Schneider's (2002b) research on disclosing secrets reported:

Each member of the couple has his or her own agenda for therapy. For the addict or unfaithful person, items on the agenda may include maintaining the ongoing problematic behavior, preventing the betrayed partner from leaving, limiting further disclosure as damage control against multiple losses, and assuaging guilt by revealing everything. The partner's agenda typically includes obtaining information to validate her or his fears and suspicions in hopes of feeling sane again and getting the addict to stop the behavior. Additionally, the partner is hoping to learn every single detail of the acting out in hopes of figuring out *why* it happened to preserve the relationship or to gain ammunition for future retaliation. Finally, the partner wants to assess the risk of having been exposed to a sexually transmitted disease (STD) or other health risks. (para. 4)

Clinical notes. Exercise 29 explores the role of complete honesty to promote a deeper relationship with one's spouse. Ask the addict to discuss how sexual disclosure and honesty will affect his or her recovery. Ask how it will affect the relationship with his or her spouse.

During disclosure, detail is necessary and other times it can be harmful. The therapist must judge how much information is needed but, in general, disclosure of details is greater in individual therapy than in group or marital therapy. For example, in marital therapy acting-out details that preceded the marriage relationship are best kept in general terms.

The objective is to encourage the addict to practice total honesty with spouse and children as an aid to sexual sobriety.

Exercise 29: Sexual Honesty

Sexual honesty supports a new relationship with one's spouse and pierces the veil of shame, denial, and lack of trust. Disclosure of sexual secrets may occur at the time of discovery, during therapy, or during step-one of a 12-step program. Not only does complete honesty involve disclosing past sexual secrets but may include disclosing current transgressions and temptations. Therapy does not end before disclosure of sexual secrets is addressed.

Addiction therapists are divided as to the degree of disclosure required. Is it prudent for an addict to unveil all his or her past behavior? Many therapists believe, until complete honesty defines the marriage, no true restoration occurs. Others believe it opens wounds that continue for a lifetime and full disclosure allows the addict to offload his or her guilt and shame but inflicts unnecessary pain on his or her partner. Some therapists place emphasis on disclosing transgression that occurred during the marriage and only broadly disclose transgression that occurred before the marriage. Disclosure should be as complete as reasonable and it is best accomplished in a therapy setting.

There is no getting around the pain, which is part of the process. Experiencing the pain of betrayal, the loss of esteem, the anger, shame, and fears that accompany the honesty are extremely difficult. At the same time, this process is required for addicts to remain sober and for relationships to heal enough to start a new journey based on honesty and shared goals. The FSLA (Female Sex and Love Addict) who insists that to tell would hurt too much or harm the recipient wants to avoid pain. (Campling et al., 2012, p. 181)

Another consideration is how honesty can change the marital relationship. Unfortunately, most addicts are dishonest. They lie to hide their dual lives; to hide their aberrant sexual behavior, to shield their ego from the pain of discovery, and they lie out of sheer habit…even when lying is unnecessary. Committing to a new life of complete honesty is a far greater challenge than just disclosing of past transgressions. Accountability for honesty deserves considerable discussion during therapy.

Do you consider yourself an honest or a deceitful person? What role does you addiction play in your answer?

_____

_____

_____

_____

Explain why honesty with yourself and others promotes sexual sobriety (not only about sex).

_____

_____

_____

_____

Do you fear the consequences of disclosure? Explain.

_____
_____
_____
_____

What does full disclosure mean to you?

_____
_____
_____
_____
_____
_____

What does being sexually honest in recovery mean to you?

_____
_____
_____
_____

What benefits do you perceive from maintaining total honesty in your relationships?

_____
_____
_____
_____

What does it mean for you to commit to sexual honesty in your day-to-day relationship with your spouse?

_____
_____
_____
_____

How would complete honesty change your life?

_____
_____
_____
_____

Therapist Introduction to Exercise 30:
Spirituality

A man in group therapy perceived his father as a harsh and unforgiving man. When asked how he viewed his Higher Power, he was surprised to hear himself characterize his Higher Power in the same terms as he described his father. Because of his feelings of shame, he also saw his Higher Power as punishing. Because he feels bad about himself, he rationalized, "Why would my Higher Power feel any different?"

If a Higher Power is viewed as punitive, the addict will have difficulty with the 12-step concept, "Made a decision to turn our will and lives over to the care of God, as we understood Him." Many 12-step participants find that recovery is only possible after choosing a committed relationship with their Higher Power where the love of the Higher Power is accepted as unconditional, even as the addict struggles with the pain of addiction.

Clinical notes. Exercise 30 explores forming a new relationship with the one's Higher Power. Ask the addict to discuss how the recovery journey will or will not include their Higher Power. Ask if s/he plans to change the relationship with his or her Higher Power.

The objective is to decide if ultimate recovery includes a closer relationship with their Higher Power.

Exercise 30: Relationship with Their Higher Power

The term *Higher Power* comes from the 12-step tradition. It refers to a supreme being or deity, or the individual's concept of someone greater than self.

A man in group therapy perceived his father as a harsh and unforgiving man. When asked how he viewed his Higher Power, he was surprised to hear himself depict his Higher Power in the same terms as he described his father. Because of his feelings of shame, he also saw his Higher Power as punishing. Since he feels bad about himself, he rationalized, "Why would my Higher Power feel any different?"

If a Higher Power is viewed as punitive, the addict will have difficulty with the 12-step concept, "Made a decision to turn our will and lives over to the care of God, as we understood Him." Changing one's relationship with spouse, friends, and particularly one's Higher Power requires a new outlook on life. It is a living at 40 task.

How do you perceive your Higher Power? Because of your addiction, do you fear His or Her wrath?

_____
_____
_____
_____

If your family of origin's love was conditional, is it reasonable to expect that your Higher Power will be different? What are your feelings?

_____
_____
_____

Is it likely that addiction has robbed you of the capacity to love in your human relationships? Was your childhood model of your parents love deficient? Explain how it was deficient.

_____
_____
_____
_____

The difference between a committed relationship and one that lacks commitment is faith. It cannot be forced, but the 12-step participants have a convincing way.

Henslin (1995) described the committed and genuine relationship this way:

No authentic and long-lasting change occurs without God's aid and the work of the Holy Spirit in a person's life. A committed and genuine spirituality is an essential foundation for recovery. By genuine I mean spirituality that is biblically based and authentic—a real experience with God, not going through the motions. By committed I mean a relationship with God in which you dedicate yourself to godly living as far as it lies in your power... By committed and genuine I do not mean a perfect spirituality (whatever that is). God begins with us where we are. (pp. 43-44)

Engaging in a committed and genuine relationship with one's Higher Power is paramount to finding peace. After the pain and misery of addiction, His embrace for many is finding the Holy Grail.

In *Addiction and Grace,* May (1988) talks about the importance of a relationship with one's Higher Power. He notes that only through His grace do humans have hope for quelling addiction.

The first and greatest commandment for both Judaism and Christianity is, "You shall have no other gods before me." Similarly, Islam's basic creed begins with "There is no god but God." It is no accident that these three great monotheistic religions share this fundamental assertion. "Nothing," God says, "must be more important to you than I am. I am the Ultimate Value, by whom the value of all other things must be measured and in whom true love for all other things must be found." We have already mentioned the two commandments that Jesus called the greatest, You shall love the Lord your God with all your heart, with all your soul, and with all your strength, and you shall love your neighbor as yourself. It is addiction that keeps our love for God and neighbor incomplete. It is addiction that creates other gods for us. Because of our addictions, we will always be storing up treasures somewhere other than heaven, and these treasures will kidnap our hearts, souls, and strength. (p. 16)

Grace is the invincible advocate of freedom and the absolute expression of perfect love.

Do you find the thought of a new relationship with your Higher Power scary or exhilarating?

_____
_____
_____
_____

Do you want your Higher Power as a friend? Why? When?

_____
_____
_____
_____

What is your relationship with your Higher Power? What are the characteristics of your Higher Power?

My Higher Power for me is:

_____
_____
_____
_____

My Higher Power for me is:

_____
_____
_____
_____

My Higher Power for me is:

_____
_____
_____
_____

Your Higher Power is sad when you fail but never ceases to love you. Do you agree with the above premise? If so, why or, if not, why?

_____
_____
_____
_____

Twelve-step programs teach addicts they are powerless over their addiction. Although your Higher Power will not do your recovery work, your Higher Power will provide aid sufficient for you to persevere. Do you agree with the above premise? If so, why or, if not, why?

_____
_____
_____
_____

**Therapist Introduction to Exercise 31:
Support Network**

An important part of the addict's journey to sexual sobriety includes a support network.

Clinical notes. Exercise 31 provides a list of the 12-steps as well as a list of major 12-step programs that support recovery. Twelve-step programs are strongly endorsed.

Attending 12-step programs and working the steps are an important part of recovery and relapse prevention. Ask the addict to research which of the 12-step programs will best serve him or her in recovery.

Ask the addict to write a support plan, which includes components of his support network and a description of how the addict's network will be used to support recovery.

During check-in at each sessions, ask the addict to share his or her attendance at 12-step meetings and other network support.

The objective is to support the addict's recovery journey through the 12-step program.

Exercise 31: Twelve-Step Programs

In part, the 12-step program helps you to recognize what caused your addiction, how it took over your life, and how living in emotional isolation adversely affects your recovery. Accept that recovery is not a solo journey. It requires the support of fellow travelers and your Higher Power. Twelve-step programs are proven interventions and they support the addict's recovery.

The 12-steps are the foundation of the program. They provide basic principles for living. With attendance at 12-step meetings, often weekly, the principles become part of the addict's thoughts, feelings, and behavior. The following are the sexual addiction version of the 12-steps adapted from the alcohol anonymous tradition.

The Twelve Steps

1. We admitted we were powerless over addictive sexual behavior - that our lives had become unmanageable.

2. Came to believe that a Power greater than ourselves could restore us to sanity.

3. Made a decision to turn our will and our lives over to the care of God as we understood God.

4. Made a searching and fearless moral inventory of ourselves.

5. Admitted to God, to ourselves, and to another human being the exact nature of our wrongs.

6. Were entirely ready to have God remove all these defects of character.

7. Humbly asked God to remove our shortcomings.

8. Made a list of all persons we had harmed and became willing to make amends to them all.

9. Made direct amends to such people wherever possible, except when to do so would injure them or others.

10. Continued to take personal inventory and when we were wrong promptly admitted it.

11. Sought through prayer and meditation to improve our conscious contact with God as we understood God, praying only for knowledge of God's will for us and the power to carry that out.

12. Having had a spiritual awakening as the result of these steps, we tried to carry this message to other sex addicts and to practice these principles in our lives. (Sex Addiction Anonymous, 2015, p. Our Program)

An Accountability Partner or Sponsor

Coming out of isolation includes being able to call a friend when you are experiencing temptation—a friend who neither judges nor condemns. You will want an accountability partner or a 12-step sponsor, if you do not already have one. The relationship between you and your accountability partner/sponsor is one of loving but firm support. Your accountability partner/ sponsor have your permission to question, challenge, admonish, and, in particular, encourage you in your recovery.

An accountability partner/sponsor is a friend who has chosen to love you even when you fail. Your accountability partner/sponsor is empowered to help you to think clearly about your choices. However, your accountability partner/sponsor is not your keeper; recovery work is your responsibility. When you select an accountability partner/sponsor, you need a person who is well into recovery, a person who has worked his or her 12-steps.

Form a Support Program

Twelve-step work and individual therapy go hand in glove. They reinforce each other. Twelve-step programs (as well as group therapy) provide a communal environment where each member supports the group.

In addition to attending 12-step meetings, the need for a support network is a given. Commit to writing a support plan and include components of your proposed network. Also, include how you will call upon your network to support your recovery. Below are some other support activities or programs.

- Family counseling
- Marriage counseling
- Targeted reading
- Bible study programs
- Celebrate Recovery
- One Man's Battle Program
- Serving others

The following is a list of the 12-step and related programs that are available to those who seek recovery from sexual addiction. The list contains the name, link to an Internet web page, and a brief description of the purpose of each organization. It is for you to decide which 12-step program best fits your needs. You may wish to try more than one program. The narrative descriptions originated with each entry's web page.

Twelve-Step Programs for the Sexual Addict

Christians in Recovery - The Web site is http://christians-in-recovery.org/wp/

Christians in Recovery (CIR) is dedicated to mutual sharing of faith, strength, and hope as we live each day in recovery. We work to regain and maintain balance and order in our lives through active discussion of the 12 Steps, the Bible, and experiences in our own recovery from abuse, family dysfunction, depression, anxiety, grief, relationships, and/or addictions of alcohol, drugs, food, pornography, sexual addiction, etc.

Sex Addicts Anonymous (SAA) - The Web site is http://www.sexaa.org/

Sex Addicts Anonymous is a fellowship of men and women who share their experience, strength and hope with each other so they may overcome their sexual addiction and help others recover from sexual addiction and dependency. Membership is open to all who share a desire to stop addictive sexual behavior. There is no other requirement. Our common goals are to become sexually healthy and to help other sex addicts achieve freedom from compulsive sexual behavior. Sex Addicts Anonymous is a spiritual program based on the principles and traditions of Alcoholics Anonymous. We are grateful to A.A. for this gift, which makes our recovery possible.

Sexaholics Anonymous (SA) - The Web site is http://www.sa.org/

Sexaholics Anonymous is a fellowship of men and women who share their experience, strength, and hope with each other that they may solve their common problem and help others to recover. The only requirement for membership is a desire to stop lusting and become sexually sober. Our primary purpose is to stay sexually sober and help others to achieve sexual sobriety. Sexaholics Anonymous is a recovery program based on the principles of Alcoholics Anonymous.

Sexual Compulsives Anonymous (SCA) - The Web site is http://www.sca-recovery.org/

Sexual Compulsives Anonymous is a fellowship of men and women who share their experience, strength and hope with each other, that they may solve their common problem and help others to recover from sexual compulsion. SCA is a 12-step fellowship, inclusive of all sexual orientations, open to anyone with a desire to recover from sexual compulsion. We are a spiritual program that provides a safe environment for working on problems of sexual addiction and sexual sobriety.

We believe we are not meant to repress our God-given sexuality. Members are encouraged to develop a sexual recovery plan, defining sexual sobriety for themselves. Our primary purpose is to stay sexually sober and to help others to achieve sexual sobriety. The only requirement for membership is a desire to stop having compulsive sex. We are self-supporting through our own contributions.

Sex and Love Addicts Anonymous (SLAA) - The Web site is http://www.slaafws.org/

Sex and Love Addicts Anonymous is a 12 step—12 tradition oriented fellowship based on the model pioneered by Alcoholics Anonymous. We draw on is our willingness to stop acting out in our own personal bottom line addictive behavior on a daily basis. In addition, members reach out to others in the fellowship, practice the 12- steps and 12 traditions of S.L.A.A. and seek a relationship with a higher power to counter the destructive consequences of one or more addictive behaviors related to sex addiction, love addiction, dependency on romantic attachments, emotional dependency, and sexual, social, and emotional anorexia. We find a common denominator in our obsessive, compulsive pattern, which renders any personal differences of sexual, or gender orientation irrelevant.

Sexual Recovery Anonymous (SRA) - The Web site is http://www.sexualrecovery.org/

Sexual Recovery Anonymous (SRA) is a fellowship of men and women who share their experience, strength and hope with each other that they may solve their common problem and help others to recover. The only requirement for membership is a desire to stop compulsive sexual behavior. There are no dues or fees.

Our primary purpose is to stay sexually sober and help others achieve sobriety. Sobriety is the release from all compulsive and destructive sexual behaviors. We have found through our experience, that sobriety includes freedom from masturbation and sex outside a mutually committed relationship. We believe that spirituality and self-love are antidotes to the addiction.

Survivors of Incest Anonymous (SIA) - The Web site is http://www.siawso.org/

Survivors of Incest Anonymous (SIA) is a self-help group of women and men who are guided by a set of 12 Steps and 12 Traditions. There are no dues or fees. Everything that is said in the program must be held in strict confidence. The only requirement for membership is that you are a victim of child sexual abuse, and you are not abusing any child. We believe we were affected by the abuse whether it occurred once or many times since the damage is incurred immediately.

Incest Survivors Anonymous (ISA) - The Web site is http://www.lafn.org

Incest Survivors Anonymous (ISA) is a 12-step and 12-tradition spiritual program for incest survivors and pro-survivors. It is an anonymous fellowship, which provides unconditional love and self and peer-help for men, women, teens.

Recovering Couples Anonymous (RCA) - The Web site is http://www.recovering-couples.org/

Recovering Couples Anonymous (RCA) is a 12-Step Fellowship. The primary purpose of RCA is to help couples find freedom from dysfunctional patterns in relationships. We are couples committed to restoring healthy communication, caring and greater intimacy to our relationships. We suffer from many addictions and co-addictions; some identified and some not, some treated and some not. We also come from different levels of brokenness. Many of us have been separated or near divorce. Some of us are new in our relationships and seek to build intimacy as we grow together as couples.

Twelve-Step Programs for the Partner or Significant Other

Codependents of Sexual Addiction (COSA) - The Web site is http://www.cosa-recovery.org

Codependents of Sexual Addiction (COSA) is a recovery program for men and women whose lives have been affected by compulsive sexual behavior. In COSA, we find hope whether or not there is a sexually addicted person currently in our lives. The COSA recovery program has been adapted from the 12 steps and 12 traditions of Alcoholics Anonymous and Al-Anon. COSA is open to anyone whose life has been affected by compulsive sexual behavior. There are no dues or fees for membership.

S-Anon Family Groups - The Web site is http://www.sanon.org/

The S-Anon Family Groups are a fellowship of the relatives and friends of sexually addicted people who share their experience, strength, and hope to solve their common problems. Our program of recovery is adapted from Alcoholics Anonymous and is based on the 12-steps and the 12 traditions of Alcoholics Anonymous. There are no dues. S-Anon's primary purpose is to recover from the effects upon us of another person's sexaholism and to help the families and friends of sexaholics.

CHAPTER TWELVE: STAGE V - RELAPSE PREVENTION

Therapist introduction. The focus of relapse prevention is long term sexual sobriety.

Clinical notes. A relapse plan is an essential part of sexual addiction recovery. The following five exercises outline possible material that may be part a relapse plan.

A fill in the blanks relapse plan is not provided. The material presented is intended to challenge the addict to think through what elements would effectively support his or her sexual sobriety. Relapse plans are intended to meet the needs of the individual addict.

An addict must resolve all forms of trauma experienced before preparing a relapse plan. Unresolved trauma directly relates to the potential for relapse.

The objective is to promote long-term sexual sobriety trough an effective relapse plan (Carnes 2001, pp. 154-190; Bissette, 2013, background).

Exercises 32 through 36: Relapse Prevention

Relapse Plan

A relapse prevention plan sharpens the addict's awareness of the pitfalls that inhibit the recovery journey. Formulating a relapse plan is usually undertaken after the addict achieves a period of sobriety. It provides the addict with reminders of his or her acting-out triggers and a multitude of strategies to help the addict reject an urge to act out.

A relapse plan includes a Relapse Contract that solidifies the recovery commitment made by the addict. It defines the addict's intentions and commitment to follow an agreed upon recovery script. The plan may be shared with one's sponsor and spouse.

Relapse happens. Likely, the addict will face unexpected cravings to repeat previous behavior. A well thought-out plan, written and discussed in advance with his or her therapist, or sponsor/accountability partner is intended to cause the addict to pause, consider options, and choose to refrain from acting out when faced with temptation.

Why prepare a relapse plan? Relapse is not certain. However, it is not unusual either. If a relapse prevention plan assists the addict to forgo temptation most of the time, it is valuable. One of the more important attributes of a relapse action plan is that it motivates the addict to reject temptation to binge after a slip.

Relapse or a Slip?

A slip is a onetime act; relapse is bingeing. A relapse plan encourages the addict to resume sobriety without bingeing.

The addict may not cross back over his or her recovery line and let one slip grant him or her permission to binge. If the addict acts out after a period of sobriety, s/he may be tempted to reason, "I slipped; I might as well act out again. I miss my old friend." Such reasoning ends the period of sobriety. Alternatively, the addict can reason, "I fell off my horse—I must get back-up and continue my journey." In a month or so the addict can say, "I have been sober for 'x' with a slip at week 'x.'" To reconcile the slip, the addict must share the slip with his or her sponsor/accountability partner and resume honesty with self and others (Carnes, 1994, pp. 259-265).

A slip has the following characteristics:

* Upon awaking in the morning, the addict did not plan to slip. It may have taken the addict by surprise—a build-up, a ritual, which resulted in a slip.

* A slip is a onetime act; relapse is bingeing. Talking to a fellow traveler will normalize the event.

- A victory occurs when the addict determines what caused the slip and has an interdiction ready for the next time s/he is tempted to engage in a similar sexual activity.

Albert's story. I have not acted out for three months. I have found my urge to act out is less over time, that is, until my friend who wanted me to go with the boys to a strip club called me. I told him no, but he insisted. It was too much stimulation for me and I masturbated that night. I am ashamed and feel bad. Even worse, I feel like I want to do it again. I no longer have my three months of sobriety; I might as well act-out again.

One of the action items in Albert's relapse plan is to talk to his sponsor daily. He had not called his sponsor. He was embarrassed to admit he had acted out. His sponsor recognized the signs of trouble and called Albert. They talked about Albert's trigger, his slippery slope, and what his relapse plan called for in this situation. Albert agreed to call his relapse a *slip*. The key for Albert was not to give up and fall back into his addictive behavior, but to recognize, while relapse happened, it was possible for him to continue his recovery journey. With his sponsor, his high-level commitment to sobriety, his 12-step meetings, and his relapse plan, he was in the position to resume his recovery journey.

A treatment plan is prepared by the therapist whereas the relapse plan is prepared by the addict and reviewed by the therapist. The content of the relapse plan will include many of the elements from a detailed treatment plan but in greater detail.

There is no hard and fast rule as to when a relapse prevention plan should be created. It is often a part of concluding therapy as a guide to maintain sobriety in the future. It also serves to raise the addict's awareness of the conditions that led him or her to act out in the past. However, the plan can be prepared earlier in therapy; in this case, it is used as a recovery tool.

Dean's story. I prepared my plan early in therapy. It included, among other steps, my approach to recovery, my commitment to awareness, and 10 changes in my life that I call behavioral objectives. The objectives, in my words, included:

- Active participation in 12-step programs.

- Find a sponsor.

- Continue individual therapy and work on it between sessions.

- Document acting-out rituals and write them down when they occur.

- Prepare strategies for triggers (persons, places, feelings, thinking, or things) that lead me to act out.

- Put a pornography filter on my computer.

- Reduce time spent alone, especially when doing mental or computer work. Engage in more non-sexual intimacy with my partner.

- Get out sexual tension with partner.

- Exercise regularly.

Dean formulated an action statement to accompany each of the above objectives. Each action includes how it will be accomplished and a time frame for the action. He also analyzed the risks that posed a threat to the completion of the goals in his plan. Two of his risks were *procrastination* and *difficulty being truthful*.

During succeeding sessions, Dean used his plan to review his progress. It was his therapy map.

Exercise 32: Emotional States

Be aware in the present moment of emotional states that lead you to act out.

When you are in a negative place emotionally, you are at risk of going down your slippery slope. The longer you are emotionally hampered, the greater is the possibility you will act out. Like an airplane that reaches a point of no return in its take off; you can reach a place where you cannot stop yourself. This is called your acting-out ritual, *slippery slope*, or *trance state*. Understanding your toxic emotional states can help you avoid passing through a point of no return.

For example, emotional states for which you need a relapse plan include:

- Depressed mood

- Anxiety

- Anger

- Procrastination

- Self-pity

- Loneliness

- Codependency

- Isolation

When you are aware of your behavior in the present moment, you are progressing in your recovery. Your *awareness* of emotional states allows you to evaluate the health of your sobriety status. It enables the addict to follow a relapse plan where awareness trumps temptation

Select five emotional toxic states that apply to your life and explain how you will minimize their effect on your recovery.

An emotional toxic state for me is:

_____
_____
_____
_____

An emotional toxic state for me is:

_____
_____
_____
_____

An emotional toxic state for me is:

_____
_____
_____
_____

An emotional toxic state for me is:

_____
_____
_____
_____

An emotional toxic state for me is:

_____
_____
_____
_____

How will your relapse plan portray your emotional toxic states? For example, list and describe your emotional toxic states along with corresponding strategies to diffuse them?

_____
_____
_____
_____
_____
_____
_____
_____
_____
_____
_____
_____

Exercise 33: Nurturing Activities, Toxic States, and Triggers

Sexual addiction is an intimacy disorder; the frequent inclusions of nurturing activities in your life enhance the outlook for long-term recovery. For example, engaging in 40 activities on a consistent basis is a proven nurturing activity.

Activities That Nurture You

Maltz (2001) believes that communication is the key to healing. Many of the problems and difficulties that couples encounter can be remedied by honestly talking out feelings and brainstorming ideas for change together. Nonsexual activities with a partner foster healthy communications (p. 228).

Long-term sexual sobriety depends on living a healthy life style. Nurture creates positive self-esteem and replaces past deficits. In the parlance of the 12-step program, they are called outer circle activities. On the other hand, sobriety is threatened in the face of deprivation. Negativity, anxiety, boredom, and procrastination often contradict sobriety.

Choosing and committing yourself to engage in *nurturing activities* is part of your relapse plan. Examples of nurturing activities are:

- Exercise.
- Spiritual activities.
- Meditation.
- Eating healthy.
- Reading uplifting literature.
- Engaging in hobbies/recreation.
- Talking daily to your spouse.
- Taking a weekend trip with your spouse.
- Attending your child's sports activities.
- Engage in weekly planning and in 40 activities.
- Going out to dinner with one's spouse.
- Follow your abstinence plan.

- Improving your spirituality.

- Sharing feelings and experiences of the day with your spouse.

- Playing tennis, golf, racket ball or another healthy sports activity.

- Attending 12-step programs and working the steps.

- Talking daily to your 12 step sponsor or accountability Partner.

- Engaging in healthy activities with one's family (spouse and children).

- Coming out of isolation by establishing healthy relationships with a same-sex friend, with family of origin, spouse and children, and extended family.

- Program time to communicate with your partner.

Select five to ten *nurturing activities* that apply to your life and explain how you will maximize their contribution to your recovery.

A nurturing activity for me is:

_____
_____
_____
_____

A nurturing activity for me is:

_____
_____
_____
_____

A nurturing activity for me is:

_____
_____
_____
_____

A nurturing activity for me is:

_____
_____

A nurturing activity for me is:

_____
_____
_____
_____

How will your relapse plan include nurturing factors? For example, list and describe your nurturing factors along with strategies to employ them in your life. How will you use them to counteract toxic states and acting-out triggers?

_____
_____
_____
_____
_____
_____
_____
_____
_____

Risky State Activities

Risky states are activities you consider questionable or signal that you are on dangerous ground. They are behaviors in which you intend not to engage, but are very tempting. You must carefully monitor your indulgence in these in these activities to make sure they do not get out of hand. They also include behaviors that make you wonder or question whether you need to stop. . Risky states ought to be addressed in your relapse plan. In the parlance of the 12-step program, they are called middle circle activities.

Boundary activities cause you to live on the edge between sexual sobriety and acting out. When you engage in risky activities, you are taking more than a normal risk that temptation will cause you to act out. For example, a risky activity may be going to the beach where scantily clad bodies abound. Visual stimulation is almost certain and thus you have a greater than normal chance of engaging in sexual fantasy and acting out.

For example, risky activities include:

- Engaging in sexual thinking and fantasy.

- Going to the beach or pool to ogle bodies.

- Procrastinating and avoiding day-to-day responsibilities.

- Engaging in obsessive negative thinking.

- Engaging in excessive self-pity.

- Engaging in all or nothing thinking.

- Going to an 'x' rated movie.

- Watching provocative TV programs.

- Going to a bar with a tempting patron.

- Failing to nurture self (vacations, exercise, not living at 40, etc.)

Select five *risky activities* that apply to your life and explain how you will minimize their effect on your recovery.

A negative risky state for me is:

_____
_____
_____
_____

A negative risky state for me is:

_____
_____
_____
_____

A negative risky state for me is:

_____
_____
_____
_____

A negative risky state for me is:

_____
_____
_____
_____

A negative risky state for me is:

_____

_____

_____

_____

How will your relapse plan treat possible risky states, for example, list, and describe your risky states along with corresponding strategies to diffuse them?

_____

_____

_____

_____

Acting-out Triggers

Triggers are catalysts that lead you to act out. For example, if reading a porn magazine is a trigger for you, in the parlance of the 12-step program, it is on your inner circle.

For example, acting-out triggers for which you need a relapse plan include:

- Watching pornography.

- Going to a strip club.

- Going to a massage parlor.

- Excessive use of alcohol or drugs.

- Flirting with a vulnerable person.

- Attending a sex party.

- Going to an 'xxx' rated movie.

- Going to a bar in search of a tempting patron.

- Engaging in cybersex (chat rooms, phone sex, web cam, etc.)

Select five *trigger activities* you know will cause you to act out. Explain what strategies you will use to exclude them from your recovery journey.

A trigger to act out for me is:

_____
_____
_____
_____

A trigger to act out for me is:

_____
_____
_____
_____

A trigger to act out for me is:

_____
_____
_____
_____

A trigger to act out for me is:

_____
_____
_____
_____

A trigger to act out for me is:

_____
_____
_____
_____

How will your relapse plan address your acting out triggers? For example, list and describe your triggers along with corresponding strategies to diffuse them?

_____
_____
_____
_____
_____
_____

Exercise 34: Twelve-step Program Attendance

Consistently attending one or more 12-step programs is a proven recovery task. When you hear another person's story, particularly in a group setting, you know you are not alone. Realizing you are not alone reduces shame. (Shame promotes denial, isolation, and acting-out behaviors.) On the other hand, disclosure and working the 12-steps repudiates denial, isolation, and acting-out behaviors.

Since most women are relational, 12-step *fellowship* along with working the steps supports recovery and is the treatment of choice. Some 12-step programs are co-ed. However, most men and women feel same-sex meetings work better for them.

What is your commitment to attend 12-step programs(s)?

_____

_____

_____

_____

_____

_____

_____

Which 12-step programs have you tried? Which one(s) work for you? Why?

_____

_____

_____

_____

Do you have an accountability partner/sponsor? How frequently do you talk/meet?

_____

_____

_____

_____

_____

What are your goals for working the 12-steps?

_____

_____

_____

_____

_____

Do you want to attend other programs? (Marriage counseling, financial planning, social adjustment, or occupational training.)

_____

_____

_____

_____

How will your relapse plan reflect your commitment to continue attending a 12-step program? For example, how long will you attend a 12-step program and at what frequency? What is your timetable for working the 12-steps?

_____

_____

_____

_____

_____

_____

_____

_____

_____

_____

Exercise 35: Professional Help

Your relapse plan needs to address supplemental therapy. You may seek individual, group, educational classes, or martial therapy, etc.

How toxic are your wounds from childhood exposure to sexual material or abuse? Do you want to address these wounds? Explain your need. (See Exercise One - Roots of Sexual Addiction)

_____
_____
_____

How did your dysfunctional family contribute to your addiction? Do you want to address the dynamics and consequences of living in a dysfunctional family? Explain your need. (See Exercise Two - Dysfunctional Family)

_____
_____
_____

How well do you manage family of origin relationships and other important contemporary relationships? Do you want to improve these relationships? Explain your need. (See Exercise 12 - Coming out of Isolation)

_____
_____
_____
_____

Do you lack social and intimacy skills? Do you want to improve your skills? Explain your need. (See Living at 40, Exercise 23)

_____
_____
_____
_____

How effective are your emotion-management skills? Do you want to improve your skills? Explain your need. (See Exercise Nine - Anxiety and Exercise 10 - Anger).

_____
_____
_____

How will your relapse plan address additional help to continue your recovery?

_____

_____

_____

_____

Exercise 36: Ongoing Self-Care

Long-term self-care is an element of all recovery programs. The following questions are intended to clarify your thinking or highlight a condition, which needs to be addressed in your relapse plan or in therapy.

What is your vision for your life? (Include your five-year goals).

_____
_____
_____
_____
_____
_____
_____
_____
_____
_____
_____

What living conditions (home, location, and relationships) promote sexual sobriety? Do you want to make a change? Explain your need.

_____
_____
_____
_____

What are your needs/goals for social activities/friends? Do you want to make a change? Explain your need.

_____
_____
_____
_____

What career and work conditions do you want to make to promote sexual sobriety? Do you want to make a change? Explain your need.

_____
_____
_____
_____

What are spirituality goals? Do you want to make a change? Explain your need.

_____
_____
_____
_____

What are your nutrition, exercise, sleep goals? Do you want to make a change? Explain your need.

_____
_____
_____
_____

What are your recreation, hobbies, and vacation goals? Do you want to make a change? Explain your need.

_____
_____
_____
_____

What are your holiday, vacations, and family time practices? Do you want to make a change? Explain your need.

_____
_____
_____
_____

What is your accountability partner or sponsor arrangement? Do you want to make a change? Explain your need.

_____
_____
_____
_____

In addition to support groups, what learning opportunities will you seek to better face obstacles and solve problems?

_____
_____
_____
_____

What are you romance/marital relations expectations?

_____

_____

_____

_____

What challenges do you face in opposite sex relationships? (See Chapter Six - Marriage and Addiction).

_____

_____

_____

_____

_____

_____

_____

_____

_____

What will trigger your need to attend more meetings or re-enter therapy?

_____

_____

_____

_____

_____

How often will you review this plan to keep it current?

_____

_____

_____

_____

Include in your plan of on-going self-care efforts how you will program physical exercise, healthy diet, planned recreation, etc. Include a description of your on-going, self-care activities and how they will affect your recovery program.

_____

_____

_____

_____

_____

_____

_____

_____

_____

_____

_____

_____

_____

_____

_____

_____

_____

PART V: RESOURCES

APPENDIX A: THE SEXUAL ADDICTION SCREENING TEST (SAST)

The Sexual Addiction Screening Test (SAST), designed by Carnes to assist in the assessment of sexually compulsive behavior, may indicate the presence of sex addiction. The SAST provides a list of questions, which help to discriminate between addictive and non-addictive behavior.

Please indicate gender: Male Female

Indicate Orientation: Heterosexual Bi-sexual Homosexual

Please check any of the following, which apply:

I have no concerns about my sexual behavior but am curious how I would score.

I have no concerns about my sexual behavior but others are concerned.

I am having problems with my sexual behavior but do not consider myself a sex addict.

I know I am a sex addict.

I have sought therapy because of my sexual problems.

To complete the test, answer each question by placing a check in the appropriate yes/no column.

1. Were you sexually abused as a child or adolescent?
   Yes   No

2. Did your parents have trouble with sexual behavior?
   Yes   No

3. Do you often find yourself preoccupied with sexual thoughts?
   Yes   No

4. Do you feel that your sexual behavior is not normal?
   Yes   No

5. Do you ever feel bad about your sexual behavior?
   Yes   No

6. Has your sexual behavior ever created problems for you and your family?
   Yes   No

7. Have you ever sought help for sexual behavior you did not like?
   Yes   No

8. Has anyone been hurt emotionally because of your sexual behavior?
   Yes   No

9. Are any of your sexual activities against the law?
   Yes   No

10. Have you made efforts to quit a type of sexual activity and failed?
    Yes   No

11. Do you hide some of your sexual behaviors from others?
    Yes   No

12. Have you attempted to stop some parts of your sexual activity?
    Yes   No

13. Have you felt degraded by your sexual behaviors?
    Yes   No

14. When you have sex, do you feel depressed afterward?
    Yes   No

15. Do you feel controlled by your sexual desire?
    Yes   No

16. Have important parts of your life (such as job, family, friends, leisure activities) been neglected because you were spending too much time on sex?
    Yes   No

17. Do you ever think your sexual desire is stronger than you are?
    Yes   No

18. Is sex almost all you think about?
    Yes   No

19. Has sex (or romantic fantasies) been a way for you to escape your problems?
    Yes   No

20. Has sex become the most important thing in your life?
    Yes   No

21. Are you in crisis over sexual matters?
    Yes   No

22. Has the Internet created sexual problems for you?
    Yes   No

23. Do you spend too much time online for sexual purposes?
    Yes   No

24. Have you purchased services online for erotic purposes (sites for dating, pornography, and fantasy and friend finder)?
    Yes   No

25. Have you used the Internet to make romantic or erotic connections with people online?
    Yes   No

26. Have people in your life been upset about your sexual activities online?
    Yes   No

27. Have you attempted to stop your online sexual behaviors?
    Yes   No

28. Have you subscribed to or regularly purchased or rented sexually explicit materials (magazines, videos, books or online pornography)?
    Yes   No

29. Have you been sexual with minors?
    Yes   No

30. Have you spent considerable time and money on strip clubs, adult bookstores and movie houses?
    Yes   No

31. Have you engaged prostitutes and escorts to satisfy your sexual needs?
    Yes   No

32. Have you spent considerable time surfing pornography online?
    Yes   No

33. Have you used magazines, videos or online pornography even when there was considerable risk of being caught by family members who would be upset by your behavior?
    Yes   No

34. Have you regularly purchased romantic novels or sexually explicit magazines?
    Yes   No

35. Have stayed in romantic relationships after they became emotionally or physically abusive?

Yes   No

36. Have you traded sex for money or gifts?

Yes   No

37. Have you maintained multiple romantic or sexual relationships at the same time?

Yes   No

38. After sexually acting out, do you sometimes refrain from all sex for a significant period?

Yes   No

39. Have you regularly engaged in sadomasochistic behavior?

Yes   No

40. Do you visit sexual bath-houses, sex clubs or adult video/bookstores as part of your regular sexual activity?

Yes   No

41. Have you engaged in unsafe or risky sex even though you knew it could cause you harm?

Yes   No

42. Have you cruised public restrooms, rest areas or parks looking for sex with strangers?

Yes   No

43. Do you believe casual or anonymous sex has kept you from having more long-term intimate relationships?

Yes   No

44. Has your sexual behavior put you at risk for arrest for lewd conduct or public indecency?

Yes   No

45. Have you been paid for sex?

Yes   No

Scoring the Test and Assessment of the Results

After you've answered all the SAST questions, add the numbers you selected for each response to obtain a final score.

Here's a general scale to help interpret your score:

Remember that no self-test can absolutely and accurately determine the nature of your problem, or the solution. Please use it as a marker to help guide you along your own path. This is a screening device that can be helpful in deciding whether you need help or not. Feelings of concern, shame or fear created by answering these questions may indicate the need to contact a professional for guidance. Checking several, yes, items usually indicates a need to address these issues.

1-3 these symptoms may be an area of concern. You may want to consider openly discussing this with a friend or family member.

3-10 consultation with a professional can be helpful in deciding if you have a sexual addiction problem. Based on your responses, you may benefit by seeking help from appropriate professional who is knowledgeable about addiction.

10-13 scoring within this range may mean that you have done some things you regret or it may mean that you are in early stage of addiction. Based on your responses, you would benefit by seeking help from a professional knowledgeable about addiction and addiction-related issues and/or join a support group.

>13 if you scored over 13 points your answers parallel other sex addicts. A high score indicates issues of sexual addiction and a need to further explore this area with a professional clinician and/or join a support group.

Developed by: Patrick Carnes, PhD & Robert Weiss, LCSW, CAS

Carnes, P. (2012). SAST: Sex addiction screening test. (ITAP). Retrieved June 19, 2014 from
http://www.sexhelp.com/addiction_tests.cfm

APPENDIX B: WOMEN SELF-TEST FOR SEXUAL/RELATIONSHIP ADDICTION

1. Have you ever thought you needed help for your sexual behavior or thinking?

2. Have you tried to stop or limit what you felt was wrong in your sexual or relationship behavior?

3. Do you use sex to escape, relieve anxiety or as a coping mechanism?

4. Do you feel guilt, remorse, or depression afterward?

5. Has your pursuit of sex or a particular relationship become more compulsive?

6. Does it interfere with relations with your spouse?

7. Do you have to resort to fantasies or memories during sex to be aroused or satisfied?

8. Do you keep going from one relationship or lover to another?

9. Do you feel the right person would help you stop lusting, masturbating, or being promiscuous?

10. Do you have a destructive need—a desperate sexual or emotional need for someone?

11. Does the pursuit of sex or a relationship make you careless for yourself or the welfare of your family or others?

12. Has your effectiveness or concentration decreased as sex or a relationship has become more compulsive?

13. Have you experienced negative consequences as a result of your sexual or relational behavior?

14. Are you depressed?

15. Were you sexually abused as a child or adolescent?

These questions are adapted from the Women's Sexual Addiction Screen Test (W-SAST) developed by Sharon O'Hara and Patrick Carnes and the self-test is used by Sexaholics Anonymous.

Carnes, P. & O'Hara, S. (n.d.). Women's self-test for sexual/relationship addiction, Bethesda Workshops and ITAP. Retrieved from

http://www.bethesdayworkshops.org/sex-addiction/self-test/ or from http://www.sexhelp.com/addiction_tests.cfm

Scoring the Test and Assessment of the Results

If the client answered yes to even a few of the questions, it is likely she is sexually addicted.

APPENDIX C: WHAT IS PERSISTENT DEPRESSIVE DISORDER, DYSTHYMIA?

A. Depressed mood for most of the day, for more days than not, as indicated either by subjective account or observation by others, for at least two years. Note: In children and adolescents, mood can be irritable and duration must be at least one year.

B. Presence, while depressed, of two (or more) of the following:

   (1) Poor appetite or overeating

   (2) Insomnia or hypersomnia

   (3) Low energy or fatigue

   (4) Low self-esteem

   (5) Poor concentration or difficulty making decisions

   (6) Feelings of hopelessness

C. During the two-year period (one year for children or adolescents) of the disturbance, the individual has never been without the symptoms in Criteria A and B for more than two months at a time.

D. Criteria for major depressive disorder may be continuously present during for two years.

E. There never has been a manic episode or a hypomanic episode, and criteria have never been met for a cyclothymic disorder.

F. The disturbance is not better explained by a persistent schizoaffective disorder, schizophrenia, delusional disorder, or other specified or unspecified schizophrenia spectrum and other psychotic disorder.

G. The symptoms are not attributable to the psychological effects of a substance (e.g., a drug of abuse, a medication) or other medical condition (e.g., hypothyroidism).

H. The symptoms cause clinically significant distress or impairment in social, occupational, or other important areas of functioning.

Note: Because the criteria for a major depressive episode include four symptoms that are absent from the symptom list for persistent depressive disorder (dysthymia), a very limited number of individuals will have depressive symptoms that have persisted longer than two years but will not meet criteria for persistent depressive disorder. If full criteria for a major depressive episode have been met at some point during the current episode of illness, they may be given a diagnosis of major depressive disorder. Otherwise, a diagnosis of other specified depressive disorder or unspecified disorder is warranted (APA, 2013, pp. 168-169).

American Psychiatric Association. (2013). Diagnostic and statistical manual of mental disorders (5th ed). Arlington VA: American Psychiatric Publishing.

APPENDIX D: THIRTY TASKS OF SEXUAL ADDICTION RECOVERY

Developed by Patrick Carnes, Ph.D.

Task/Goal	Performables	Life Competency
1. Break through denial.	Make a full disclosure to therapist all forms of sexual acting out. Complete a list of examples of powerlessness and unmanageability. Address thinking errors.	Recognize self-delusion.
2. Understand the nature of the illness.	Read at least one book on sexual illness addiction/ anorexia. Complete the First Step. Complete a Sexual History. Complete a consequences Inventory.	Have knowledge of Addiction and Recovery.
3. Surrender to the process.	Complete a Second Step and Third Step.	Know personal limits.
4. Admit damage from behavior.	Write a Damage Control Plan and implement it.	Be an expert in self-care, crisis avoidance and crisis.
5. Establish sobriety.	Write a Sobriety Statement. Complete a Celibacy Contract of eight weeks or more. Write a Relapse Prevention Plan. Complete Fantasy Contamination Exercise.	Manage life without dysfunctional sexual behavior.
6. Ensure Physical Health/Integrity.	Complete a physical exam.	Be an expert in physical self-care.
7. Participate in a culture of support.	Attend Twelve Step sex addiction meetings regularly. Attend other Twelve Step meetings as appropriate.	Build a functional health support system.
8. Reduce Shame	Complete Step 4 and Step 5.	Recognize and manage shame.
9. Grief Losses.	Define clear grieving strategies and use them.	Recognize grief and have skills for grieving.

10. Understand multiple addictions and sobriety.	Complete an Addiction Interaction Disorder screen. Complete a Multiple Addiction Relapse Prevention Plan.	Remain relapse free from all concurrent addictions.
11. Acknowledge cycles of abuse.	Complete Survivors weeks. Complete Abuse Inventory.	Identify abuse and exploitation.
12. Bring closure and resolution to addiction shame.	Complete Step Eight and Step Nine.	Keep current on shame, resentment and relationship issues.
13. Restore financial viability.	Save within financial means (spend less than earned). Work recovery financial plan.	Maintain financial viability.
14. Restore meaningful work.	Establish a meaningful career path.	Have meaningful works.
15. Create lifestyle balance	Use a Personal Craziness Index for 8 weeks.	Live in balance and harmony.
16. Build supportive personal relationships.	Find and use a sponsor. Attend therapy group for 175 hours. Be a sponsor to others.	Initiate and sustain enduring life relationships.
17. Establish healthy exercise and nutrition patterns	Have a weekly aerobic exercise pattern. Remain in appropriate weight range for age and height.	Stay physically fit
18. Restructure relationship with self	Complete eighteen months of individual therapy. Clarify boundaries, goals and needs.	Have a workable, compassionate relationship with self to be self-determining and autonomous
19. Resolve original conflict wounds.	Do therapy specific to family of origin or trauma issues.	Identify and manage recurring dysfunctional patterns
20. Restore healthy sexuality.	Write a sex plan and keep it updated.	Have sexual health.
21. Involve family members in therapy.	Family members attend Family Week. Family members attend therapy sessions.	Capacity to ask help from immediate family.
22. Alter dysfunctional family relationships.	Full disclosure to primary partner and immediate family as appropriate.	Remain true to self in the presence of dysfunction.
23. Commit to recovery for each family member.	Family members/spouses enter a recovery program for themselves.	Take responsibility for self.

24. Resolve issues with children.	Share secrets and make amends to children when appropriate.	Resolve conflict in dependent relationships.
25. Resolve issues with extended family.	Share secrets and make amends to extended family when appropriate.	Resolve conflict in interdependent relationships
26. Work through differentiation/healthy boundaries.	Write a "Fair Fight" contract.	Sustain intimacy without loss of self.
27. Recommit/commit to primary relationship.	Commit to a primary relationship, or recommit to primary relationship.	Capacity to maintain a committed relationship.
28. Commit to couple-ship.	Attend Twelve Step meeting for couples regularly.	Participate in a community of couples.
29. Succeed in primary intimacy	Have a primary relationship which is satisfying.	Be vulnerable and intimate.
30. Develop a spiritual life.	Find and use a spiritual director or mentor. Join a spiritual community.	Be spiritual conscious.

See Also:

Facing the Shadow: Starting Sexual and Relationship Recovery (Carnes, 2001b, pp. 270-273)

Carnes, P. (1998). 30 tasks for addiction recovery. 1-19. Retrieved June 19, 2014 from http://www.iitap.com/documents/Tasksl-30-Detailed.pdf)

Sexual Addiction Recovery Generally Requires:

1. Individual therapy.

2. Couple/Family therapy.

3. 12 Step support group work

4. Group therapy

APPENDIX E: ASSESSMENT INSTRUMENTS

Attachment Style Assessment

Adapted by M. Deborah Corley from Bartholomew, K. & Horowitz, L M. (1991). Attachment styles among young adults: A test of a four-category model. *Journal of Personality and Social Psychology*, 61, 226-244.

Compulsive Sexual Behavior Inventory (CSBI)

Available through Dr. Eli Coleman, *Center for Sexual Health*. 1300 2nd Street S., Suite 180, Minneapolis, MN 55454. Phone 612-625-1500. Available at http://www.uofmmedicalcenter.org

Hypersexual Behavior Inventory (HBI)

Reid, R., Garos, S., Carpenter, B. (2011). Reliability, validity, and psychometric development of the hypersexual behavior inventory in an outpatient sample of men. *Addiction & Compulsivity*, 18, 30-5 1. Available at http://wsvw.rory.net/Pubs/HBI.pdf

Internet Sexual Screening Tool Revised (ISST-R)

Delmonico, D. L., & Miller, J. (2003). The Internet Sex Screening Test: A comparison of sexual compulsives versus non-sexual compulsives. *Sexual and Relationship Therapy*, 18(3), 261-276. Available at http://www.internetbehavior.com/isst

Love and Relationship Addiction Questions

Available through Brenda Schaffer's website http://www.loveaddiction.com

Sexual Addiction Screening Test Revised (SAST-R) (Carnes, 2012, ITAP).

Women's Sexual Addiction Screening Test (W-SAST)

Psychometrics of both are reviewed in: Carnes, P., Green, B., and Carnes, S. (2010). The same yet different: Refocusing the sexual addiction screening test (SAST) to reflect orientation and gender. *Sexual Addiction & Compulsivity*, 17(1), 7-30. Both instruments and the article are available on the IITAP website: http://www.iitap.com/documents/SDI-R%20 The%2OSame%2OYet%2ODifferent.pdf

Sexual Compulsivity Scale (SCS)

A copy and psychometric information is located in: Kalichman, S. C., Rompa, D. (1995). Sexual sensation seeking and sexual compulsivity scales: Reliability, validity and HIV risk behavior. *Journal of Personality Assessment*, 65, 586-60 1.

Sexual Dependency Inventory (SDI-R)

Delmonico, D., Bubenzer, D. & West, J. (1998). Assessing sexual addiction with the sexual dependency inventory-revised. *Sexual Addiction & Compulsivity*, 5(3), 179. Restricted in use. Contact the International Institute for Trauma and Addiction Professionals at http://www.iitap.com

Ferree, M. (Ed.). (2012). Making Advances: A Comprehensive Guide for Treating Female Sex and Love Addicts. Royston, GA: Society for the Advancement of Sexual Health. (pp. 72-74)

Diagnostic Considerations

In addition to a diagnosis related to sexual behavior there are a host of medical, substance, and mental disorders to consider. Co-addiction is common among sexually addicted clients. These conditions need to be ruled-out for each client. Some of the conditions to consider are:

- Delusional disorders, NOS – Erotomania can exhibit as a sexual fixation on a public figure or an inappropriate age differential sexual relationship–between a teacher and student or the jealous type where the client maintains a fixed belief that a partner is engaged in an affair.

- Sexual disorders - Concern about sexual orientation or the ability to perform sexually.

- Neuropsychological issues–for example, learning disabilities that mask the client's ability to focus on recovery tasks.

- Drugs and Medical Conditions Related to Acting out. Some prescriptions medications foster sexual thinking or behavior.

- Medical Conditions – Examples include Syphilis and traumatic brain injury or tumor.

Co-occurring Disorders – Psychiatric disorders including:

- Depressive Disorders – Dysthymia Disorder or low grade depression lasting at least two years.

- Dissociative Disorders - Dissociative fugue, depersonalization, dissociative identity disorder, and dissociative disorder NOS. (Disconnects with reality).

- PTSD – Trauma induced abnormal behavior.

- Substance abuse - abuse of alcohol, addictive recreational drugs, and medical prescriptions such as tranquilizers (Xanax), crack cocaine, marijuana, opioids, coffee, and nicotine.

- Disorders of Extreme Stress – Examples include prolong sexual abuse, chronic illness, or extreme physical or emotional abuse.

- Eating Disorders – Anorexia or bulimia.

- Somatic Disorders – Chronic constipation, ulcers, and other stress related somatic symptoms.

- Personality Disorders – Rule out multiple behavioral personality disorders.

- Impulse Control Disorder – Gambling.

- Obsessive Compulsive Disorder – Anxiety driven behavior.

- Bipolar Disorder- Irresponsible sexual behavior during the manic phase.

Note: APPENDIX E was adapted from *Making advances: A Comprehensive Guide for Treatment Female Sex and Love Addicts*, Chapter three, Diagnosing Sex and Love Addiction in Women, provides an instructive chapter for assessing and diagnosing sexual addiction and co-existing disorders.

Ferree, M. (Ed.). (2012). Making Advances: A Comprehensive Guide for Treating Female Sex and Love Addicts. Royston, GA: Society for the Advancement of Sexual Health.

APPENDIX F: SUGGEST READINGS

Note: Book descriptions originated from book-seller Web sites and were edited for this APPENDIX.

Books by Dr. Patrick Carnes

Carnes, P. (1992). *Don't Call It Love: Recovering From Sexual Addiction*. New York: Bantam.

This book describes sexual addiction and its characteristics based on the testimony of more than one thousand recovering sexual addicts. It is the first major scientific study of the disorder. It includes the findings of Dr. Carnes' research with recovering addicts as well as advice from the addicts and co addicts themselves as they work to overcome their compulsive

Carnes, P. (1994). *A Gentle Path Through the Twelve Steps: A Guidebook for all People in the Process of Recovery.* (rev. ed.). Center City, MN: Hazelden.

This workbook provides a unique set of structured forms and practical exercises to help recovering people integrate the 12- steps into all aspects of their lives. It is the first workbook on the 12- steps specifically designed with sex addicts and co addicts in mind.

Carnes, P. (1994). *Contrary to Love: Helping the Sexual Addict.* (rev. ed.). Center City, MN: Hazelden.

This book provides counseling professionals with a resource for understanding and helping sexual addicts. Subjects include stages and progression of the illness, family structures, boundaries, assessment, and strategies. The book presents a Sexual Addiction Screening test, useful to therapists and addicts alike. The book is a sequel to Out of the Shadows.

Carnes, P. (1997). *Sexual Anorexia: Overcoming Sexual Self-Hatred*. Center City, MN: Hazelden.

This book is a first-time examination of sexual anorexia: the extreme fear of sexual intimacy and obsessive avoidance of sex. It examines its causes, and then describes concrete tasks and plans for exploring intimacy and restoring healthy sexuality.

Carnes, P. (1997). *The Betrayal Bond: Breaking Free of Exploitive Relationships*. Deerfield Beach, FL: Health Communications Inc.

This book presents an in-depth study of exploitive relationships: why they form, who is most susceptible, and how they become so powerful. It explains to readers how to recognize when traumatic bonding has occurred and provides a checklist so they can examine their own relationships. Included are steps readers can take to safely extricate themselves or their loved ones from these situations.

Carnes, P., Laaser, D., & Laaser, M. (1999). *Open Hearts: Renewing Relationships with Recovery, Romance and Reality.* Carefree, AZ: Gentle Path Press.

This book will guide the reader along a pathway of self-assessment, discovery, and fulfillment. Proven techniques from Recovering Couples Anonymous help couples overcome anger, resentment, and dysfunctional patterns, thus allowing them to enjoy the intimate, fulfilling relationship for which they long. It is a book a couple does together. It takes techniques Carnes and Laaser developed in their psychotherapy practices and weaves them into a series of individual and joint exercises. It looks at tough issues: shame, anger, money, betrayal, sex, and parenting. It encourages fun like drawing up a family motto, expressing spirituality together, and taking gentleness breaks.

Carnes, P., Delmonico, D. & Griffin, E. (2001). *In the Shadows of the Net: Breaking Free of Compulsive Online Sexual Behavior.* (2nd ed.). Center City, MN: Hazelden.

This book explains how the anonymity of online access, the ability of people to use their computers in private, and the powerful rationalization that virtual interactions are not "real." It can combine to entice people to spend hours online, sacrificing real relationships and increasing their sense of loneliness. The book provides an Internet Screening Test to help people decide if they have a problem with their use of sexual material on the Internet.

Carnes, P. (2001). *Out of the Shadows: Understanding Sexual Addiction.* (Rev. 3rd ed.). Center City, MN: Hazelden.

This book, the first to describe sexual addiction, is the standard for recognizing and overcoming this destructive behavior. It outlines how to identify a sexual addict, recognize the way others may unwittingly become complicit or codependent, and change the patterns that support the addiction.

Carnes, P., & Adams, K. (2002). *The Clinical Management of Sex Addiction.* New York, NY: Brunner-Routledge.

This is the first comprehensive volume of the clinical management of sex addiction. Collecting the work of 28 leaders in this emerging field, the editors provide a long-needed primary text about how to approach treatment with these challenging patients. The book serves as an introduction for professionals new to the field as well as serving as a useful reference tool. The contributors are pioneers of addiction medicine and sex therapy.

Carnes, P. (2009). *Recovery Zone, Volume 1: Making Changes that Last, The Internal Tasks.* Carefree, AZ: Gentle Path Press.

This workbook notes that recovery from addiction is a work in progress and that many things must change simultaneously for recovery to work. The book shares strategies for maintaining and nurturing recovery, in the early days and beyond.

Carnes, P. & Harkin, M. (2005). *Facing the Shadow: Starting Sexual and Relationship. Recovery.* (2ⁿᵈ ed.). Carefree, AZ: Gentle Path Press.

This workbook is designed as a companion to *Out of the Shadows, Don't Call It Love,* and *Sexual Anorexia.* It includes exercises to help work through such subjects as denial, understanding the addictive cycle, and identifying compulsive behaviors.

Other Readings

Arterburn, S., Stoeker, F., & Yorkey, M. (2000). *Every Man's Battle: Winning the War on Sexual Temptation One Victory at a Time.* Colorado Springs, CO: WaterBrook Press.

This book describes the challenge every man faces—the fight every man can win… sexual temptation. From the television to the Internet, print media to videos, men are constantly faced with the assault of sensual images. The book denies the perception men are unable to control their thought lives and roving eyes. The book shares the stories of men who have escaped the trap of sexual immorality and presents a practical, detailed plan for any man who desires sexual purity-perfect for men who have fallen in the past, those who want to remain strong today, and all who want to overcome temptation in the future. It includes a section for women, designed to help them understand and support the men they love.

Arterburn, S., Stoeker, F., &Yorkey, M. (2002). *Every Man's Battle Workbook: The Path to Sexual Integrity Starts Here.* Colorado Springs, CO: WaterBrook Press.

This book is a practical guide for individuals and men's groups designed to help men win the war on sexual temptation. It is a companion workbook to *Every Man's Battle.*

Beattie, M (1992). *How to Stop Controlling Others and Start Caring for Yourself.* (2nd ed.). Center City, Mn: Hazelden.

The author asks: Is sometheir problem your problem? If, like so many others, you've lost sight of your own life in the drama of tending to someone else—you may be codependent. The healing touchstone of millions, this modern classic holds the key to understanding codependency and to unlocking its stultifying hold on your life. With instructive life stories, personal reflections, exercises, and self-tests, *Codependent No More* is a simple, straightforward, readable map of the perplexing world of codependency-charting the path to freedom and a lifetime of healing, hope, and happiness.

Becker, P. (2012a). *Why Is My Partner Sexually Addicted? Insight Women Need.* Bloomington, IN: AuthorHouse.

A woman rarely has a need to understand the origin and consequences of sexual addiction until someone close is found to exhibit sex addiction behavior. Each of the chapters in this book reveal aspects of sexual addiction, all to help a women understand her partner's betrayal and to enable her to decide how she will live her life in the future. If you are confounded by the discovery of your partner's aberrant sexual behavior and need to understand why this is happening to you and your family, this book is for you!

Becker, P. (2012b). *Recovery From Sexual Addiction: A Man's Guide.* Bloomington, IN: AuthorHouse.

This book takes men through a structured educational process to identify the characteristics of sexual addiction, why and how addictive behavior took hold of their lives, challenges to ending addictive behavior, and an examination of the role of anger, anxiety, codependency, and depressed mood in addiction.

Becker, P. (2012 c). *Recovery From Sexual Addiction: A Man's Workbook.* Bloomington, IN: AuthorHouse.

Through interactive questions and answers men are invited to gain an in-depth understanding of their own sexual addiction story. With greater insight into the why, how, when, and consequences of addictive behavior, men are strengthened to select choices to maintain a high-level sexual sobriety commitment. With the investment in sexual sobriety, men are empowered to form new and improved family relationships. Men can turn addiction into a joy filled life.

Becker, P. (2013d). *Clinical Guide for the Treatment of Male Sexual Addiction.* Bloomington, IN: AuthorHouse.

This book serves as a syllabus for a group program with Recovery from Sexual Addiction books.

Black, C. (2002). *It Will Never Happen to Me: Growing Up With Addiction As Youngsters, Adolescents, Adults.* (2nd ed.). Center City, MN: Hazelden.

This book identifies common issues faced by children who grew up in alcoholic families—shame, neglect, unreasonable role expectations, and physical abuse. Using narratives and profiles, Black describes the survival techniques characteristic of children raised in alcoholic families, including the unspoken laws of don't talk, don't trust, and don't feel.

Black, C. (2000). *A Hole in the Sidewalk: The Recovering Person's Guide to Relapse Prevention.* Center City, MN: Hazelden.

The journey along the road to recovery may be a glorious and fulfilling adventure, but there are dangers and pitfalls along the way. The person recovering from any addiction needs to be aware of the hazards that lead to relapse. A Hole in the Sidewalk points out ways to avoid the holes; as one travels the path of recovery.

Black, C. (2009). *Deceived: Facing Sexual Betrayal Lies and Secrets.* Center City, MN: Hazelden.

No matter the 'drug' of choice, men who act out sexually leave their partners reeling in fear, rage, incredible shame, and isolation. Deceived was written expressly to help women better understand what is happening in their lives, garner validation for their experiences, and find a path that offers clarity, direction, and voice.

Black, C. (2010). *Intimate Treason: Healing the Trauma for Partners Confronting Sex Addiction.* Las Vegas, NV: Central Recovery Press.

Those in an intimate relationship with someone struggling with sex addiction will find hope and relief as they work through the exercises in this self-help workbook. They will also develop a better understanding of what is happening in their lives and find a path to healing and recovery.

Bradshaw, J. (1988). *Bradshaw on: The Family.* Deerfield Beach, FL: Health Communications.

This book focuses on the dynamics of the family, how the rules and attitudes learned while growing up become encoded within each family member. It guides the reader out of dysfunction to wholeness and teaches bad beginnings can be remedied.

Brisch, K. H. (2002). *Treating Attachment Disorders: From Theory to Therapy.* New York, NY: Guilford Press.

Attachment theory and research have greatly enhanced our understanding of the role of parent-child relationships in the development of psychopathology. Yet until now, little has been written on how an attachment perspective can be used to actively inform psychotherapeutic practice. Brisch presents an attachment-oriented framework for assessing and treating patients of all ages

Carnes, S. (Ed.). (2011). *Mending a Shattered Heart: A Guide for Partners of Sex Addicts.* 2nd ed. Carefree, AZ: Gentle Path Press.

This book is for the partner who needs an answer to the question: "Where do I go from here?" Many discover their loved one, the one person that they are supposed to trust, has been living a life of lies and deceit because they suffer from sex addiction.

Carnes, S., Lee, M. & Rodriguez, A. (2012) *Facing Heartbreak*. Carefree, AZ: Gentle Path Press

This is the first available workbook that follows the Patrick Carnes 30 task model to help partners of sex addicts cope and recover from discovering their loved one has compulsive sexual behaviors.

Cassidy, J., & Shaver, P. R. (2008). *Handbook of attachment: Theory, Research, and Clinical Applications* (2nd ed.). New York, NY: Guilford Press.

This comprehensive work includes the origins and development of attachment theory; biological and evolutionary perspectives; and the role of attachment processes in personality, relationships, and mental health across the lifespan.

Cooper, A. (Ed.). (2001). *Sex and the Internet: A Guide for Clinicians*. New York, NY: Brunner-Routledge.

Sex and the Internet is the first professional book on Internet sexuality. This book is a clinician's guide that addresses Internet sexuality by both informing and providing practical and concrete suggestions and directions. The book is compilation of contributions by international experts in the field of sexuality including Patrick Carnes

Corley, D., & Schneider, J. (2002a). *Disclosing Secrets: When, to Whom and How Much and to Reveal*. Carefree, AZ: Gentle Path Press.

This book is a guide to revealing sexual addiction secrets to their partner and others. The book takes the reader through the painful process of revealing addiction related secrets—what, where, when to tell and who to involve.

Crow, G., Earle R., & Osborn, K. (1989). *Lonely All the Time: Recognizing, Understanding and Overcoming Sex Addiction, for Addicts and Codependents*. New York, NY: Pocket Books (Div. of Simon & Schuster).

This book is a comprehensive and practical approach to recovery for the addict. It explains what sex addiction is and how to recover from sex addiction. The book explores the causes and symptoms of sex addiction. It also includes a practical approach to recovery for the addict and family.

Ferree, M. (Ed.). (2012). *Making Advances: A Comprehensive Guide for Treating Female Sex and Love Addicts*. Royston, GA. Society for the Advancement of Sexual Health.

Making Advances is the first book to offer a targeted approach for effectively treating women who struggle with sex and love addiction. *Making Advances* describes the problem, explores its bio psychosocial roots, and thoroughly outlines the assessment and diagnosis process. The text emphasizes the importance of the therapeutic relationship and describes how treating female sex and love addicts is different from treating men.

Ferree, M. (2010). *No Stones: Women Redeemed from Sexual Addiction*. Downers Grove, IL. (2nd ed.). InterVarsity Press.

This book offers a unique resource for women struggling with sexual addiction. Ferree distills her clinical expertise on female sexual addiction accessibly and gently, providing a much-needed resource for women struggling with any degree of relational or sexual addiction. Ferree details the roots of addiction in family trauma and offers clear-eyed advice as both a counselor and a "grateful recovering sex addict" on how to achieve sobriety and healing.

Gordon, J. R., & Marlat, G. A. (Eds.). (1985). *Relapse Prevention: Maintenance Strategies in the Treatment of Addictive Behaviors.* New York, NY: Guilford Publications.

This book analyzes factors that may lead to relapse and offers practical techniques for maintaining treatment gains.

Gottman, J. M. (2011). *The science of Trust: Emotional Attunement for Couples*. New York, NY:WW. Norton.

Gottman draws from his longitudinal research and theory to show how emotional attunement can down regulate negative affect, help couples focus on positive traits and memories, and even help prevent domestic violence. He offers a detailed intervention devised to cultivate attunement, thereby helping couples connect, respect each other, and show affection.

Hendrix, H. (2007). *Getting the Love You Want: A Guide for Couples.* (20th anniversary ed). London: St. Martin's Griffin.

This book presents relationship skills to help couples replace confrontation and criticism with a healing process of mutual growth and support. It describes the techniques of Imago Relationship Therapy, which combines a number of disciplines—including the behavioral sciences, depth psychology, cognitive therapy, and Gestalt therapy, among others—to create a program to resolve conflict and renew communication and passion.

Hope and Recovery: A Twelve-Step Guide for Healing From Compulsive Sexual Behavior. (1987). Minneapolis, MI: CompCare Publishers.

This was one of the first books to comprehensively describe the application of the 12- Steps of Alcoholics Anonymous to sexual addiction and compulsivity. It also includes a wide range of personal stories in which recovering sexual addicts share their experience, strength, and hope.

Kasl, C. D. (2002). *Many Roads, One Journey: Moving Beyond the Twelve Steps.* Saint Helens, OR: Perennial Press.

This book, from the author of Women, Sex, and Addiction, is a timely and controversial second look at 12- Step programs. It is intended to help readers draw on the steps' underlying wisdom and adapting them to their own experiences, beliefs, and sources of strength.

Kasl, C. S. (1990). *Woman, Sex, and Addiction: a Search for Love and Power.* New York, NY: Harper & Row.

Sex is the price many women pay for love and the illusion of security. A woman who seeks a sense of personal power and an escape from pain may use sex and romance as a way to feel in control, just as an alcoholic uses alcohol; but sex never satisfies her longing for love and self-worth. In this book Kasl shows women how they can learn to experience their sexuality as a source for love and positive power and sex as an expression that honors the soul as well as the body.

Laaser, M. (2004). *Healing the Wounds of Sexual Addiction.* Grand Rapids, MI: Zondervan Publishing Company.

This book is written by a former sex addict. It offers help and hope for regaining and maintaining sexual integrity, self-control, and wholesome, biblical sexuality.

Leahy, M., (2008). *Porn Nation: Conquering America's #1 Addiction* (new ed.). Northfield Publishing;

Porn is a $100 billion a year industry worldwide. Even bigger when you consider the fact that porn is now the norm in our mainstream media. But have you ever stopped to think about why, when it comes to porn, we just can't seem to get enough? And are we certain this "cheap form of harmless entertainment" isn't changing the way we see ourselves and act towards others in relationships?

What you feed grows, and what you starve dies.

Maltz, W. (2001). *The Sexual Healing Journey: A Guide for Survivors of Sexual Abuse.* (rev. ed.). New York, NY: Harper Perennial.

This comprehensive guide will help survivors of sexual abuse improve their relationships and discover the joys of sexual intimacy. Maltz takes survivors step-by-step through the recovery process using groundbreaking exercises and techniques.

Maltz, W. & Maltz, L. (2009). *The Porn Trap: The Essential Guide to Overcoming Problems Caused by Pornography.* (rep ed.) New York, NY: William Morrow Paperbacks.

This book sheds new light on the compelling nature and destructive power of today's instantly available pornography. Weaving together poignant real-life stories with innovative exercises, checklists, and expert advice, this groundbreaking resource provides a comprehensive program for understanding and healing porn addiction and other serious consequences of porn use.

Melody, P. & Freundlich, L. S. (2004). *The Intimacy Factor: the Ground Rules for Overcoming the Obstacles to Truth, Respect, and Lasting Love.* New York, NY: Harper Collins.

The author shares her profound wisdom on what it takes to sustain true intimacy and trusting love in our most vital relationships.

Mellody, P. (1989). *Facing Codependency: What It Is, Where It Comes from, How It Sabotages Our Lives.* New York, NY: Harper & Row.

The author creates a framework for identifying codependent thinking, emotions and behavior and provides an effective approach to recovery. The book sets forth five primary adult symptoms of this crippling condition, and then traces their origin to emotional, spiritual, intellectual, physical and sexual abuses that occur in childhood. Central to the approach is the concept that the codependent adult's injured inner child needs healing. Recovery from codependence, therefore, involves clearing up the toxic emotions left over from these painful childhood experiences.

Milkman, H., & Sunderwirth, S. (1998). *Craving for Ecstasy: How Our Passions Become Addictions and What We Can Do About Them.* (rep. ed.). San Francisco, CA: Jossey-Bass.

The book describes the variety of addictive ways individuals lose control of their lives while striving for pleasure and escape. Addictive behavior goes beyond the compulsive use of drugs and alcohol. It is possible to become addicted to what may seem a harmless pleasure such as sex, jogging, watching television, and eating. This book explains the biology, chemistry, and psychology of the universal desire for pleasure and escape. For example, it reveals how the brain produces "mind-altering" substances and what the skydiver has in common with the heroin addict. With the use of a self-assessment test and a guide for treatment, the book shows what steps one can take to regain control of their life.

Schaumburg, H. (1997). *False Intimacy: Understanding the Struggle of Sexual Addiction.* (rev. ed.). Colorado Springs, CO: Navpress Publishing Group.

This book, set in a Christian context, examines the roots behind destructive sexual behaviors and offers realistic direction to those whose lives or ministries have been impacted by sexual addiction.

Schneider, J. (2001). *Back from Betrayal: Recovering from His Affairs.* (2nd ed.). Recovery Resources Press.

This book provides practical help for women involved with sex addicted men. The second edition is expanded and updated, with a new chapter for men whose partner is a sex addict, and another new chapter on living with a cybersex addict.

Schneider, J. & Weiss, R. (2001) *Cybersex Exposed: Simple Fantasy or Obsession?* Center City, MN: Hazelden Publishing & Educational Services.

Examining the negative consequences of Internet sex addiction on health, career, intimacy and family relationships, and this guide provides a test to help readers evaluate their own behavior. The guide also discusses the negative impact of cybersex on partners and presents stories of recovery.

Schneider, B., & Schneider, J. (2004). *Sex Lies and Forgiveness: Couples Speaking Out on Healing from Sex Addiction.* (3rd ed.). Recovery Resources Press.

In this book, 88 couples talk about how they have coped with the problem of addictive sexual behavior.

Steffens, B. & Means, M. (2009). *Your Sexually Addicted Spouse: How Partners Can Cope and Heal.* Far Hills, NJ: New Horizon Press.

This book shatters the stigma and shame that millions of men and women carry when their partners are sexually addicted. They receive little empathy for their pain, which means they suffer alone, often shocked and isolated by the trauma. Barbara Steffens' ground breaking new research shows that partners are not codependents but post-traumatic stress victims, while Marsha Means' personal experience provides insights, strategies, and critical steps to recognize, deal with, and heal partners of sexually addicted relationships. Firsthand accounts and stories reveal the impact of this addiction on survivors' lives.

Struthers, W (2009). *Wired for Intimacy: How Pornography Hijacks the Male Brain*, (6th print ed.) Downers Grove, IL: IVP Books;

This book scientifically quantifies what those of us who work in the field of sexual addiction have observed. *Wired for Intimacy* presents "brain" connection to understanding how pornography powerfully impacts the brain.

Weiss, D. (2000). *Steps to Freedom.* (2nd ed.). Colorado Springs, CO: Discovery Press.

This book follows the tradition of the 12-steps from a Christian perspective. It breaks down the various principles to help the reader experience freedom from sex addiction.

Weiss R. & Schneider, J. (2006). *Untangling the Web: Sex, Porn, and Fantasy Obsession in the Internet Age*. Boston MA: Alyson Books.

With personal stories from addicts and their significant others, this updated edition offers realistic healing strategies for anyone experiencing the devastating impact of Internet pornography and sex addiction on intimacy, relationships, career, health, and self-respect.

Weiss R. & Carnes, P. (2013). *Cruise Control: Understanding Sex Addiction in Gay Men.* (2nd ed.), Carefree, AZ: Gentle Path Press.

The author focuses on the clinical approach, asking the question, "Is your sexual behavior causing problems in other areas of your life?" *Cruise Control* leads men to a better understand the difference between sexual compulsion and non-addictive sexual behavior within the gay experience, and it explains what resources are available for recovery. *Cruise Control* provides understanding, empathy and encouragement to gay men seeking healthy sexual expression.

APPENDIX G: REFERENCES

American Psychiatric Association. (2013). *Diagnostic and statistical manual of mental disorders* (5th ed.). Arlington VA: American Psychiatric Publishing.

American Psychiatric Association, (2013). Anxiety. In *Diagnostic and statistical manual of mental disorders* (5th ed.). Retrieved June 30, 2014 from http://www.apa.org/topics/anxiety/

Arterburn, S., Stoeker, F., & Yorkey, M. (2000). *Every Man's Battle: Winning the War on Sexual Temptation One Victory at a Time*. Colorado Springs, CO: WaterBrook Press.

Beattie, M (1987). *Codependent No More: How to Stop Controlling Others and Start Caring for Yourself.* (2nd ed.). Center City, MN: Hazelden.

Becker, P. (2012a). *Why Is My Partner Sexually Addicted? Insight Women Need*. Bloomington, IN: AuthorHouse.

Becker, P. (2012b). *Recovery from Sexual Addiction: A Man's Guide*. Bloomington, IN: AuthorHouse.

Becker, P. (2012c). *Recovery from Sexual Addiction: A Man's Workbook*. Bloomington, IN: AuthorHouse.

Becker, P. (2013). *Clinical Guide for the Treatment of Male Sexual Addiction*. Bloomington, IN: AuthorHouse.

Bissette, D., (n.d.). Relapse prevention plan. *HealthyMind.com*. Alexandria VA. (n.p.) background, Retrieved December 17, 2013 from http://www.healthymind.com/

Black, C. (2014). Trauma in the addicted family. *Addiction in the Family*. Familial trauma section, para 2. Retrieved from http://addictioninfamily.com/family-issues/trauma-in-the-addicted-family-by-claudia-black/

Bradshaw, J. (1988). *Bradshaw On: The Family: A Revolutionary Way of Self-Discovery*. Deerfield Beach, FL: Hazelden, Health Communications, Inc.

Bradshaw, J. (2005). *Healing the Shame that Binds You*. Deerfield Beach, FL: Hazelden, Health Communications, Inc.

Burnham, T., Chapman, J., Gray, P., McIntyre, M., Lipson, S., & Ellison, P. (2003). Men in committed, romantic relationships have lower testosterone. *Hormones and Behavior 44*, no. 4 (2/15): 1-4, Abstract section, para 1. Retrieved July 21, 2014 from http://www.ncbi.nlm.nih.gov/pubmed/13129483

Campling, S., Corley, D., Ferree, M., & Hudson, L. (2012). Best practices for arresting acting out. In M. Ferree (Ed.), *Making Advances: A Comprehensive Guide for Treating Female Sex and Love Addicts* (p.181). (pp. 72,74,80) Royston, GA. Society for the Advancement of Sexual Health.

Campling, S., Corley, D.,, Katehakis, A., Valenti-Anderson, A., & Weedn, S., (2012). Diagnosing sex and love addiction in women. In M. Ferree (Ed.), *Making Advances: A Comprehensive Guide for Treating Female Sex and Love Addicts* (pp.156-159,181). Royston, GA. Society for the Advancement of Sexual Health.

Carnes, P. (1991). 18.2 Sexual addiction. *International Institute for Trauma and Addiction Professionals.* (6) 4, 6-7. Retrieved February 17, 2014 from: http://www.iitap.com/documents/ARTICLE_18.4%20Sexual%20Addiction%20-%20Patrick%20Carnes.pdf

Carnes, P. (1992). *Don't Call it Love: Recovery from Sexual Addiction.* New York: Bantam.

Carnes, P. (1994). *Contrary to Love: Helping the Sexual Addict.* Center city, MN: Hazelden

Carnes, P. (1997a). *Sexual Anorexia: Overcoming Sexual Self-Hatred.* Center City, MN: Hazelden.

Carnes, P. (1997b). *The Betrayal Bond: Breaking Free of Exploitative Relationships.* Deerfield Beach, FL: Health Communications Inc.

Carnes, P. (1998). The making of a sex addict. (Adapted from "The Obsessive Shadow.") *International Institute for Trauma and Addiction Professionals.* 1-3. Retrieved March 2, 2014 from http://www.iitap.com/documents/ARTICLE_The%20Making%20of%20a%20Sex%20Addict_PCarnes.pdf

Carnes, P. (2000). Sexual addiction and compulsion: Recognition, treatment & recovery. *CNS SPECTRUMS, 5* (10), 3 and 6, 63-72. Retrieved July 27, 2014 from http://www.recoveryonpurpose.com/upload/article_sexualaddictionandcompulsion_pcarnes.pdf

Carnes, P. (2001a). *Out of the Shadows: Understanding Sexual Addiction.* (3rd. ed.) Center City, MN: Hazelden.

Carnes, P. & Harkin, M. (2001b/2005). *Facing the Shadow: Starting Sexual and Relationship Recovery.* Carefree, AZ: Gentle Path Press.

Carnes, P. (2003). Pornography and the internet in today's world. *Enrichment Journal.* 1, Trauma and Sex Addiction section, para 1, Background section, para. 1, Characteristics section, para. 3. Retrieved March 2, 2014 from http://enrichmentjournal.ag.org/200504/200504_022_internet.cfm

Carnes, P. (2010). Women and sex addiction. [PowerPoint presentation]. *International Institute for Trauma and Addiction Professionals.* Slides 2, 3, 6. Retrieved March 2, 2014 from www.iitap.com/

Carnes, P. (2012). SAST: Sex addiction screening test. (ITAP). Retrieved June 19, 2014 from http://www.sexhelp.com/addiction_tests.cfm

Carnes, P. & O'Hara, S. (n.d.). Women's self-test for sexual/relationship addiction, *Bethesda Workshops*, Nashville, TN. Retrieved from http://www.bethesdayworkshops. org/sex-addiction/self-test/

Carnes, P. (n.d.). 30 tasks for addiction recovery. 1-19. Retrieved June 19, 2014 from http:// www.iitap.com/documents/Tasks1-30-Detailed.pdf.

Carter, D., Henslin, E., Townsend, J., Cloud, H. & Brawand A. (1991). *Secrets of Your Family Tree: Healing for Adult Children of Dysfunctional Families.* Chicago, Il: Moody Press.

CASA. (2013). Ending addiction changes everything. *Addiction Prevalence.* 1 CASAColumbia. Retrieved February 10, 2014 from http://www.casacolumbia.org/ addiction?gclid=CNPnrrSy2LwCFW8V7AodHjgA6w

Corley, D., Ferree, M., & McDaniel, K., (2012). Systemic issues in treating female sex and love addicts. In M. Ferree (Ed.), *Making Advances: A Comprehensive Guide for Treating Female Sex and Love Addicts. (*p.220). Royston, GA. Society for the Advancement of Sexual Health.

Corley, D. & Schneider, J. (2002a). *Disclosing Secrets: When, to Whom and How Much and to Reveal.* Carefree, AZ: Gentle Path Press.

Corley, D. & Schneider, J. (2002b). Disclosing secrets: guidelines for therapists working with sex addicts and co-addicts. *Sexual Addiction & Compulsivity 9:*43-67, para 4. Retrieved July 28, 2014 from http://www.jenniferschneider.com/articles/disclosing_secrets_5_02. html

Covenant Eyes. Last retrieved January 28, 2015 from www.covenanteyes.com/Accountability

Duckworth, K. (2009). Women and depression. *The National Alliance on Mental Illness.* para.4. Retrieved July 17, 2014 from http://www.nami.org/Template. cfm?Section=Women_and_Depression&Template=/ContentManagement/ ContentDisplay.cfm&ContentID=89194

Enth (2001, May 1). Dopamine, Delta-FosB, and the nature of addictive drugs. *Everything 2. 2.* Retrieved January 25, 2014 from http://everything2.com/title/Dopamine%252C+Delta-Fo sB%252C+and+the+nature+of+Addictive+Drugs

Ewald, R. (2003, May 13). Sexual addiction. *All psych Journal.* para. 4-7. Retrieved March 3, 2014 from http://allpsych.com/journal/sexaddiction.html

Ferree, M. (2010). *No Stones: Women Redeemed from Sexual Addiction.* Downers Grove, IL: (2nd ed.). InterVarsity Press.

Ferree, M., Campling, S., Cato, R., Corley, D., Hudson, l., Katehakis, A., McDaniel, K., Valenti-Anderson, A., Vermeire, J., & Weedn, S., (2012). In M. Ferree (Ed.) *Making Advances: A Comprehensive Guide for Treating Female Sex and Love Addicts.* Royston, GA: Society for the Advancement of Sexual Health.

Ferree, M., Hudson, L., Katehakis, A., McDaniel, K.,& Valenti-Anderson, A., (2012). Etiology of female sex and love addiction. In M. Ferree (Ed.) *Making Advances: A Comprehensive Guide for Treating Female Sex and Love Addicts.* (pp 47-49, 52-54, 47, 49, 50). Royston, GA: Society for the Advancement of Sexual Health.

Framingham, J. (2011). Minnesota Multiphasic Personality Inventory. *PsycCentral.* Para. 1. Retrieved from http://psychcentral.com/lib/minnesota-multiphasic-personality-inventory-mmpi/0005959

Goodman, A. (1998, October 1). Sexual addiction: Diagnosis and treatment. *Psychiatric Times.* 25(10):15-17. Retrieved February 15, 2014 from http://www.psychiatrictimes.com/articles/sexual-addiction-update-assessment-diagnosis-and-treatment/page/0/3

Goodman, A. (2001). What's in a name? Terminology for designating a syndrome of driven sexual behavior. *Sexual Addiction & Compulsivity*, 8, Issue 3-4, 191–213. Abstract, 195-196. Retrieved July 27, 2014 from http://www.tandfonline.com/doi/abs/10.1080/107201601753459919

Goodman, A. (2009, May 26). Sexual addiction update assessment, diagnosis and treatment. *Psychiatric Times.* Psychiatric Pharmacotherapy section, para. 2. Retrieved February 15, 2014 from http://www.psychiatrictimes.com/sexual-addiction/sexual-addiction-diagnosis-and-treatment

Hastings, A.S. (1998). *Treating Sexual Shame: A New Map for Overcoming Dysfunction, Abuse, and Addiction.* Northvale, NJ: Jason Aronson.

Hayden, D. (2012, February 2). Sex addiction therapy: an integrated approach. *Self Help; Go articles.com.* The Problem of Sex Addiction section, para. 7. Retrieved March 3, 2014 from http://goarticles.com/article/Sex-Addiction-Therapy-An-Integrated-Approach/6038272/

Helpguide.org (n.d.). Understanding addiction: How addiction hijacks the brain, para.11. Retrieved January 2015 from http://www.helpguide.org/harvard/how-addiction-hijacks-the-brain.htm

Hendrix, H. (2007). *Getting the Love You Want: A Guide for Couples.* (20th anniversary ed). London: St. Martin's Griffin.

Henslin, E. (1995). David and his family tree. Chapter one. In D. Carter, (Ed.). *Secrets of Your Family Tree: Healing for Adult Children of Dysfunctional Families.* (pp. 43-44). Chicago, IL: Moody.

Herkov, M. (2006). What causes sexual addiction? *PsyCentral.* para 7. Retrieved February 26 2014 from http://psychcentral.com/lib/what-causes-sexual-addiction/000744

Hughes, D. R. (September, 1998). Protecting children in cyberspace. *Probe Ministries*, 1. Retrieved November 25, 2014, from Http://www.protectkids.comeffects/patternofaddiction.htm

Introduction to the Genogram (2014). *Genpro.* 1. Retrieved March 2, 2014 from http://www.genopro.com/genogram/

Kastleman, M. (2007*). The Drug of the New Millennium, the Brain Science Behind Internet Pornography Use* (2nd ed.). 39-57. Orem, UT: Power Thinking Publishing.

Kasl, C. S. (1990). *Woman, Sex, and Addiction: a Search for Love and Power.* New York, NY: Harper & Row.

Kathehakis, A. (2012). Best practices for addressing attachment injuries. In M. Ferree (Ed.). *Making Advances: A Comprehensive Guide for Treating Female Sex and Love Addicts.* (p. 188). Royston, GA. Society for the Advancement of Sexual Health.

Keirsey, D. & Bates, M. (1978). *Please Understand Me: Character & Temperament Types.* Del Mar, CA: Prometheus Nemesis.

Laaser, M. (2002, Feb). The pornography trap. *Wineskins Archives.* Para 1-2. Retrieved January 28, from http://archives.wineskins.org/article/pornography-trap-jan-feb-2002/

Laaser, M. (2006). The secret sin: sex addiction. *Growthtrac.* Para. 9. Retrieved December 10, 2013 from http://www.growthtrac.com/the-secret-sin-sex-addiction/#.Uqd_y8RDvDU

Laaser, M. & Carnes, P. (2008). Sexual addiction. *Christian Counseling Today, Vol 16,* No. 1. Prevalence section, para 2. Retrieved March 15, 2014 from http://www.faithfulandtrue.com/Resources/CCT-Sex-Addiction2008-vol16no1.aspx

Lee, P. (2014, March 5). Thirty percent of women, 70 percent of men confess to looking at online porn: study. *Daily News.* Para 1. Retrieved March 5, 2014 from http://www.nydailynews.com/life-style/percent-women-70-percent-men-confess-online-porn-study-article-1.173109#ixzz2v8ySAMxF

Maltz, W. (2001). *The Sexual Healing Journey: A Guide for Survivors of Sexual Abuse.* (rev ed.). New York, NY: Harper Perennial.

May, G. (2007). *Addiction and Grace: Love and Spirituality in the Healing of Addictions.* (Reissue ed.). New York, NY: HarperOne.

McDaniel, K., Valent-Anderson, A.,Ferree, M., Hudson, L., & Katehakis, A., (2012). Definition and understanding of female sex and love addiction. In M. Ferree (Ed.). *Making Advances: A Comprehensive Guide forTreating Female Sex and Love Addicts.* (pp. 19, 28, 30, 27-28, 37-38, 40-41). Royston, GA. Society for the Advancement of Sexual Health.

Means, M. (2003). *Living with Your Husband's Secrete Wars*, Grand Rapids, MI: Fleming H. Revell

Minwalla, O. (2012, July 23). Partners of sex addicts need treatment for trauma. *The National Psychologist.* Para. 3, 7. Retrieved May 25, 2014 from http://nationalpsychologist. com/2012/07/partners-of-sex-addicts-need-treatment-for-trauma/101713.html

Morris, D (2001), Addictions restrict our ability to dream beautiful dreams. *Kavod Addiction Recovery*, Rochester, N.Y: Retrieved from http://www.kavodrecovery.com/about-kavod. html (No longer posted to Kavod website.)

Nestler, E., Barrot, M., & Self, D. (2001, September 25). Your brain on porn. *National Academy of Science*, USA. 1. Retrieved January 25, 2014 from http://yourbrainonporn. com/book/export/html/120

O'Hare, S. (2012, June 1). How are female sex addicts different from males? *Psych Central.* para. 2,6,7. Retrieved February 26 2014 from http://psychcentral.com/blog/archives/2012/06/01/how-are-female-sex-addicts-different-from-males/

Pornography Statistics (1998-2104). *Family Safe Media*, Nextphase, Inc., Salt Lake City, UT: (n.p.) Retrieved from http://www.familysafemedia.com/pornography_statistics.html

Potter-Efrom, R. & Potter-Efrom, P. (1989). *Letting Go of Shame*, Center City, MN: Hazelden.

Rettner, R. (2012, October 10). Sex 'addiction' is a real disorder, study suggests. *LiveScience.* para 6. Retrieved July 17, 2012 from http://www.livescience.com/23860-sex-addiction-real-disorder.html

Sbraga, T. & O'Donohue, W. (2003). *The Sex Addiction Workbook.* Oakland, CA: New Harbinger Publications.

Sexual Addiction, (2014). *Society for the Advancement of Sexual Health*, screen 2. Royston GA: Retrieved July 27, 2014 from http://www.sash.net/?q=sexual-addiction.

Schneider, J., Corley, M. & Irons, R. (1998). Surviving disclosure of infidelity: Results of an international survey of 164 recovering sex addicts and partners. *Sexual Addiction & Compulsivity,* 5,3, 189-217. Retrieved November 4, 2014 from http://www.jenniferschneider.com/articles/surviving_disclosure.html

Sex Addiction Anonymous (SAA) (2007-2014). *International Service Organization of SSA, Inc.* Para 4. Houston, TX: Retrieved January 20, 2015 from https://saa- recovery.org/IsSAAForYou/AreYouASexAddict/ and https://saa-recovery.org/OurProgram/TheTwelveSteps/

Sexaholics Anonymous [SA] (1989). SA Literature

Statistics on pornography. (1998-2014). *Family Safe Media.* Retrieved March 16, 2014 from http://www.familysafemedia.com/pornography_statistics.html

Steffens, B. & Means, M. (2009). *Your Sexually Addicted Spouse: How Partners Can Cope and Heal.* Far Hills, NJ: New Horizon Press.

Struthers, W. M. (2009). *Wired for Intimacy. How Pornography Hijacks the Male Brain.* Downers Grove, IL: Inter Varsity Press.

U.S. *Attorney General's Commission on Pornography.* (July 1986). A*ttorney General's Report on Pornography: Final Report.* Washington D.C., U.S. Government Printing Office. Retrieved July 8, 2013 from http://www.porn-report.com/202-history-of-pornography.htm 2/3/09

Weiss, D. (1998). *The Final Freedom: Pioneering Sexual Addiction Recovery.* Fort worth, TX: Discovery Press.

Weiss, D. (2000). *Steps to Freedom.* (2nd ed.). Colorado Springs, CO: Discovery Press.

Weiss, D. (Feb 12, 2012). Women don't look at pornography. Do they? *Citizenlink.* Pornography and girls section. Para. 1. Retrieved March 5, 2014 from http://www.citizenlink.com/2012/02/21/women-dont-look-at-pornography-do-they/

Wilson, G. (May 16, 2012). The great porn experiment. [Video File] *TEDxGlasgow.* Viewed January 25, 2014 http://www.youtube.com/watch?v=wSF82AwSDiU and retrieved http://www.youtube.com/watch?v=wSF82AwSDiU&goback=%2Egde_112401_member_5830762512437501955#%21

Zoldbrod, A. (1998). *Sex Smart, How your Childhood Shaped Your Sexual Life and What To Do about It.* 147. Oakland, CA: New Harbinger Publications, Inc.

INDEX

Non-sexual intimacy 46, 191, 217, 238, 243,
248, 249, 252, 253, 254, 269, 288
Relapse contract 286
Relapse prevention 93, 98, 100, 278, 286, 287
Rigorous honesty 57
Risky states 293, 295
Searching and fearless moral inventory 57,
248, 279
Selective Serotonin Re-uptake Inhibitor 190
Self-sacrificing love 27, 29, 75
Sexual honesty 272, 273
Sexual sobriety 63, 93, 94, 98, 99, 102, 150,
197, 215, 215, 221, 222, 226, 232, 236,
238, 244, 245, 263, 272, 278, 281, 282,
285, 291, 302
Spirituality 29, 105, 243, 276, 292
Strategies 59, 94, 190, 195, 196, 209, 211, 213,
217, 221, 222, 223, 236, 239, 243, 286,
287, 290
Substituting new behaviors 58, 89, 195,
259, 260
Supplemental therapy 10, 300
Support network 237, 280
Thirty Tasks of Sexual Addiction
Recovery 318
Three second rule 226, 238
Twelve-step programs 57, 97, 245, 277, 279,
280, 281

S

Sex addict's world
Acting-out cycle 93, 157, 166, 167, 168, 171,
172, 211, 212
Acting-out ritual 97, 101, 157, 166, 167, 170,
173, 174, 175, 176, 212, 213, 226, 237,
259, 287, 289
Addict's life scale 177, 178, 179, 181, 202,
250, 251
Anonymity 6, 66
Arousal 4, 5, 6, 13, 20, 22, 29, 37, 39, 55, 58,
59, 60, 63, 65, 66, 68, 70, 71, 75, 107,
108, 117, 128, 131, 145, 151, 159, 167,
169, 186

Body parts 21, 38, 86, 160, 161, 186, 207,
211, 212
Boredom 130, 173, 197, 199, 211, 212, 291
Co-addict 19, 24, 47, 77, 79, 80, 95, 283, 324
Compartmentalization 25, 58, 79, 243, 265,
266, 267
Core beliefs 13, 18, 55, 99, 105
Double life 21, 134, 137, 141, 149, 152
Dreams die 13
Dual images 46
Euphoric 12, 62, 233, 251, 159, 178
Habit 12, 21, 39, 44, 53, 58, 61, 74, 93, 98, 106,
146, 155, 169, 181, 195, 196, 227, 228,
259, 272
Inventory of sexual practices 129
Low self-esteem 12, 16, 51, 86, 178
Object 4, 21, 22, 59, 60, 68, 69, 86, 99, 103,
226, 229, 238
Orgasm 6, 10, 11, 12, 18, 20, 60, 61, 179, 181,
184, 211, 251
Secrets 27, 40, 41, 46, 80, 84, 85, 87,100, 112,
129, 149, 228, 229, 248, 271, 272
Sexual fantasy 10, 17, 22, 58, 60, 86, 98, 130,
131, 146, 147, 158, 159, 160, 161, 162,
163, 164, 165, 169, 237, 263, 293,
Sexual stimulation 9, 11, 13, 16, 32, 37, 39, 40,
59, 65, 68, 69, 71, 77, 85, 107, 121, 149,
169, 178, 195, 208, 226, 227
Sexual thinking 11, 21, 32, 51, 58, 59, 93, 99,
157, 158, 159, 160, 164, 165, 167, 169,
174, 221, 222, 223, 228, 236, 245, 263,
264, 293
Slippery slope 170, 173, 174, 175, 212, 225,
226, 227, 237, 287, 289
Triggers 46, 60, 70, 97, 112, 157, 168, 183, 211,
212, 213, 227, 237, 286, 287, 291, 293,
295, 296
White-knuckling 220, 221, 222, 235